# Schoolmarms:

## Women in America's Schools

Edwina Walsh

**Schoolmarms:**
**Women in America's Schools**

By Edwina Walsh

Copyright 1995 by Edwina Walsh

Published by Caddo Gap Press
   3145 Geary Boulevard, Suite 275
   San Francisco, California 94118

Represented overseas by
   Drake International Services
   Market House, Market Place
   Deddington, Oxford OX15 0SF
   United Kingdom

Cover design by Mason Jones

List price $19.95 US

ISBN 1-880192-14-4

Library of Congress Cataloging-in-Publication Data

Walsh, Edwina.
    Schoolmarms : reflections on women in America's schools / Edwina
Walsh.
       p.    cm.
    Includes bibliographical references and index.
    ISBN 1-880192-41-1 (pbk.)
    1. Women teachers--United States.  2. Women teachers--United
States--Social conditions.  3. Teachers--United States.  4. Sex
discrimination in education--United States.  5. Educational change-
-United States.  I. Title.
LB1775.2.W25  1995
371.1'0082--dc20                                        95-16118
                                                           CIP

# Table of Contents

# Acknowledgements

I want to thank my husband, Ken, who provided the place and the peace for the writing of this book, my sisters and brothers, who provided the discussions and encouragement, and Agnes, who sponsored the book.

# Introduction

**R**eforms in American education have been typically generated by economic crises. Russia launched a Sputnik into space and the United States launched school reform in science and math. Japan threatens megapower in world trade and the United States castigates the public school system. But the schools cannot be jump-started and reform will not happen on demand.

The recent panic over education has given us an "Education President," a governors' education summit, and .new programs sprouting in the schools like dandelions on the front lawn. In all the frenzy, however, the main issue is clouded. To paraphrase the Clinton campaign, "it's the teachers, stupid."

Until we address the needs of the teachers, we can forget about improving education for the children. Richard Branson, a young entrepeneur who made millions in the recording industry and is now starting Virgin Airlines, revealed on CSPAN the secret of his immense success. "Staff comes first, customers second, stockholders last."[1]

We could well apply that to the schools. Teachers come first, students second, then parents and the rest of society. School reform should concentrate on the teaching profession because the surest way parents and society will get what they want for the children is through high caliber teachers who have the autonomy to do their job. Much of the education reform literature today focuses on the children. Right motivation, wrong emphasis.

An important fact mostly ignored in the debate on education is that the majority of teachers are and have been women. Public schools survived and thrived on the undermined labor of women without much of a crisis until now, when rising crime, poverty, and competition in world trade magnify the problems of the schools and when the schools can no longer depend on attracting a large portion of the nation's top women as they have for centuries.

Despite the women's movement, little attention has been drawn to the plight of women teachers and the fact that schools have been designed on the abasement of teachers. Teachers have been subjugated for so long, it has come to be expected, even accepted, often by teachers themselves.

The first purpose of this book is to demonstrate that reform in education is futile without the redefinition of teachers because their plebeian status shaped the course of the American public school, led to its present crisis, and continues to stymie the movement for reform. In this book, teacher means teachers in elementary and secondary schools, as we say in education jargon, "grades K through 12."

The second purpose is to show how the present status of teachers not only cripples their work but also denies parents and students real impact on education in the schools.

The final purpose is to sift the major criticisms of the schools and respond to them from the viewpoint of a school teacher. In the past decade, publishers spewed volumes of solutions to the problems of education, hundreds of treatises delineating teachers' ineffectiveness. Columnists like Thomas Sowell call teachers "dummies" and

declare that teachers come from the "dregs" of the college population. University professors claim that the schools are failing because
teachers are not working, but simply showing up to receive un-
earned paychecks. The study of public schools done by the Association of American University Women declares that teachers, specifically women teachers, shortchange girls.

The first chapters of *Schoolmarms* trace the evolution of the
American teacher, describe the plight of teachers today, and outline
the options for change. The last two chapters demonstrate how the
redefinition of teachers will strengthen the role of both parents and
students.

Critics claim that teachers have not been heard in the national
education forum because they have no recommendations to offer.
The reality is that teachers are not heard because they do not enjoy
the prestige of a Secretary of Education like William Bennett, or
chancellor of schools like Joseph Fernandez, or president of the
Carnegie Foundation like Ernest Boyer. Women do not serve in
these prestigious education positions; they serve in the classrooms—
and women who teach in the classroom are not likely to have access
to the national forum. It's a pity.

I wanted to write this book years ago, as soon as I realized that
the debate on education reform ignored women teachers, but I was
too busy teaching. As a classroom teacher, I worked a minimum of
eleven hours a day, part of many weekends and all of some. Jonathan
Kozol, John Holt, and Herbert Kohl had to quit teaching to write
their books. Speaking of the junior high where he taught, James
Herndon said that it was a place where he had no time to think at all.
Geri Stern, a teacher interviewed in Susan Dichter's *Teachers:
Straight Talk from the Trenches,* went into teaching so she could find
time to do her art work. "That was a fallacy," she admitted, "teaching doesn't provide you with any time to do anything."[2]

I had to retire to write this book.

The school district wanted me to retire anyway because I was
too expensive. After thirty-five years teaching, I earned all of $44,000,
about ten thousand less than the median income of the town in
which I taught. I earned that much because I had a masters degree in
English and an additional thirty credits, some of which I had to earn
if I wanted to teach special education. And I wanted to. My student
load in a regular class was one hundred sixty. In special ed, it was

fifteen to twenty-eight. When I went back to teaching in regular education (we really called it that) I had two hundred and ten students. It was time to retire. As an incentive, the district offered me a golden handshake, two years retirement credit, and a wooden plaque.

Having heard that teachers burned out, a favorite student of mine asked, "What does that mean, Ms. Walsh? Is that what happened to you?"

Burnout is commonly used to describe teachers who can't take it anymore. City teachers are described as shell-shocked. At our school, the teacher who went up in flames, so to speak, was the youngest teacher in the school. One Friday afternoon she drove her Bronco clear across campus to her classroom door, loaded up her paraphernalia, and rode off into the sunset.

I did not leave teaching because I was burned out. I left because I was burned up. I have taught in both New York and California; in the inner city, the suburbs, and a rural town; in public and parochial schools; at the elementary, junior, and senior high school levels; in special education and regular classes.

This is not a book sponsored by grants, nor is it based on years of research from the university. It is the simple testimony of a classroom teacher based on thirty years of observations and conclusions. Much of the book comes from my teaching experience from 1970 to 1992 in the Anaheim Union High School District in the shadow of Disneyland. I taught at Walker Junior High in La Palma, a town with a profile typical of southern suburban California. The population was fifteen thousand, twenty-eight percent of which was foreign born. Eighty-nine percent of the parents graduated from high school and thirty-two percent held college degrees. Eighteen percent of the nine hundred twenty students were Asian, fifteen percent Hispanic, and four percent African American.

Like the schools of the majority of American children, Walker is a suburban school. Although suburban schools like Walker do not suffer the poverty, violence, and drugs prevalent in inner city schools, they have similar problems in weaker dimensions which intensify every year.

# Chapter 1

# Out of the Loop

During the past decade, an aggressive campaign for reform in public elementary and secondary schools barreled its way across the country. The media spewed a multitude of bright ideas on school renewal from businessmen, politicians, professors, union leaders—everyone but the teachers.

Every document in the debate declared that raising teacher status is essential to education reform and not one addressed the contradiction of trying to raise teacher status while excluding teachers from the debate.

## Exclusion of Teachers in School Reform

Patricia Albjerg Graham, in her *S.O.S.: Save Our Schools*, writes that educators as a group are not leaders in the reform, and accepting that, she expounds ways to reform the schools despite them.[1] Tracy Kidder, whose bestseller was a book on building a house, spent nine months in a Massachusetts school to write the book *Among School Children.*[2] Emily Sachar worked for a year as an eighth-grade public school teacher to research for *Shut Up and Let the Woman Teach.*[3] Samuel Feldman spent three years in the public schools of Chicago to produce his poignant *Small Victories.*[4] Noteworthy as they are, reports of the classroom from non-teachers are views from the rear window.

Journalists Catherine Collins and Douglas Frantz published a collection of interviews with teachers,[5] as did Susan Dichter.[6] Both books give actual views of teachers on poignant issues. What is needed next is teachers' own unedited discussion of the schools.

I read *A Nation at Risk, A Nation Prepared, Who Will Teach Our Children, Caught in the Middle,* and *Horace's Compromise.*[7] I read discourses from professors at the universities, researchers from the institutes, businessmen on Wall Street, observers in Japan. All the reports presented material about classroom teachers; few of them presented material from classroom teachers.

Albert Shanker has probably done more to raise the economic status of classroom teachers than any other single individual, but his achievements as a union leader do not make him an authority on teaching. When reporters cite him as an expert in curriculum or classroom organization, they undermine classroom teachers whose undiluted opinions ought to be the stuff of their reports.

In the introductory notes to *Savage Inequalities,* Jonathan Kozol admits that it was a long time since he'd been with children in the public schools.[8] Theodore Sizer in *Horace's Compromise* says that although he has a historian's training and experience in higher education, his point of view is that of schoolteacher.[9] But the point of view of a schoolteacher must come from a schoolteacher. The Paideia Group of the famous *Paideia Proposal* for the public schools included not one teacher.

In the foreword to his report on secondary education in America, Ernest Boyer said that he asked the help of a national panel of teachers, principals, superintendents, university administrators, parents, school board members, and citizen representatives.[10] But while the published list includes four principals, a superintendent, and two union leaders, it does not have a single classroom teacher, unless, of course, to be included, classroom teachers must be named by more prestigious titles.

Bruce Romanish, a professor of education at St. Cloud State University in Minnesota, wrote *Empowering Teachers: Restructuring Schools for the 21st Century* to advise teachers of their nonexistent role in the renewal of education.[11] A perusal of the major reform documents proves him correct.

The commission for *Who Will Teach Our Children*: A *Strategy For Improving California's Schools* was composed of seventeen members, six of whom were women, two of whom were classroom teachers.[12] Their list of forty-three witnesses includes six classroom teachers.

*Caught in the Middle* was presented to California middle schools as a manual for reform designed by classroom teachers. The credits page, however, clearly lists administrators.[13]

In the national spotlight, the schools do not reflect the fact that they are predominantly a female occupation. Standing amid a circle of men, in a room full of men, President Clinton accepted philanthropist Walter Annenberg's $500-million dollar contribution to the schools. The money, he said, would support the work and programs of men like Sizer and David Kearns.[14]

In his book *Why Johnny Can't Tell Right from Wrong*, William K. Kilpatrick declared that teachers are not reliable in education reform because their idyllic imagination prevents them from seeing what is really needed in the schools.[15] According to Kilpatrick, most of the problems in the schools stem from the desire of teachers to avoid the hard work of teaching; yet, after a single year in the schools, Kilpatrick left to become a university professor. Now he's in the university department of education teaching future teachers, his idyllic imagination apparently cured.

## History of Excluding Teachers in School Reform

Not only are classroom teachers excluded in the reform literature today, but they have also been ignored in virtually every reform since the beginning of American education. This is evident in histories such as Diane Ravitch's *The Great School Wars* which traces the cycles of reform in New York City's public schools from

1805 to 1973. As Ravitch notes in her preface, parallels to the history of school reform in New York City can be found in the history of national school reform. In New York City then, and one can assume in most American school districts, university and business people, not teachers, had the power in school reform.[16]

According to Ravitch, in 1893 a "well-bred," upper-class group of mostly men started the Good Government Club E to reform the schools.[17] They were joined by the PEA (Public Education Association), an assortment of wealthy ladies including the mayor's wife. Ravitch calls the PEA's mission to tell the teachers how to run the schools "blatantly patronizing."[18]

The situation is typical of American education: the powerful and the wealthy from outside the schools impose change upon the menial teachers. In 1893, a teacher wrote to the *School*, a teachers' magazine, "Why should we be invited to their 'teas' and waited on by these estimable ladies? [Their] children do not come to our schools. We do not expect that Mrs. Levi P. Morton will drive up to our schools in the governor's open barouche to take us on a ride in the Park of an afternoon."[19] Teachers knew the score then and they know it now.

Both the PEA and Club E developed into political bastions for Nicholas Murray Butler, the first president of the teacher training institution that later became Teachers College of Columbia University. Butler also patronized the teachers. As president of a teachers' college, you would think that he would want to work for the professionalization of teachers so they could better run the schools. On the contrary, he lobbied for a central board of professionals to run the schools. Butler's condescension toward teachers cultivated the division that prevails today between the teachers who labor in the schools and the university professors who consider them incapable of either evaluating the schools or participating in education reform.[20]

One of the most powerful education reforms was progressive education. Its most prominent document, *The Cardinal Principles*, was written in 1918 by professors of education, secondary principals, educational bureaucrats, and a college president. Ravitch indicates that this group was more representative of the schools than earlier education committees.[21] Representation of the schools, however, never meant representation of the teachers. Progressive education, like every education reform before or since, was formulated without teacher input and foisted upon the schools without teacher preparation.

Progressive education, ironically enough, was designed to foster democratic principles in children, stressing their dignity and their right to choose. Hollis Caswell, dean of Teachers College, Butler's old haunt, suggested that principals fire teachers who refused to follow the progressive goals set up for them. One principal fired half the faculty and replaced them with teachers who knew better than to disobey orders. So much for democratic principles and freedom of choice.[22]

The point is not the educational value of progressive education; the point is that it was imposed upon the schools without the input of classroom teachers. Had teachers been involved in its evaluation, progressive education would have been less radical and far more sensibly applied to the schools.

Ravitch's entire history reads like a litany of school agendas designed to exclude teachers. When in 1893 a state commission was established to reform schools, Mayor Thomas Gilroy refused to let teachers have a representative on it.[23] In 1897, Charles Bulkley Hubbell, president of the New York City board of education, started three high schools but refused to allow any teachers in the city's schools to serve as principals. In 1910, a city committee appointed to scrutinize school operations declared that teachers had no part in designing curriculum or choosing texts. In 1915, Mayor John Purroy Mitchel adopted the Gary Plan into the schools without consulting school personnel.[24]

Ravitch's *Troubled Crusade* describes teacher resistance to the National Science Foundation (NSF) and Richard Nixon's Experimental Schools Program. NSF had assembled the nation's best scholars, revised courses of study to reflect the latest knowledge and the best methodology, yet the schools remained essentially untouched.[25] Local officials could order teachers to participate in inservice training, but they could not force them to support the program. NSF did not know that, nor did ABC, nor XYZ, nor the countless reformers of the schools.

The universities have tried to reform schools without teacher input throughout history; they do it today. Speaking about the recent Boston University/Chelsea School District partnership, James

Nehring, a high school teacher, remarks that, "What B.U. proposed, and got, was essentially carte blanche to reorganize the schools in exchange for money and 'expert' management. This was not a partnership. It was a hostile takeover."[26]

Not only the university reformers, but also school administrators have excluded teachers from school reform. School districts throughout the land imposed innovation much the way it was imposed on the Anaheim school district. In 1961, the Anaheim school board implemented the new flexible scheduling originated by Lloyd Trunk of Stanford University. Louise Booth, district historian, notes that under the principal, Gardner Swenson, the new scheduling "burst like a bombshell" at Brookhurst Junior High.[27] Knowing the scheduling was imminent, twenty-seven of fifty-nine teachers chose not to return to the school. The following year, another twenty-seven teachers did not return, the next year seventeen, and the next eleven. The teachers not only knew that their opinion and concern mattered about as much as the color of a new textbook, but also that any opposition on their part would bring recriminations. Booth, a teacher herself, writes that some of the "braver ones" dared to voice their frustrations.

Flexible scheduling required another administrator on campus, a program coordinator, and entirely new planning procedures by the teachers, for which they received no training. Not only the teachers but also the parents were unhappy with the new program, claiming that their children were too young to choose their own courses and flexibly scheduled themselves out of a solid education. The board was as unresponsive to the parents as it was to the teachers. It maintained flexible scheduling at Brookhurst until Principal Swenson accepted a position out of the district. By then, Trunk's colleagues over at Stanford had decided that his theory was good but the practice uncertain.

Joseph Fernandez relates that as assistant principal in his Florida high school he had the clout he needed to push similar scheduling but it failed there, too.[28] In my opinion, it failed because the "clout" didn't come from the teachers. It was not that flexible scheduling was wrong; something has to be done with the traditional scheduling that carves the school day into brittle pieces. The problem was the implementation of change without regard to teachers.

❋   ❋   ❋   ❋   ❋

*In planning a grant project for Walker, I suggested teaching half of the students science and math the first semester and English and social studies the second. In this way, students would have four academic classes instead of six. Each teacher would halve her student load and lesson preparation. The media center and the science and math labs would halve the number of students using them. Most of all, since this is always a primary concern in the schools, the plan would require no extra dollars.*

*Before school one morning, I called a voluntary meeting to discuss the idea. All of those who showed at the meeting, including our innovative principal, were supportive. We wanted and needed to know a great deal more than could be explored in a half-hour faculty meeting, but we were teachers eager to find new ways to improve the learning of our students.*

*Since we didn't get the grant or the time to study the schedule proposal, we never determined whether it was feasible. But if we had received the grant, the Walker program would have had teacher input from the planning stage until the implementation, unlike the Brookhurst flexible scheduling which was imposed upon teachers who had no vote in its introduction, no training in its procedures, and no part in its success evaluation.*

## Exclusion of Women in School Reform

Nearly three-fourths of public school teachers are women. A survey by the National Educational Association found that the percentage of male teachers is at its lowest point since the NEA first measured the female-male ratio in 1961.[29] Romanish says that teachers would be startled to know that of the 132 people who sat on the six major school reform panels of the 1980s, only three were teachers. I am not startled. My guess is that of those three teachers, two or more were men and that's a conservative guess. The *AAUW Report* declares that of the thirty-five commissions, task forces, or board of directors that they studied, only two groups had at least fifty percent female representation.[30]

Ninety percent of the literature for education reform presented to classroom teachers in schools of education and in inservice training is written by men and has been since the days of Horace

Mann and John Dewey. Kidder notes that a surprising number of education reform books were written by men.[31] Ravitch lists the education reformers of the 1960s: Paul Goodman, Herbert Kohl, Edgar Friedenberg, Nat Hentoff, John Holt, and Kozol. If I listed all the names she cites in her 160-year history of New York City's schools, I might find three women. *The Great School Debate* lists ninety-two people in its "Who's Who in the Great Debate." Fourteen of those people are women and, of course, none are teachers.[32]

Men who write books about change in education write with the advice and support of men. In *A Place Called School*, John I. Goodlad credits an "Advisory Committee to A Study of Schooling."[33] The committee's six members are all men, two administrators and four university professors. Of the twenty-seven members of the Paideia Group, three are women. Their book is dedicated to three great teachers, all of whom, of course, are men.[34]

Reform literature written by men reflects the bias of men. It was the male authors of *Cardinal Principles* who declared college-preparatory studies particularly incongruous with the actual needs and future responsibilities of girls, while they deemed homemaking equal to any other school work.

Reform literature written by men reflects the experiences of men as if the schools are predominantly male. Sizer's Horace, as in Horace "Man," is a male, as are most of the teachers Sizer uses to illustrate his arguments. The only able woman teacher in his book worth noting at all is a nun. Mark and Dennis, the students he describes at length to illustrate students' predicaments, are boys, as are most of his student examples. In *Horace's School* the movement for reform is led, of course, by "Horace Smith, who had been vocal and persuasive about the need to re-evaluate his school." Horace is supported by Patches, the history teacher who is "smart and influential, though exasperating." Women teachers are arranged along the sidelines in cheerleader fashion. One is "tall, silver-haired, a woman stuffed with sense and principle [who] had a small smile on her face, but her eyes were focused on the vast crochet project that spilled around her feet." Another, Green, "looked down as she spoke...the older talkative faculty, particularly the males, threatened her."[35]

There is a distinct impression throughout the reform literature that schools are failing, but that they are failing male children more.

The number of recently proposed educational programs designed specifically for African-American male children say exactly that. President George Bush gave support for such schools, even though the Office for Civil Rights in 1989 declared them illegal in Dade County, Florida. For years statistics showed that girls did not do well in science and math, but until the *AAUW Report* no one advocated science programs for girls.

## Devaluation of Women in Reform Literature

Not only are women excluded in the reform literature, but they are also degraded in it. Rita Kramer spent two years observing four university education departments across the country. Her observations indicate that if there's any hope at all of education reform, it must come through male educators. Every woman she meets, whether professor or student, is of inferior quality. "Professor Klein has an image problem as a professor. She does not seem professorial. She is—no other word will do—cute." Kramer further remarks, "Perhaps it was a coincidence, but one of the liveliest and most interesting classes I visited was also the one with the largest number of young men."[36] Of another class with more male students she observed, "It seemed to me the students were more alert, more focused, than the elementary group I'd seen earlier...they were more intelligent, more articulate.... Perhaps the students in this class and others like them would be the new monks, keeping learning alive in a new kind of academic dark age."[37] Maybe so, but it was the women who kept learning alive in American elementary and secondary education through most of its history.

In books on school reform, women teachers embody the traditional negative stereotypes of teachers: they are weak, meek, and narrow-minded. Nehring suggests that men teachers seek reform more aggressively. In his *Schools We Have, Schools We Want,* "a tale, not a report," two male teachers press for school innovation despite disheartening obstacles. By the end of the book, only the male protagonist has the stamina to continue. Ellie Gross Hartig, the sole female teacher to get involved, did it "as a friendly gesture toward the new principal."[38]

Kilpatrick evinces a condescending attitude towards teachers in general and women in particular. He professes a respect for the

Catholic church and its schools; yet he attributes the decimation of a well-respected Catholic teaching order to the influence of one man, as if the nuns were fatuous school girls disappointed by a leading man on campus. He says it was Carl Rogers and his education project who caused 600 Sisters of the Immaculate Heart of Mary to leave the order. In fact, the nuns did not simply leave the order. They became a lay community in order to implement reforms without the restrictions of the Congregation of Religious Institutes, a Vatican governing body. Kilpatrick doesn't discuss the influence of the second Vatican council on these women, nor the effect of the women's movement, nor the fact that nuns were deserting the monastic life in droves around the world.[39]

## Devaluation of Experienced Teachers in the Reform

Male professions ennoble age. Senators and lawyers increase in prestige as they grow old. Judges are granted positions for life and enjoy them through their eighth decade. Supreme Court justices begin their terms at an age when most people retire. Byron J. White retired from the Supreme Court at age eighty-five. At age seventy, Senator Robert Dole is running for president in the next election. In politics, the first assessment made is whether the candidate has experience in foreign affairs, domestic issues, any issue. Society considers these men, despite their age, capable of contributing to their field—but teachers with many years experience are considered a liability.

Every professor of education I ever met, whether on the pages of a book, in a school of education, or at a dais during a convention, believed that classroom teachers who taught for many years were the major obstacles for progress in education. Professors' most common flattery to teachers-in-training was that they would become a breed apart from those presently in the schools. Their cleverest witticisms ridiculed the methods and ideas of those with many years in the classroom.

Disregard for experienced teachers explains why it is difficult to make advances in education. The people who become the experts after years of experience are the first to be rejected and the last to be heeded. Even Nehring, a teacher himself, reflects that attitude. He describes recruitment of teachers for a renewal proposal. "Joe had been teaching for twenty-five years. It would not serve the cause to tell him he just needed to have vision, to see the possibilities." Joe's vision was "clouded" and "stacked the odds against the possible in favor of the status quo."[40]

During my teaching career the same belief prevailed throughout the school district among administrators and teachers themselves, even though every new program from technology to the writing process to cooperative learning to back to the basics was implemented by those who had been teaching for years.

❋ ❋ ❋ ❋ ❋

*For five years, for example, I badgered the district and the union to initiate what I've since learned is called shared decision-making. Mostly as a lark, but also to start discussion, I sent a form to every teacher in the district asking her to rate her principal on shared decisions. Every school but one returned the forms signed from about 30 percent of the teachers. I declared the highest scoring administrator "principal of the year," figuring that if the administrators could choose teacher of the year, we could repay in kind. It turned out that the winning principal was one several teachers considered as willing to share decisions as a poker player holding four aces. Elizabeth Jackman, the principal at Walker, who should have won, came in second. She was energetic, charismatic, and valued not only her own creativity but that of those around her. So my survey wasn't scientifically exact (I had no access to the Rand Corporation), but it convinced me that teachers, young and old, wanted shared decision-making.*

*In typical bureaucratic fashion, both the district and the union declared that before shared decision-making could be implemented a study had to be made by a joint committee and the committee had to be negotiated in the teachers' contract. In 1990, the contract stipulated the right to establish a teacher/administrator committee to study the feasibility, not the implementation, of shared decision-making. In 1992, after an entire school year and seven meetings, the committee concluded that because many of the teachers in the district had been teaching for twenty years or more they were not ready for something as radical as shared decision-making. The committee recommended a pilot program at one school.*

## Teacher Evaluation of Reform

The problem is not that experienced teachers resist reform; it's that experienced teachers are not recognized as evaluators of reform. When they reject change, experienced teachers have valid reasons. Recently, Alice Sullivan, a thirty-year teacher, called me for information on technology in the elementary classroom. She was eagerly gathering resources and would probably give hours of her own time to the project. She was also enthused about the "writing process," a contemporary method of teaching writing. About "inventive spelling," a program newly introduced to the school, she was not so sure. She was not trained in inventive spelling and no one had convinced her of the wisdom of encouraging second graders to invent spelling for words instead of learning how to spell sounds. She didn't think a child would learn by osmosis what "ch" sounds like. She supported change where she saw the need, resisted it where she saw peril.

An example of how experienced teachers' evaluation of reform is ignored is the installation of assertive discipline at Walker and hundreds of districts throughout the country.

✳   ✳   ✳   ✳   ✳

*Picture it.*

*At seven-fifteen, on a hot October morning, with the temperature expected to reach the high nineties, the principal calls for a faculty meeting of two hours instead of the usual forty-five minutes. He gets the extra time by declaring a shortened day, which means the students will come in an hour later. Teachers will not get less work to compensate for this meeting. Teachers never get less work; they merely get delayed work. Instead of seeing six classes for forty-five minutes, today I will see six for thirty minutes with a three-minute break between each class. I am disposed to reject this early morning faculty meeting, whatever it is about.*

*I have no agenda before time, although I've heard sinister rumors. The guest speaker, a businessman with an attaché case, shows a film called "Assertive Discipline" starring an eloquent salesman named Lee Cantor.*[41] *In a well-modulated voice, he slowly explains the film to us. He says that Cantor's Assertive Discipline has been implemented in schools across the country with remarkable success. It is based on a set of rules which are posted in every classroom. Every time a student breaks a rule, his name goes on the board as a warning. For the second offense, the offender gets a check mark. After the third one, the offender is assigned a punishment, like detention, which the teacher shall arrange on her own time. If a student repeatedly interrupts the class, he may be dismissed from the room to the office, but only with notification in writing.*

*"How can a teacher interrupt a lesson to jot names on the board?" someone asks.*

*"Very simple," says our guest, and sure enough he demonstrates by jotting down the names of the next three people who interrupt his spiel.*

*Lest anyone think the program totally negative and confining, there are also rewards to students who obey all the rules. They get "catch them doing something right" coupons. Using any method she has time to devise, the teacher observes who is obeying the rules and awards them a coupon which may be redeemed for soda at the student store, or a raffle ticket for a monthly drawing, or some other equally valuable prize.*

*As wonderfully comic as the entire presentation is, no one laughs. Three-fourths of the faculty believe it's an asinine idea. One-fourth say so and the speaker continues.*

*"With this method, the entire school will be uniform in its discipline. Students will not get confused or be able to feign ignorance of the rules in any class."*

*And more of the same.*

*The principal tells us he will establish a schoolwide detention hall with teachers taking turns so that everyone can share detention duty and not have to stay after school all the time. But I am remembering that when I stay after school it's to meet with students who want help or who hang around because they have nothing better to do.*

*"The program will help the weaker teachers" he tells me when I object. But most of Walker's faculty has been teaching at least fifteen years. If they weren't strong by now, I say, give it up. If it's the few new teachers who are weak, they need fieldwork with an experienced peer, not fancy footwork from Cantor.*

*During the thirty-minute lunch, I trade protest strategies with my buddy, Fil Forsyth, the foreign language teacher, and others of our cadre, but I have already determined my plan of action. I will simply ignore Cantor and his discipline.*

*Within the week, however, a large laminated sign with the class rules in bold black print is carried to my door by a student office assistant who has been directed to post it somewhere in the room. I give it a spot conveniently obstructed by a file cabinet. The "catch them doing something right" coupons I use as rewards for class races like memorizing the highest number of lines in a favorite poem, devising a Logo program with the lowest number of steps, preparing to leave with the least amount of disorder. The coupons become so popular, I often need to replenish my store. The student store advisor thinks I'm over my quota.*

*My resistance to Assertive Discipline stemmed from my indignation that we teachers had never been afforded time or opportunity to analyze what was wrong with the classroom management already in existence. If the time and opportunity had been granted, I think we would have recognized that asking students to sit still all day in periods of forty-five minutes did not work as it used to and other new approaches would have been explored.*

*When I left Walker, the rolled-up rules chart lay somewhere on a dusty shelf in a back cupboard next to a box of unused "catch them doing something right" coupons.*

## Movement for Technology in the Schools

Despite all the planning, research, and mandates that went into education reforms, few of them had any more lasting effect than did Cantor's Assertive Discipline. That's because few of them were designed with teacher involvement. Even as reformers analyzed the reasons for the failures of education reform, teachers continued to be systematically excluded in the formation of change in the schools.

The movement towards technology further illustrates my point. The *Investor's Business Daily* recently declared that despite all the energy, time, and money devoted to computers, most schools give computer use in the schools an F.[42] I consider that a generous grade. As computer coordinator at Walker, I worked and shared notes with teachers from all over California. My time with them convinced me that the Anaheim experience was typical.

❈    ❈    ❈    ❈    ❈

*About ten years ago when the Anaheim district moved to implement computer technology, a number of teachers already had computer expertise. Several of them worked closely with Computer Using Educa-*

*tors (CUE) and were leading training workshops. At Walker, Don Geldbach had been teaching mentally gifted minors computer programming in collaboration with the Digital Company. The district didn't assign any of these teachers to be Administrator of Educational Technology. Instead, it gave that position to a librarian who had no experience at all in computers. One of the first things that administrator did was ask a group of these teachers to write guidelines for computer implementation in the schools.*

*The task was programmed to fail. First of all, the teachers were given only two weeks during the summer to create this district plan. Secondly, the teachers had difficulty communicating with the administrator who, although she was one of the most cordial people in the district, didn't understand the technology. Third, although they owned and operated computers themselves, and completed the cost analysis, the teachers had no control over the budget. Lastly, once the guidelines were written, the teachers lost all responsibility for the plan. They were not expected to evaluate its success or empowered to mandate changes.*

*During the next few years, the district spent over a million dollars to incorporate technology in administration, for recording grades, reporting absences, and forwarding mail from the district office to the sites. Technology was helping us track, tally, and penalize students, but it was not inspiring learning or helping teachers teach. Every secretary in the district had a computer on her desk, but no money was allocated to put computers in the hands of teachers or students.*

*Money for classroom computers had to come from fundraisers initiated by teachers or grants also written by teachers. Both fundraising and grant writing required hours of time for which neither the principal nor the teachers were compensated. More than that, teachers had to make time on top of an already crowded day. Sometimes substitute teachers were hired to give teachers time during the school day, but, as usual, such days do not give teachers less work, only shifted work. First of all, teachers have to prepare lesson plans for substitute teachers. Secondly, they need to review any work the students have done for the substitute teacher which, in effect, is holding a day's work on the shelf until the teacher gets to it.*

*At the state level, California educators recognized the need to include teachers in planning technology implementation. Every state technology grant application required evidence of site staff support. Since 1983, when Walker received several grants and bought its first computers, we struggled to finance and maintain technology on campus. In 1990, the superintendent summarily decided that only seven schools in the district would be allowed to apply for a particularly attractive grant. Walker was not among them. Because at least eighty percent of the Walker staff wanted to try for the grant, including the principal who didn't know why Walker had been excluded, I called the superintendent to seek an explanation.*

*"I want to see more accountability at Walker," she told me.*

*It seems Walker's writing scores on some standard test had gone down. It didn't matter that the scores had not gone down for years before, when the school had been given no compensating privileges. It didn't matter that Walker was now absorbing a larger number of non-English-speaking students. It didn't even matter that the technology grant had no direct relation to the test scores.*

*Other sources at the district office told me that the superintendent wanted to eliminate Walker and several other successful grant-writing schools so that less fortunate schools could have a better chance. But that was the very scenario the state tried to eliminate: schools applying for grants at the impetus of the district rather than that of the site staff.*

*Two years ago, and eight years too late, the Anaheim district devised a master plan for the implementation of technology throughout the district. Eight committees were formed. Only teachers recommended by administrators were invited to serve on the committees. The planning team was composed of ten administrators and two teachers, only one of whom had been involved in technology on the school site.*

✳  ✳  ✳  ✳  ✳

In short, the technology reform in education is crippled, as are most other education reforms, because teachers who have the most responsibility for its implementation have the least to say in its planning.

## How Women Teachers Are Silenced in the Reform Movement

Why women teachers have not vociferously objected to the condescending attitude of education reformers and why they have not demanded to be heard in the reform movement can be understood in the light of writings like Gerda Lerner's *The Creation of*

*Feminist Consciousness.* She declares that the unending familial obligations imposed on them made concentrated attention to professional writing difficult if not impossible for women.[43] Most education reformers have wives who take care of their personal and family needs so they could exert their powerful influence on the schools. Most of them admit this in their acknowledgements and introductions. Fernandez, for example, is unstinting in his thanks to his wife, Dolores. The women educators I've known, although they held full-time jobs, were also fully responsible for family and housework. This was true even if both husband and wife were teachers. It was true thirty years ago and it is true today.

Studies like Betty Friedan's *The Feminine Mystique*,[44] Susan Faludi's *Backlash*,[45] and Nan Robertson's *The Girls in the Balcony*[46] describe how the voices of women have been muted in politics, business, and entertainment. The same forces have silenced women in the schools.

Women in education are, as President Bush would have said, "out of the loop," because the positions of power belong to men. The roster of powerful names in American education down through the years reads like the Senate roll call: Horace Mann, John Dewey, Ernest Boyer, Theodore Sizer, John Goodlad, and on and on.

There have been six Secretaries of Education since the position was inaugurated and only one of them was a woman, Shirley Hufstedler. Although she is an education advocate, it is significant that Hufstedler is a distinguished lawyer, not an educator. The Association of American University Women reports that in 1991 only nine of the fifty chief state school officers were women.[47]

As much as I delight in the rags to riches Fernandez story, I suspect that partnership in the typical school male club boosted his efforts. He became friends with his first principal, who made him department head at his next school. Fernandez in turn hired his buddy from the faculty softball team. When he became superintendent another buddy became his number one aide. It is not that there's anything wrong with hiring one's buddies. It's that buddies tend to be of the same sex. Fernandez's story is filled with the names of men who form circles of power that spin the wheels of Dade County's schools. There are a couple of women who rise, one of whom he wants to succeed him when he leaves, but of course she doesn't, not having access to the circles of power that her competitor has.

Districts thrive on the traditions imposed on them through the decades by superintendents. In honor of its bicentennial, the Albany (New York) School District published its history: the story of nine superintendents, all of whom were male, all of whom served as administrators for two decades or more.[48] They left an enduring, totally male legacy, which for years promoted only male administrators, especially at the district level.

As Faludi notes, "Women, feminist or otherwise, account for a mere ten percent of the tenured faculty at all four-year institutions (and a mere three to four percent at Ivy League colleges)—a rise of only six percent from the 1960s."[49] Jane White in *A Few Good Women* summarizes the same sad facts. "What boggles the mind," she says "is that even in the realm of academia—the 'accepted' environment for women—the numbers are just as dismal.... Although approximately two-thirds of all public school teachers are women, only five percent of the nations's superintendents are female."[50]

Cynthia Grennan is one of the five percent. She became Anaheim's first female superintendent in 1979. After her appointment, it wasn't safe to assume that every woman in the district office was a secretary. During her tenure more women became administrators than under the combined tenure of the five superintendents before her and it is possible that many of those she chose were friends, part of her buddy system.

## Devaluation of Teachers in the Schools

Another major reason why teachers have not been heard in the reform is their subordinate position in the schools. While Grennan moved toward equity by appointing women to administration, she did little to dissolve the inequity imposed on women as well as men in the classroom.

Until Grennan, the teachers who were department chairs elected one of their members to serve as district department chair. Grennan decreed that instead of teachers electing one of their own for the job, an assigned administrator would do it. Special education teachers, for example, met with a junior high principal, a former coach with no experience in special ed and no time in his busy job as principal to get any.

Anaheim district standard procedures undermine teachers. The district's newspaper, *Reporter*, for example, clearly demonstrates teachers' status. Almost every front page article features the superintendent. My favorite is the issue of the smiling superintendent holding a golden school bell presented annually by the California School Boards Association for the "most creative and effective instructional programs in the state."[51] The teacher responsible for the program is mentioned in the last line of the second paragraph.

When students receive prestigious scholastic trophies and honors for outstanding programs, the school board recognizes them at a public meeting. One year, three of our high schools placed first, second, and third in Orange County's "Mock Trial" program. In the light of news cameras, the participating students accompanied by the school principal came forward to receive congratulations from the school board and superintendent. The classroom teacher responsible for inaugurating and nurturing the program was neither present nor acknowledged. Incidentally, under the same circumstances, I have never seen a sports team honored without notable recognition of its coach.

All district school newsletters feature a column by the principal and often his or her photo. Individual teachers may or may not be featured. It could be argued that the school newsletters are vehicles of the principals, just as the district newspaper is the vehicle of the superintendent, and therefore are intended to inform the public about the people in charge. That message seems clear.

❋　❋　❋　❋　❋

*In the Walker Junior High School Parent-Teacher-Student Association Program and Directory for the 1991-1992 school year, the faculty is listed after the PTSA Board, the Board of Trustees, the administrators, the counselors, the clerical staff, the special services staff, the custodial staff, and the cafeteria staff.*

*At the end of the school year Walker teachers, like teachers across the nation, honor outstanding students at an awards assembly. On each certificate of award a line is printed for the principal's signature. I had to draw a line on each certificate for my signature, which I thought was at least as important as the principal's, since I was conferring the award.*

*During the end of the year promotion exercises, the final highlight of the school year, the principal, assistant principal, and the counselors go on stage before the community, parents, and promotees to call out the names of the students and present the certificates of promotion. The teachers remain in the classrooms to supervise the seventh graders, direct lines to the cafetorium, and assume crowd control on the school grounds.*

*In its evaluation of teachers, the public takes its cue from the districts. When the local Chamber of Commerce, for instance, wants to hear from the schools, it calls upon a school administrator, or if they want more stature, the superintendent. A classroom teacher as guest speaker minimizes the event.*

*When the town of Brea built a new high school, the* Brea Community Accents, *a paper distributed at the town mall, featured an issue on the school. The paper published photos and interviews of some students and seven school personnel: the principal, assistant principals, and counselors. Not one classroom teacher was highlighted.*[52]

*Some effort has been recently made by business, political, and media leaders to counteract the low status of teachers. The president greets the National Teacher of the Year. Disney hosts an annual televised awards ceremony for outstanding teachers. It is as effective as* Queen for a Day.

❋   ❋   ❋   ❋   ❋

William Bennett, former Secretary of Education, declared that "the most striking feature of education reform today is the relative lack of progress—the relative lack of results."[53] Considering the enfeebled position of its teachers, it is remarkable that the schools make any progress at all.

# Chapter 2

# Raising Hell

Belittling education is as popular an American pastime as honoring baseball. Nostalgia for the old school house is replete not with love of learning but with the wild antics of its schoolboys and the blackboard caricatures of its wicked school teachers. In Betty Ballantine's essay on Charles Wysocki's painting of one, she calls the one-room school house a place in which to "raise a little hell once in a while" and to beware of the "dragon who headed it."[1]

Unwittingly, Ballantine has described the basic American attitude towards school: its teachers are subjects of ridicule and its disrupters are merry mischief-makers. Ruth S. Freeman in *Yesterdays' Schools* fondly notes that the propensity which distinguished the American schoolboy was carving on the old wooden desks, sometimes with markings that would make heathens blush.[2] Typically modest about their scholastic achievements, Americans boast most about their own hell raising in school.

*Even as he proffered utmost cooperation, every father I ever talked to about his son's antics in class admitted a bit proudly that the boy was a chip off the old block:*
*"You think he's bad. You should've seen me in school."*
*No matter how bright or academically competent students are when I teach them, whenever they come back to reminisce they sound like classmates of the Dirty Dozen.*
*"Do you remember how awful we were, the worst kids in the school, weren't we? Didn't we drive you clear out of your mind?"*
*I hate to disappoint them with the truth, but I do.*

In short, no matter how much they learn there, Americans see school primarily as a place where they evaded learning. Americans scorn schooling. Their most popular heroes have been self-made, unschooled men, starting with that giant of colonial America, Benjamin Franklin. Franklin started school at age eight and quit at ten, but he did more with his two years of schooling than any ten Yale graduates do with twenty. Abe Lincoln had less than a year of schooling, studied law from a book he found in the bottom of a barrel, and with not a single course in public speaking beat in debate the erudite Stephen Douglas. Without book learning, Andrew Carnegie built a fortune for which business majors would cheerfully risk prison twice. We could as soon picture Daniel Boone and Davy Crockett in a school house as we could an eagle nesting in a bird house.

Those who would reform the schools need to consider the paradox of American culture: it praises education but scorns schooling. The predicament of American teachers is that they are expected to educate a population that mocks school. When he states that Americans have always valued education, William Bennett seems to imply that respect for schooling is inherent in American culture.[3] Wrong, wrong, wrong, incontestably wrong. Americans respect education that comes without schooling.

## Schooling in American Literature

That derision of schooling inherent in American culture is demonstrated in American literature. Ichabod Crane, that early American schoolmaster, is a bungling buffoon, myopic, eccentric, inept. His very name means "inglorious" and he is not an attractive fellow:

> His head was small, and flat at the top, with huge ears, large green glassy eyes, and a long snipe nose, so that it looked like a weathercock, perched upon his spindle neck, to tell which way the wind blew. To see him striding along the profile of a hill on a windy day, with his clothes bagging and fluttering about him, one might have mistaken him for the genius of famine descending upon the earth, or some scarecrow eloped from a cornfield.[4]

His fondest hope is to be rich enough to get out of teaching. "Then, he thought, how soon he'd turn his back upon the old schoolhouse; and kick any itinerant pedagogue out of doors that should dare to call him comrade!"[5]

Huckleberry Finn, that favorite American boy, echoes that favorite American feeling: "At first I hated the school, but by and by I got so I could stand it."[6] Huck learned far more on a raft than he could as a schoolboy, who is exemplified less by the clever Tom Sawyer than by his obnoxious brother, Sidney. While the noble figures of Huck's world, like himself and Jim, are unlettered, the nefarious characters are those with book-learning, like the duke and the king.

In *Catcher in the Rye,* Holden Caulfield's saga starts when he plays hooky from the hated and hateful prep school, Pencey.[7]

## Schooling in the Popular Culture

Neil Postman in *Teaching As a Conserving Activity* defines television as the second curriculum. While television's place in the curriculum is debatable, its role as purveyor of the common culture is not.

From Fonzy to the boys of *Welcome Back Kotter* to Mike in *Growing Pains,* television's most popular youths have been those who have had the least respect for schooling. The wonder of Michael J. Fox is that he rose to stardom playing an attractive, smart Alex on a family sitcom. Usually smart children are clumsy oddballs in thick rimmed glasses like Paul in *The Wonder Years* or brazen brats like *Mr. Belvedeere's* Wesley who charm us with their adorable disruption of school and the delightful torment they heap upon imbecilic principals and naive teachers. The epitome of the hell-raising mentality is Bart Simpson, neither animal nor human, wearing a t-shirt emblazoned with his coat of arms, "Underachiever and Proud of It." His sister, Lisa, is Miss Goody Two-Shoes. She does well in school and is hated equally by Bart and his admirers.

A television special designed, I think, to inspire young people, featured Bill Cosby, Howie Mandel, and Roseanne returning to their old schools. Much of what they said was inspirational indeed, but all of it undermined by their witty anecdotes about what great clowns they were in school and what mighty havoc they imposed upon the unsuspecting faculty.

The humor of many cartoon characters lies in their relentless struggle against schooling. Dennis the Menace battles the studious Margaret, Archie confronts the battle-axe Miss Grundy, and for Calvin it is the pointer-armed ogre, Miss Wormwood, who continually snatches him from his vibrant world.

## Disparagement of Teachers

Cultural derision of schooling established the demeaning image of teachers. Americans who haven't a glimmer of George Bernard Shaw's ideas on education gleefully quote his witty adage, "Those who can, do; those who can't teach." The Albany school district history records similar sentiments. "Teaching offered no rewards sufficient to attract men of education or capacity, and it sometimes seemed as if a master's chief reason for taking up teaching was inability to earn anything in any other way."[8]

In his book, *Our Children and Our Country,* every time Bennett speaks positively about teachers he says **good** teachers as if most of them are **bad**. Theodore Sizer speaks of the parent prototype at the corner bar who cannot bear the shame of admitting his son is a teacher. "He's just temporarily a schoolteacher," the father says. "He's really earning money to become a lawyer."[9]

Joseph Fernandez, recent Chancellor of New York City's public schools, in his own crusade to rescue American education, declares on the one hand that we should be for almost anything that will give teachers more standing. On the other hand, he gloats in the luck that got him out of teaching. "If everything had turned out the way I intended, I might be growing old teaching geometry in Tucson today."[10]

Susan Dichter's interviews with them illustrate public school teachers' bitterness at their status.[11] Many of them relate how they were encouraged to become teachers by the very parents who now commiserate with them because they are still in the classroom.

## Disparagement of Women Teachers

American culture mocks teachers, but it reserves utter abjection for women teachers. Women teachers are still the frequent subject of warped humor in the way mothers-in-law used to be. Because most of them are women, ridicule is aimed directly at elementary and secondary teachers, not college or university professors who are mostly men. The professor is lovable and intelligent, albeit absent-minded. While it is true that university teachers get more respect because they have a higher degree of autonomy, it is nonetheless true that they get more respect because they do men's work. Professors work with young adults while teachers work with children. The first is dignified work, the second is trivial.

In *The Learning Gap*, their comparison of American education to Japanese education, Harold W. Stevenson and James W. Stigler note that *sensei*, the word for teacher in Japanese, is a term of respect and deference for those who teach first-graders as well as those who teach university students—an interesting contrast to the differential in status implied in the terms **teacher** and **professor** as they are used in the United States.[12] Early American male teachers were called schoolmasters, a term *Webster's* defines as "one who disciplines or directs." Female teachers were called schoolmarms, defined in *Webster's* as a person who exhibits strict adherence to arbitrary rules.

In American culture, women teachers are forlorn spinsters who have either the wit and weight of the proverbial schoolmouse or the ugliness and disposition of a bulldog. Dichter remarks that for the women teachers in *Main Street,* teaching is a poor second to a husband and places very definite limits on their social importance.

"Teachers are tolerated, even liked, as long as they know their place—like any servant."[13] In *The Color Purple,* Alice Walker reinforces the stereotype. "Pa say, Whoever listen to anything Addie Beasley have to say. She run off at the mouth so much no man would have her. That how come she have to teach school."[14] In Virginia Woolf's *A Room of One's Own,* we feel poignant sadness for the women "destined to become schoolteachers."[15]

The strong teacher roles on television from *Mr. Novak* to *Room 222* to *Welcome Back Kotter* to the *Head of the Class* are male. Mr. Peepers was easily intimidated and poorly named but at least he was sincerely interested in education, whereas our Miss Brooks spent all her time trying to entrap the science teacher into marriage. In the film, *Teachers,* the strong role is played by Nick Nolte, and despite the large faculty in his big city high school, no other teacher comes close to matching his courage.

In *Backlash,* Susan Faludi notes that screen strong women were displaced by good weak girls like Debbie Reynolds and Sandra Dee.[16] She could have included the wispy-voiced Sandra Dennis, who plays the bewildered teacher who can't cope in *Up the Down Staircase.* Given the same circumstances in *To Sir with Love,* Sidney Poitier not only copes but prevails. The magnetism of Miss Jean Brodie as a teacher pales beside her sexual encounters, whereas Robin Williams in *Dead Poets' Society* astounds solely with his strength as a teacher.

My morning's newspaper quoted Kenneth Cooper, author of *Kid Fitness*: "The stereotype of the physical education teacher is a fifty- to fifty-five-year old woman...overweight, a chain-smoker, and I'm sorry, but when I go to conventions and schools, that's exactly what I see."[17]

I, too, have known many gym teachers over the years and met many more at conventions, meetings, and workshops. Some were overweight, male as well as female, and I'm sorry, but I can't think of a more pertinent image for fitness than the California female gym teacher. I met her many times. She is anywhere from twenty to sixty. She is slim, tan, with shiny bobbed hair.

Even when men teachers write about teachers, they reserve their worst images for the female of the species. James Herndon in *The Way It Spozed to Be* describes a female teacher: "This Mrs. X was white, elderly, tall, stringy, wore a print dress—the very picture, I must say, of the old-lady schoolteacher."[18]

In *Schools We Have,* James Nehring's fictitious lecturer of a program called A1A presents slides of teachers before and after. The before image, of course, is "the traditional image of the old-fashioned schoolmarm, recalled in the mind's eye by the wagging index finger, the hand on hip, the forward-leaning torso.... The tight lips...and the furrowed brow." The after image is a man, "Jonathan...assertive/concerned (erect posture, left fist on rear quarter hip, right hand, also in fist, to chin, eyes wide, eyebrows raised)."[19]

On second thought, that lecturer is not fictitious. I have met him at almost every education class or teachers' workshop I attended. Lecturers assign negative qualities to women teachers, positive traits to men teachers.

✳    ✳    ✳    ✳    ✳

*My sister, Dianne Walsh-Hampton, who is an elementary school administrator, lunched with an assistant superintendent at a fine hotel during a school convention. Their waiter, trying to be friendly as waiters do, asked them what grade they taught. When they told him their positions, he said, "Oh, I'm sorry. I thought you were just schoolteachers."*

✳    ✳    ✳    ✳    ✳

*In Anaheim when I called the district office, before the secretaries would forward my call or answer my question, they would frequently ask, "Are you a librarian or just a teacher?"*

✳    ✳    ✳    ✳    ✳

The low status of women teachers has been intensified today by the influx of women into other professions, glass ceilings notwithstanding. Up until two decades ago, teaching was one of the two career options for women; nursing, the second. Today if a woman chooses teaching rather than the new options available, she is even less respected than her predecessors.

## Women and the Common Culture

Bennett declares that the critical responsibility of teachers is to preserve and transmit to each generation the nation's "common culture." But when he lists the towering figures of the common culture, he mentions not a single woman. When he lists events that have shaped the nation's identity, not one is testament to the history of women. Of the books he terms the highest kind, none is written by a woman. He mentions Martin Luther King, Jr., who fought for the civil rights of an entire people, but he has not a word for the women who suffered degradation and imprisonment that half the population could have the first civil right of suffrage.[20]

If teachers are to transmit the common culture as Bennett suggests, they have to see themselves as part of it. But throughout the two hundred pages of his own book on American education, Bennett mentions only fourteen women, four in one paragraph, and four because they are related to Martin Luther King, Jr. The book, of course, refers to over two hundred men, a good number quoted at length. Bennett finds two women worth citing, and one of them is a teenager who talks about virginity. I'm not saying Bennett hasn't a perfect right to quote whomever he chooses; I'm saying he doesn't choose to quote women. When he discusses the common culture, Bennett cannot conjure up references to women because women are not common in the common culture. If they were, as powerful an intellectual as Bennett would know it.

The absence of women in the common culture is especially mortifying for women teachers. Just as Japanese women prepare a feast for men while they themselves meekly feed on leftovers, so women teachers transmit a male common culture that buries their own heritage under fanciful characters like Betsy Ross and her needle.

## Devaluation of Child Care

One of the reasons teachers have little status in American culture is that they work with children. Columnist Suzanne Fields says that in the United States the status of woman is determined "more by what she does away from her children than with them."[21] Anna Quindlen says that in other countries "the care of children is an honorable profession. In America, it is treated like scut work."[22] Molly Ivins voices the same sentiment. "Because child care is a 'woman's problem,' it has precious little attention."[23]

Americans often hear the adage, "the hand that rocks the cradle rules the world." Two failed nominations for attorney general clearly demonstrate the conflict that ensues when the hand that rocks the cradle tries to rule. The fact that the first woman attorney general is a woman without children happened because the first two candidates were interrogated about child care. The question is not whether what Zoey Baird did was illegal; it was. The question is why weren't attorney generals in the past, or military generals, or any other government officials now or then ever asked about child care. No government official discussed his children or their care, and not one senator ever asked, until Baird.

Teachers' work will not be respectable until women's work, rocking the cradle, becomes respectable, or to put it somewhat colloquially, until both men and women rock and rule.

## Effeminization of Schooling

Since schooling is women's work, it is considered effeminate. Men who teach in the lower grades tell of being suspected of homosexuality. A male teacher interviewed by Dichter believes that fear of being labeled gay keeps men from teaching in the lower grades even when they prefer to work with young children.[24]

Never has the image of the teacher matched the appeal of the cowboy, nor even that of the railroad engineer. The American male paragon is a bodybuilder, barely articulate, and poised to protect his turf. He is best embodied in the *Terminator* and he is as out of place in a classroom as a *Kindergarten Cop*. The macho mentality of frontier cowboys did not fade away, it just moved to Marlboro country where there are no children. Down on the farm and home on the range, real men teach children how to play baseball or pitch a tent but not how to read a poem or write a sentence.

By the time they are eight, boys know that carrying a book is not masculine. Homework, if it is to be done at all, must be accommodated on a piece of paper that can be folded unobtrusively into a pocket that doesn't interfere with the macho strut. I have seen boys go through the entire seventh and eight grade without ever carrying a book. And I know of at least three who were pounded on the school yard for the crime of hauling books either in a backpack or on a bike.

The African-American and Hispanic machismo cultures of today are no different from the sexist cultures of the Polish, Irish,

Italian, German, Chinese, all the immigrants who filled the public schools of yesterday. Women teachers have always had students whose native culture considered women inferior and boys who accept orders or instruction from women unmanly. Today the problem is exacerbated by the increasing degradation and violence against women in the culture of film, rock music, and music videos. In her study, *Boys Will Be Boys,* Marilyn Miedzian articulates precisely this phenomenon. She notes that the split between the TV set and the school reflects the dichotomy between masculine and feminine values. On the one hand, there are the powerful, wealthy broadcasters and advertisers—mostly male—who care primarily about making money and are rewarded with prestige and admiration. On the other hand there are the nice, caring teachers—mostly female—who look out for the welfare of children and enjoy low salaries and low prestige.[25] Patricia Albjerg Graham says pretty much the same thing: "In the male-dominated world of CEOs, schooling is women's work."[26] The children in the schools know this. Their choice is to do well in school and accept second place or reject school and gain prestige.

## Nerd Syndrome

Ridiculing and effeminizing education in America gave birth to the concept of the "nerd," a student ridiculed for being out of style, out of sync, and devoted to academic excellence. A significant television nerd is Arvid in *Head of the Class.* His pants are too short, his face acned, his pockets jammed with pen protectors. He wears thick glasses and talks in nasal tones except in the presence of girls where he can't talk at all. Steve Urkel on *Family Matters*—the kid with the brain of a genius and the voice of Donald Duck—out nerds all nerds, making him the TV kid American kids love to laugh at most.

Evidence of the nerd appears early in American education. *Yesterdays' Schools* records that every school had its "smart Aleck," a bright boy. "He was conceited, vain, and egotistical, and the scholars would regard him only as a source of innocent amusement."[27]

The nerd syndrome saps the educational aspirations of elementary and secondary school children and undermines learning schoolwide. It is the peer pressure parents and teachers are up against when they try to encourage learning in a child that dreads peer ridicule. It is the symptom cited in studies showing that many teenagers today show little purposive striving toward goals of intellectual development, and they invest little mental effort in learning.

\* \* \* \* \*

*Almost every scholastic event is vulnerable to symptoms of the nerd syndrome. The year I came to Walker, for example, the awards assembly was moved from the cafetorium to the quad outside the gym.*

*"We had to move it outside," the math teacher informed me. "Inside, the noise was unbearable."*

*Outside the noise just seemed more bearable because it didn't bounce off the walls. Every time a name was called, the students shouted boos and catcalls while the staff controlled the derision by policing the crowd. Although they will scream themselves hoarse cheering an outstanding pitcher or star quarterback, American students reserve only scorn for the successful scholar.*

*Since the arrival of Jan Billings, Walker's first female administrator, Walker holds its award assembly after school or in the evening. Held by invitation only for the honorees, their parents, and supporters, it was my favorite event of the year. To the accompaniment of the school jazz band and chorus, students accepted parchment certificates ribboned in school colors from teachers who presented them with warm anecdotes and simple praise. The PTA hung banners and flowers. The honorees mingled with parents and teachers sharing kool-ade, chocolate cake, and friendly conversation.*

*The awards assemblies at Walker are now dignified because they're exclusive. The promotion ceremony at the end of the year is chaos because all students are invited. At the promotion ceremony, the most popular students, usually those who do the most hell-raising, receive the loudest cheers whether or not they have successfully completed the academic requirements. The shy children, or the scholastically successful—the nerds—accept their certificates in jeers or silence.*

*For two years now, the Anaheim Union High School District has been debating whether or not students who fail academically should be allowed to participate in the promotion exercises. On the one hand, should students who make no scholastic effort and, indeed, whose only efforts have been to sabotage the system be honored in a public ceremony primarily designed to honor scholars? On the other hand, since parents and community would be well aware of a student's absence on stage, does hell-raising merit public embarrassment? My guess is that hell-raisers will continue to disrupt promotion exercises because the custom is enshrined even at the college level.*

＊　＊　＊　＊　＊

*Whereas they used to be occasions of pomp and circumstance, today's commencement exercises on all levels are exercises in camaraderie and comic relief. During the June 1992 commencement at California State University, Fullerton, students kicked beach balls throughout the ceremonies. At West Point a couple of years ago, I was as impressed with the exercises as I was with the ability of the cadets to kick their shoes onto the marching field without losing a single step or revealing an unshod foot in the long gray line. Unfortunately, most graduates cannot raise a little hell without impeding the ceremony as well as West Point cadets can.*

＊　＊　＊　＊　＊

Trudeau's *Doonesbury* addresses the same issue. Joanie is talking with an old classmate about another.

"Remember when he showed up for our graduation?"
"Hee, Hee, yeah! What a day! Remember our graduation speaker?"
"Um...No."
"Well, me neither, but I'll bet she was inspiring!"[28]

In comparing school programs for African-American male students, Carole Ascher notes that many black youths assert their blackness by rejecting the value that whites and (blacks who supposedly want to emulate whites) place on academic achievement. But Stevenson and Stigler report that **all** American students often shy away from seeking distinction in their academic work because it isn't "cool" or because they fear they will be labeled "nerds, grinds, or bookworms."[29] In fact, the only American youth who do not find status in the rejection of education are the Asian Americans who are, therefore, the nerds.

## Nerd Syndrome and Asian Students

*One of the computer assignments I gave to my students each semester was to gather facts about a single topic for a data base. When the school library didn't have enough information sources, I suggested students use the La Palma public library which was a half block away. Most of the students looked at me as if I had suggested fireworks from rubbing rocks together. After class when most students had gone, several explained.*

*"Ms. Walsh, we can't go to the public library. No offense, but you go there, you see only Asians and nerds."*

*As a matter of fact, the students who used the school library after hours were mostly Asian and they used any other academic resources we offered. In an effort to assist failing students, most of whom were minority boys, Walker initiated an after school tutor room. As it turned out, most of the volunteer tutors were Asians. Incidents such as these lead me to easily believe Stevenson and Stigler's story of a teacher who after a lecture threw his lesson notes in a waste basket. At least three Japanese students rushed to retrieve them.*

*At Walker's annual awards assemblies, Asian students walked off with about seventy percent of the honors even though they comprised only eighteen percent of the student population. The top honors often went to Asian students who started the school year not knowing a word of English.*

✳   ✳   ✳   ✳   ✳

Some strange explanations have been suggested for the academic achievement of Asian children. I read an argument that Japanese children have higher IQs. I can't quote the source because I didn't consider it any more valid than similar studies on the brain power of blacks and women.

Stevenson and Stigler suggest yet another explanation for the academic success of Asian American children: they inherit a culture rich in legendary scholars and a long tradition of reverence for learning.[30] Whatever else it did, the television series *Kung Fu* promoted the traditional concept of an Asian warrior who honors and uses his brain to master his brawn. Little Spider was no Rocky, who inspired American youngsters both with his bulging muscles and his ability to communicate an entire sentence in a solitary grunt.

Stevenson and Stigler report what American teachers have known for years, that education does not play as central a role in the American conception of the tasks and responsibilities of childhood as it does in Chinese and Japanese societies.[31] When students in my classes discussed their out-of-school activities, Asian students mentioned numerous options: going to concerts, learning calligraphy, attending Japanese lessons, studying a musical instrument. Other students had options, too: baseball, football, soccer.

Bennett also notes that Asians inherit a tradition of love of learning. "I am told," he says, "that in Vietnam—when Vietnam was a free nation—teachers were revered. When Vietnamese are asked to describe their culture, love of learning is a characteristic frequently mentioned."[32] This time Bennett is right, incontestably right. Asian children respond to a respect for learning that American children find laughable. For that reason alone, Asians have little competition in American schools.

The Asian reverence for learning instills reverence for teachers, which in a virtuous circle instills reverence for learning. Stevenson and Stigler state that in Taiwan and Japan there is no question that teachers are considered professional; here we compare them to other city workers.

❋    ❋    ❋    ❋    ❋

*To earn money for our computer lab at Walker, we held Saturday Logo workshops for teachers from other schools. I suggested that we set aside a small part of the profits as payment for the students who gave up their Saturdays to set up the computers and give demonstrations. The Asian students immediately objected, declaring that they considered it an honor to help the teachers.*

*Of course, many non-Asians have similar attitudes towards school and learning, but if they express these attitudes they risk losing status among their friends. Asian students, however, can express respect for learning without losing status among their friends.*

## Teaching in a Fatherless Society

Because more and more single women are raising children, child care both in the school and in the home is seen as the exclusive domain of women. The adult world outside the home and the school is masculine. At earlier ages, boys are rebelling against both the school and the home.

Nina J. Easton, in her article "Life Without Father," discusses the debilitating consequences to society as more and more American men disconnect with the family. She declares that one third of American children are raised in homes without fathers. She quotes New Jersey legislator Wayne R. Bryant, who describes the difference between the boy who throws a bottle on the ground in a stable suburb and one who does the same in an almost-fatherless housing project. The first boy picks it up when challenged by the man next door; the second responds to a female neighbor's request with a menacing "Don't you tell me what to do."[33]

\* \* \* \* \*

*About 1985, Walker established a Student Intervention Team (SIT) to provide additional assistance to students who were having a difficult time. More than half of the students identified as SIT came from single-mother homes, and more than half were boys. Almost every single mother admitted that her children didn't listen to her either. Women are having difficulty coping with these children in the homes; women teachers have to cope with them in the schools, and in larger numbers.*

*I had a bright young student, I'll call Joel, assigned to my computer class. One on one at the computer Joel was fine, but when I spoke to the whole class he continually made loud interruptive noises. When I ignored both Joel and his noises, having found that in junior high strange noises often disappear if they are ignored, Joel got louder and louder until in angry frustration he shouted, "Go to hell," and other bits of advice equally appealing. When I talked to his mother, she said, "Put him in a class with a man teacher. He doesn't listen to women. His father works on a ship most of the time and when he's away, I can't get Joel to do anything."*

*My further investigation of Joel led to the information that his brother was in juvenile hall, and Joel had, in fact, no trouble with men teachers.*

*The strong handsome boy I'll call Jason was also the son of a single mother. He came into my class silent and morose. He would talk only to me, communicating with other students by elbowing past them, pushing them up against a wall, or wordlessly standing over them as they sat apprehensively at their desks. After several conversations, Jason told me how he loved to draw. I have often thought that if we would let junior high boys write in hieroglyphics, special ed classes would have to close for lack of numbers. At any rate, as his first assignment in computer class, I started Jason on a graphic program. From there things only got better. Jason did not earn any trophies, but he came in each day, did his work enthusiastically, moved on to the other assignments, and communicated civilly with his classmates, considering at least one his friend. Jason, it turned out, resented his father and did not do well in classes with men teachers.*

*Both Joel and Jason, like so many children in this society, see that their care is allotted to women. In their eyes, this makes women either weaker than men or more accessible but not equal to men and not a real force in society. It's not that single mothers cannot raise well-adjusted children; they have been doing it astonishingly well for centuries. It's that in a society where men are divorced from child care, but central to powerful positions, children see child care providers as weak.*

## The Schools and Gangs

The fact that women are raising the children of this country both in the schools and in the homes is relevant to the spread of youth gangs.

❋   ❋   ❋   ❋   ❋

*Anaheim Union High School District has a program specialist whose job it is to diminish gang activities on campus. He goes to the schools and talks to the teachers about what they can do to prevent the escalation of gangs. At one workshop he explained that a student wearing red was thought to be in danger from the gangs whose color was blue. He also listed at least seventeen different ways in which gang members display their colors.*

*"Teachers," he said, "should look for gang colors on jackets, headbands, scarves, socks, shoelaces, backpacks, lunch bags, and more."*

*"Hogwash," I said to Filomena who taught in the classroom next door to mine. "I don't even have the time to discuss the homework of each of the two hundred and ten students I see each day. I'm not about to check the color of their shoelaces."*

*"Maybe I can teach them to say the colors in French," said Fil.*

*Later, gangs became more sophisticated and used clothing rather than colors. One semester a gang insignia was a hanging suspender. Another time it was untied shoes. When Raiders jackets became the insignia, they were forbidden on campus. I was waiting for the gangs to make the red and white Walker Vikings sweatshirt their insignia. Would we forbid our students to wear them, too?*

*Personally I followed my own junior high survival technique: ignore whatever behavior is possible to ignore. When I checked with Fil, Ric, and Fran, our lunch table coterie, I discovered the insignia search was also beyond them. Whether they considered the search important or trivial, all the teachers knew it was impossible.*

\*     \*     \*     \*     \*

The reasons for the rise in gangs among teenagers are many and complex, but one need not be a sociologist to see that young people join gangs to belong, to find status. As long as schools are considered effeminate, they will not be a deterrent to gangs. On the contrary, from the time they are eight-years-old, boys know that macho status comes from disrupting school, not supporting it. The greater the disruption, the higher the status. American schoolboys progressed from putting snakes in the teacher's desk, to dipping girls' pigtails into inkwells, to playing hooky, to bullying smaller kids, to extorting lunch money, to smoking in the bathroom, to drinking on campus, to drugs on campus, to deadly weapons, to rape, to murder. The problem in the schools today is not different in kind, only in degree. Because everything has been done before, it's getting harder and harder to raise a little original hell.

Far fewer girls join gangs than do boys. One reason is that school for girls is acceptable, status-giving, and role-providing. Studies show that girls do well in the lower grades, even out-achieving their male classmates, but in the higher grades they fall behind. Several explanations have been advanced for this phenomenon, including maturity development patterns. I believe that girls do better in the lower grades because schooling in the lower grades is considered feminine, therefore safe for them. In the higher grades, especially in college and university, education is associated with adults, not children. On that level, where more men teach than women, it is not considered effeminate to succeed and boys, more than girls, are encouraged to do so.

As long as the schools are considered effeminate, not humanist, they will be targets of rebellious boys in gangs or otherwise. As long as they are degraded, not dignified, teachers will have little influence on gangs even if they spot every gang color in the schoolyard.

# Chapter 3

# History Repeats Itself

The low regard for schooling in American culture is best understood in historical perspective. Almost every writer in the debate on school reform commends American devotion to public education. They note that George Washington, John Adams, John Jay, Thomas Jefferson, Benjamin Franklin, Alexander Hamilton, and other leaders of the early republic argued for education of the masses. But in fact, American public education was a great idea that developed into an American public myth.

America's devotion to schools hinged on its economy, not on an idealistic call for informed citizens of the republic. Public education didn't prevail in the land until well into the nineteenth century, after the industrial revolution established the need for literate workers. Before the industrial revolution, when the economy was based on agriculture, schooling was belittled by rich and poor alike. Washington Irving, that witty observer of the American scene, reflected this in his legendary Sleepy Hollow:

> These magic books and the poetic scrawl were forthwith consigned to the flames by Hans Van Ripper; who from that time forward determined to send his children no more to school; observing, that he never knew any good come of this same reading and writing.[1]

Ruth S. Freeman declares that it took from 1825 to 1850 to get free schools in the north, and in the south it didn't happen until after the Civil War.[2] When public schools finally became common, attendance was irregular and didn't become nationally compulsory until the start of the twentieth century. Missouri legislated compulsory attendance as late as 1905.

## Churches and the Schools

In the beginning, before there was economic need for schools, literacy was forced on the American people by the churches to get them to read the *Bible*. While the populace considered the Good Book worth reading, they resented the time it took to learn how. In his comments on education in Pennsylvania, Sheldon Cohen relates the general reluctance of the people to devote as much time to education as William Penn considered necessary.[3]

That the churches were the impetus for American education is substantiated by historians Harry G. Good and James D. Teller, who declare that in Europe, church and school were connected for a thousand years and that it remained unchanged in the colonies.[4] Lawrence A. Cremin states that the first purpose of American schools, like English schools, was to teach piety and combat papism. He notes that the Society for the Propagation of the Gospel in Foreign Parts developed the most organized and best funded school system in provincial America.[5]

*Standing Tall*, the centennial history of the public schools of Albany, New York, records that the first schools were established by the Reformed Church with the mandate that "the patroons and colonists shall in particular endeavor as quickly as possible to find some means whereby they may support a minister and a schoolmaster, that thus the service of God and zeal for religion may not grow cool and be neglected among them."[6]

Since most school districts in the country had similar beginnings, the church-school relationship indelibly marked American education. Indeed, there was little enthusiasm for education outside the churches. Cohen cites the scientist who wrote in 1750, "Tho the Province of New York abounds certainly more in riches than any other of the Northern Colonies, yet there has been less care to propagate knowledge or learning in it than anywhere else."[7] In New Jersey in 1702, the government's interest in education was minimal, and the mandate to license all colony schoolmasters was usually ignored. That Massachusetts was a leader in literacy among the colonies is attributed to the power of its religious leaders.[8]

And so it came to pass that the first American teachers were churchmen. Whether they were ministers or priests or not, the first duty of colonial schoolmasters was religious. They were to see that all the children learned to read and understand the principles of religion. Schoolmasters were called dominies or preceptors, as was Irving's Ichabod Crane. They had to be members of the church and a skill in playing the organ was high recommendation.

The churches demanded that teachers be more virtuous, more dedicated, than the rest of society, and less interested in worldly goods. It was a code of conduct made in heaven for schools on earth: school officials not only had a superior staff that could be overworked and underpaid, but they also had divine authorization that emboldened them and intimidated the teachers.

For two centuries, it was assumed that teachers could be expected to prevail under the most dire circumstances because they were dedicated. David P. Page, the first principal of the normal school for teachers at Albany, New York, described this philosophy in *Theory and Practice of Teaching*. "To teach must be the teacher's primary purpose, not money, reputation, [nor] preparation for another profession."[9]

## Politicians and the Schools

It didn't take politicians forever to realize that there were votes "in them thar schools." Both Cremin and Diane Ravitch remark that political leaders were attracted to the schools because of the opportunities they offered as a source of patronage.[10] To better secure that patronage, politicians created districts to separate church and school.

Schools became a political concern all over the nation, but they did not achieve national support nor were they under national jurisdiction. Instead, each state controlled its own schools with its own political agenda, the most notorious being the preservation of segregation of the races. Public education thus became a pawn in the battle between states rights and the general welfare. It developed as a contradiction in terms: all citizens were to have equal education, which would be provided with unequal funds under unequal local laws.

Education reformers who invariably compare American schools to those of other countries neglect to mention that in most countries schools are national institutions. Critics of the schools who are especially fond of comparing American education to education in Asian nations fail to stipulate that education in Asia is a national commitment. American schools depend on the good will and politics of the local community.

## Poverty of the Schools

The most notable effect of local control of the schools was poverty of the schools. Americans opposed public education for three main reasons. First of all, they believed that public schools undermined the authority of the family. Secondly, they believed that public schools undermined the authority of the church. Finally, and most of all, they believed public schools cost too much. The history of its development everywhere indicates that Americans thought as much of schooling as they did snow in winter. They could live through it or live without it, but they weren't willing to pay for it.

And who could blame them? At the federal and state levels, politicians eloquently voiced support for the schools and established mandates for public education, but they refused to foot the bill. This left local communities with a tremendous burden they could not accommodate and avoided whenever possible. Massachusetts passed a law in 1647 mandating that all towns of fifty families maintain an elementary school. But by 1700, only one-third of the towns had schools.[11]

The first principle of American school districts everywhere was to save money. To avoid the expense of a school entirely, some towns shuttled a teacher back and forth between neighboring towns as frequently as was necessary to delude the authorities into believing that each town was maintaining a school. Freeman's following description fits most school boards: "Some of these men had no children to be schooled, and some of them were not interested enough in national affairs to vote in a presidential election. The one point on which all could agree was that the schoolhouse should be built where the land was as nearly valueless as possible. The main purpose of the constructors of the buildings seems to have been to see into how small a space the children could be crowded, and some school rooms not over thirty feet square accommodated a hundred pupils."[12]

One schoolmaster writes that the school buildings were crude austere edifices. The one assigned him had "the glass broke, the floor very much broken and torn up to kindle fires, the hearth spoiled, the seats some burned and others out of kilter, that had well nigh as good keep school in a hog stie as in it."[13]

The tradition of poor schools that began in the colonies persisted. An official report of Massachusetts in 1838 stated, "There is no other class of buildings within our limits, erected for the permanent or temporary residence of our native population, so inconvenient, so uncomfortable, so dangerous to health by their construction within, or without, abandoned to cheerlessness and dilapidation."[14] An 1894 school board report found the schools to be badly ventilated, cold, drafty, dark, with foul odors from badly maintained water closets. Teachers couldn't be heard above the trains and factories.[15] Similar conditions were cited in the 1945 congressional hearings on the schools. When he first became superintendent, Joseph Fernandez found comparable examples in the schools of Dade County, Florida.[16] According to Jonathan's Kozol's *Savage Inequalities,* inner-city schools today suffer similar conditions.[17]

## Funding the Schools

In early America, when each state had its own militia and each community its own school, both soldiers and teachers were poor men who could find little work elsewhere. When the country grew and prospered, and men moved to careers more lucrative than the army, the nation acted to make the military more attractive. Today, the Armed Services schools of higher education rank among the most prestigious in the land. Retired military personnel enjoy generous pensions and medical benefits. When the military faced a labor force crisis after it dropped the draft, it increased benefits to lure recruits. A recent recruiting ad featuring Colin L. Powell, former Chairman of the Joint Chiefs of Staff, calls the armed services one of the most sophisticated and technologically advanced organizations in the world and promises "excellent training, increased educational opportunities, and greater responsibility."[18]

The nation never made teaching an attractive career, as it did the military, because when men left the schools for better jobs, local communities hired women to take their places. There was no need to attract women because they were a captive labor force, politically powerless, without opportunities for work in other fields, without suffrage, without even the right to own property.

There are those who argue that the nation did not establish a federal school system because the people did not want federal control of education. But the people objected to a federal army for the same reason. They feared that a national militia would give the federal government the power to attack individual states. But arguments for local control did not impede the development of the national militia.

Just as the nation recognized the need for a federally maintained militia, so it saw the need to maintain a federal postal service despite objections in the southern states that it interfered with local control. Like the military, postal workers were assured a financially secure retirement, nationally equitable working conditions, and nationally equal pay for equal work.

Chester Finn, former Undersecretary of Education, maintains that education is a "public good, after defense, perhaps our most important form of common provision."[19] It was the only public good not included in the national common provision. The positions of Secretary of War and Attorney General were created in 1789; Postmaster General in 1732; but the Office of Education was not established until 1867, and was not made a cabinet position until 1979 under President Jimmy Carter. Federal monies were not assigned to education until the twentieth century.

If the nation could not have exploited women with impunity, a national school system would have developed as did the national militia and the national mail.

## Funding Schools through Property Taxes

The schools were the only national public service financed by property taxes, because local communities had no other resource. From the beginning, both the states and the towns knew that property taxes would not afford teachers competitive wages, but since the schools had a captive labor force in women, competitive wages were not a concern of the schools.

As it turns out, school property taxes are not only an injustice to teachers but to communities as well. In the first place, school taxes are unfair. Property owners who pay the largest share of school taxes often have the least need for a school. Today the median age of homeowners is fifty, an age when concern for the education of children takes second place to the need to provide for retirement.[20] Decisions on school expenditures, furthermore, are frequently decided by those who pay the lowest taxes.

Secondly, school property taxes are a violation of one of the first maxims of American life: no taxation without representation. Property owners do not get fair representation because no matter how many times a school bond or tax is defeated, it is repeatedly brought to the voters until it passes. In many larger cities, property owners have no vote at all on school taxes.

Finally, property taxes are inequitable, providing generous support in some districts and barely enough in others. *Savage Inequalities* by Kozol cites examples of urban school districts that yield less money for education even though they are taxed at higher rates than their suburban counterparts. Communities from coast to coast are rebelling against supporting schools by property tax and Governor John Engler of Michigan has successfully supported a bill to abolish this method of funding schools in his state.

Many of the recommendations of school reformers cannot be implemented with school property taxes. For example, Finn suggests that teachers' salaries be higher for those who teach in trying or hazardous surroundings.[21] But wealthy communities which are not trying or hazardous have more money to pay teachers while the hazardous neighborhoods have less. Property taxes are unfair to property owners, inequitable to students, and unequal in teacher compensation.

Today, national school reform is a formidable task because the crux of it is the teaching profession, which has a two hundred year history of degradation.

# Chapter 4

# Indentured Servants

Until now, teacher status was never a vital issue because for over two centuries, despite the low status of teaching, many of the nation's best women taught. Discrimination against them in almost every other field drove women into teaching and nursing as effectively as the draft marshaled soldiers into the army. The nation never had a better bargain.

## Staffing the Early Schools

Since they operated with funds wrested from begrudging property owners, the main trust of school boards was to stretch every dollar, which they did with extraordinary skill in teacher salaries. Wherever possible, and it was commonly possible in the South, teachers were indentured servants. In those early days, sea captains who transported criminals could sell them for periods of time to pay for their passage. If they could read and write, the felons were often bought to be used as schoolmasters. Among those who bought a bondsman for use as a teacher was George Washington's father. The bondsman's name was Hobby and he was Washington's first schoolmaster.[1] When indentured servants or unlucky felons weren't available, free citizens were hired at comparable wages.

Although in most places teachers' salaries were equal to that of a farm hand, many towns paid fines to the state rather than pay for a teacher. A popular custom was the shortening of school terms to lower the number of days a schoolmaster had to be paid. Today's teachers are criticized for school-free summers, as if they were inaugurated to benefit teachers.

Because families were large, there were usually a great number of children in the schools, but no matter how many the scholars, there was never any thought of providing more than a single teacher. A superintendent in New York City complained that one school had 736 pupils to ten teachers. He understood that all classes couldn't be under sixty, but he thought 100 might be too high.[2]

Teacher salaries were based not on the number of students but on the achievement of all students, regardless of their number. Student achievement, furthermore, was determined by school board committee reports and student test scores. For reasons known only to themselves, school boards often did not allow teachers to know the marks they received in the reports or in what subjects their class tested well or poorly. That such ignorance kept teachers from improving both their own and their students' performance apparently mattered not a whit.

Typical of the schools' drive to stint on teacher salaries was the adoption of the Lancaster system in many city school districts. Under the Lancaster system, the only person paid in the school was the principal, who taught students to tutor each other, bringing the cost to about two or three dollars per pupil in an enrollment of 500.[3] Wall charts were used instead of textbooks and students wrote with fingers on sand tables or with chalk on slate. Such techniques fostered memorizing from dictation, which led to a dependence upon rote learning. School boards held banquets in tribute to Lancaster and across the nation cities hired Lancaster consultants. It took decades for the regimented system to erode in the schools. As recently as the 1960s, individually and collectively, education reformers rocked the nation with their revelations of uncaring teachers who emphasized rote learning, cultivated conformity, and made school an unhappy place.

## Salary of Women Teachers

Teachers' salaries remained low or declined as women entered the field. While men earned ten or twelve dollars a month, women earned four to ten dollars. In the early schools, men were hired for winter school which paid more; women could only work in summer schools. Although in 1847 Massachusetts paid the highest teacher salary, a male teacher still earned what a farm hand did and female teachers still earned less by one-half or two-thirds.

Women were groomed and doomed to tolerate low wages by both church and society. They entered the teaching profession through the dame schools, called petty schools by the English, who know how to turn a phrase. Dame schools were supported by several families who left their children with a housewife. For a paltry sum the dame or housewife, often a widow with no other means of support, babysat and taught the children the alphabet, syllables, spelling, and reading. Dames had the same status in the school as women had in the churches—which was none—and they earned too little to be considered wage earners and certainly too little to instigate emancipation.

Today school critics like Chester Finn are still using women to rationalize the unjust salaries of teachers. Finn argues that since most teachers are women, it is to be expected that their wages will be less than other professions and that compared to other women's wages, teacher wages aren't that bad.[4] But today in the teaching profession itself, women are still paid less than men. A Labor Department study of elementary teachers, who are about eighty-five percent of all teachers, found that women earn four percent less than men doing the same job.

As the schools developed from common into elementary and secondary schools, women were allowed to teach only on the elementary level, which is why elementary schools traditionally pay less money. Later, women moved into the secondary schools, but it wasn't until the twentieth century that they were accepted at the college level. Harry G. Good states that "for some unfathomable reason the American college instructor teaches three classes a day and the high school teacher teaches five or six classes, supervises a study hall, and directs the band or another student group. The difference between the needs of the high school senior and the college freshman is not very great."[5] The reason is not unfathomable. The inequities began when women became the majority of teachers on both the elementary and secondary level and men the majority of teachers on the college level.

## Non-Academic Labor of Teachers

Because instruction of children was never considered worthy of their full attention, teachers were assigned as many other tasks as could be negotiated for the smallest fee. The semi-annual report of the Albany, New York, board of commissioners to the Common Council on December 14, 1846, allocated $423.54 to be paid to six of the teachers for fixtures and repairs to schoolhouses.[6] An administrator gave this advice to the teachers. "No matter how unclean or unattractive the interior of the school building may be, it should never seem hopelessly so to the rural teacher. Such a condition may be opportunity for him to work it with the children to make it livable and attractive."[7]

E. R. Eastman, retired Chancellor of the New York State Board of Regents, describes his work as a teacher in the early nineteen hundreds:

> I did my own janitor work in my first school, including building and keeping a fire going in the long-bodied Franklin stove. There was no library or apparatus, and I taught all the eight grades with little time for any one.[8]

Despite all the tasks allotted to them, teachers were evaluated solely on the academic performance of their students. Today teachers are still rated on the academic performance of their students and are still mandated a host of non-academic assignments. In most districts they patrol schoolyards, chaperone dances, serve breakfast, supervise lunch, collect money, and do inventory. While other professionals have secretaries to run the paper chase and accountants to crunch numbers, teachers are responsible for countless records with no help and no avenue of protest. At Albany High School, teachers not only receive no secretarial assistance, they are also required to help the secretaries in the office.

Schools allocate teacher time to countless clerical tasks which seem to be regarded as more important than teaching itself—taking attendance, for instance. Teachers are hired and fired on the accuracy of their attendance registers. Moreover, the task is designed to be as cumbersome as possible. An early state law allotted school monies "in proportion to the average number of scholars to be ascertained by the teachers keeping an exact account of the number of scholars present every school time or half day, which being added together and divided by 500, the number of half days for a year, shall be considered the average of attending scholars; which average shall be sworn or affirmed to by the teacher."[9]

Today attendance registers require adding late students, deducting students excused to leave early, and deducting with an explanation students who leave early unexcused. Guaranteed, every elementary school teacher in the land spends at least one tenth of her time taking, recording, and reporting attendance. Junior high teachers spend more. Would that time spent in actual teaching was considered as half as sacred.

* * * * *

*At Lincoln elementary school in Albany, the principal told me it was against the law to take the register home because it was school property. She never told me how one could possibly keep an accurate register in school with a special ed class of fifteen hyperactive children, all of whom demanded constant attention and one-third of whom had excused or unexcused appointments outside the class at any given time. She also told me that every teacher in the school kept a neat register. She lied. I never saw a neat attendance register in my life, and I never expect to see one. I used white-out over ink so many times the register could be read like braille. The last day of school, the principal announced over the loud speaker that the entire school would not be released on time because Ms. Walsh didn't turn in her attendance register and no one could leave the school until every last number was turned into the office.*

*My third graders looked worried. "You in trouble, Ms. Walsh?"*

*"Nah, the principal's just being funny." What do third-graders know?*

✳   ✳   ✳   ✳   ✳

The year I left, Walker inaugurated a new attendance form. Instead of reporting attendance once a day, teachers now fill out a form every period because the money allotted to the schools on average daily attendance (ADA) is now upgraded to average period attendance. If a student is in school only half a day, the schools get paid for only half a day, as if schools use less light, less heat, and fewer teachers if some kids go home early. It's one more way for the state to squeeze funds from the schools. The squeezing always means more work for teachers and it's always work unrelated to actual class instruction.

## Saving Money on Long-Term Substitutes

In 1969, when she wrote all year to me about the sunshine, my sister sent articles describing the teacher shortage in southern California. Finally her pleas and an exceptionally long February in New York drew me out there. The day before I arrived, California hired the last teacher it needed.

My teaching experience, masters in English, and fine affidavits from previous employers got me nothing until I met my sister's next door neighbor, Ray Macklin, who was a special ed teacher at Walker. He needed a temporary substitute teacher to take his place while he filled in for the counselor, who filled in for the assistant principal, who filled in for the principal, who had a heart attack.

For six months, I worked with no benefits for about one-fourth what regular teachers made. Although the salary was that of a part-time teacher, the duties were not. I taught full-time every day, took full responsibility for the class including teaching, grades, parent conferences, faculty meetings, and department chair meetings. I also had to assume extra duties like chaperoning dances and cafeteria supervision.

I was exploited then, and long-term substitute teachers are exploited today in the same way. At least I was hired for only six months in a temporary position. Today the district hires long-term substitute teachers in September for the entire year in positions that require full-time teachers. Last year the Sacramento district asked teachers who had been laid off in the spring to substitute in the fall in the same positions.

✳  ✳  ✳  ✳  ✳

*At Walker, Steve Katz, a long-term substitute, joined Fil and Ric Adonay in the foreign language department, but he also taught in the social studies department. Despite his inexperience and reduced salary, Steve, labeled "cool cat" by his students, taught six classes a day like everyone else. Because he was hired to fill the gaps in the schedule, however, he had four different courses to prepare, whereas most teachers had three. More than that, Steve's assignments included all the meetings and activities of both the foreign language and social studies departments, and the same number of supervisory assignments as any other teacher. To make ends meet, he waited tables every night on the* Queen Mary *in Long Beach and drove a Volkswagen van about twenty years old. We spent many lunchtimes listening to his expertise on how to party for under ten dollars and dine for under five.*

## Teacher Salary and the Marketplace

On the one hand, Finn declares that teaching should be paid according to the demands of the marketplace. On the other, he suggests that teachers salaries' should be viewed in the light of their other incomes, such as the earnings of their mates or summer jobs. Finn states that if she were compensated for a forty-eight-week year, the average public school teacher would be earning about $44,400. The question is, why aren't teachers hired for a forty-eight-week year? And the answer is that communities can't afford to hire them today any more than they could a century ago.

According to the dictates of the marketplace, says Finn, good teachers should be paid better than bad.[10] But bad teachers shouldn't be paid at all. The thrust of education reform should be to establish a way to weed out ineffective teachers. In the early schools, teachers were frequently dismissed for political reasons, which is why unions fought for and obtained the right to a fair hearing for teachers. Despite the fact that the means exist to do so, administrators today claim that they cannot fire bad teachers—implying, of course, that the solution is to do away with fair hearings. A more effective and just solution is to have teachers themselves responsible for the success or failure of schools, which would enable them, as the saying goes, to police their own.

Critics who repeatedly declare that teaching should be subject to the marketplace consistently describe work that can't be measured by the dollar. Finn speaks of the "superhuman efforts" of the teachers who "push back the boundaries of time and role, enmeshing themselves with the lives of their children, families, and communities...digging into their own human resources when necessary."[11] He speaks of schools open from seven to seven and staff that work around the clock and calendar. He recalls the famed teacher of *Stand and Deliver*, Jaimie Escalante, who not only monitored his students' study habits but also their eating habits and, on occasion, the drinking habits of their parents.[12]

People like Escalante will always emerge in our schools. I suspect there are many more of them than the latest barrage against teachers leads us to believe. But to envision school reform in the light of such paragons is not realistic. Teaching should be an honorable and fairly compensated profession that will attract upright and conscientious people who will do the job they're paid to do even if they don't do it in epic proportion.

Marketplace strategies, according to Finn, would give higher wages to teachers in shortage fields. That argument sounds powerful to someone who has not spent years in the classroom. Someone who has knows that, no matter what their field, all teachers do the same job: instruct children five hours a day, tally grades, attend meetings, prepare lessons, dialogue with parents. Because a teacher is teaching science instead of English does not entitle her to more pay unless she is doing more work. Furthermore, math and science, which are traditionally male fields, tend to be shortage areas in the schools because the public sector more generously compensates those areas than, for example, English. Engineers have always been better paid than journalists, but that does not mean children should have science teachers that are higher paid than English or reading teachers unless we consider science more vital than reading to children's education.

Harold W. Stevenson and James W. Stigler also offer a view of teachers in the marketplace. They note that Americans are much more willing to spend money for the training of professionals other than teachers.[13] They don't believe teachers deserve the respect and compensation of doctors and lawyers. They do not say so, but it is my belief that medicine and law command more respect because they are traditionally male professions, whereas teaching is traditionally a women's profession.

Finn cites Emily Feistritzer's survey declaring that four out of five teachers went into and stay in teaching because of the desire to work with young people. And he says let us be glad "that teachers are not motivated exclusively by financial considerations."[14] One also hopes that four out of five pilots who ferry us across the continent at dizzying altitudes like to fly, but their delight has not been used as an excuse to pay them less.

Finn argues that in the 1980s, teachers' salaries rose twenty-seven percent, improving their relationship to that of other professions such as attorneys, professors, and engineers whose income rose by eighteen, eighteen, and fourteen percent respectively.[15] He doesn't state by what percent teachers' salaries were lower in the 1970s, say, or the 1960s.

## The Japanese Competition

Stevenson and Stigler, who have been studying education in Japan since the 1970s, declare that in Japan a prospective teacher is not lured away by Mitsubishi or Toyota because of the promise of a higher salary. Elementary school teachers and corporation employees with comparable degrees of education receive equivalent salaries. Teachers' salaries in Japan are 2.4 times the national per capita income, as opposed to only 1.7 times for teachers in the United States.[16] In addition, the ratio of Japanese teachers' salaries to the average salaries of various other occupations has been shown in every comparison to be higher than it is in the United States. Young Japanese choose teaching without having to worry that they will suffer financially from their decision.

The Japanese school year is longer, but teachers are paid to design and evaluate curriculum. American teachers spend their summers doing the same work without pay. Tracy Kidder describes Chris, the teacher in *Among Schoolchildren*. Her principal asked her to teach sixth grade next year, which meant new colleagues and a new curriculum and a lot of summer vacation spent working on new lesson plans.[17]

In Asia, teachers teach two or three classes a day, meet with students two or three hours, and spend the rest of the time preparing for class. Asian teachers have time for serious discussion of educational policy and practice. Furthermore they have large conference rooms with desks for all teachers to meet and work together.

✳   ✳   ✳   ✳   ✳

*When I described my schedule to Tian Xianyu, a high school teacher in Tianjin, China, he asked when I had time to prepare for classes and meet with other teachers.*

*"I prepare whenever I can," I told him, "all hours of the night and weekends. I meet with other teachers on the last day of school, when we take inventory, unless you count the forty-five minute faculty meetings when we listen to the administrators talk."*

✳   ✳   ✳   ✳   ✳

*For the past few years, School Improvement Plan (SIP) funds provided time for teachers to meet during the day, but unless all the students were released, the meetings were another burden for the teachers. To take part in a meeting, I would get what is called a "released" day. A substitute would take my classes, but, of course, I had to prepare a plan for her anyway and if the students did any work while I was gone, I was responsible for that, too. If students didn't cooperate with the substitute, I was expected to take disciplinary action for that also. In short, the days I worked on school curriculum, I worked two jobs but was paid for one. Japanese teachers who talked to Stevenson and Stigler and those who visited Walker could not believe that American teachers met with their classes all day long.*

✳   ✳   ✳   ✳   ✳

Just as Thomas Sowell in his praise of Japanese schools neglects to compare their salaries to American teachers', so in his mocking of American teachers who claim to work at home he neglects to compare the working hours of Japanese and American teachers.[18] In Japan, the teachers have a longer day but half of it is devoted to the work American teachers take home every night after a longer teaching day. The discussions, exchange of ideas, and lectures that Japanese teachers do as part of their school day, American teachers do at the end of it on their own time. Early in this century, American garment labor unions fought the cottage industries because seamstresses were forced to work unpaid hours at home. The amount of hours school teachers spend on unpaid work at home represents the same kind of worker exploitation; yet this is precisely the dedicated work extolled by Finn.

## Salary of Administrators

In American schools, the farther a teacher gets from the classroom, the higher her salary. Typically teachers are paid less than administrators, and site administrators are paid less than district administrators. Stevenson and Stigler note that Asian ministries of education allocate little money to non-teaching positions. They report that in the United States in 1959, teachers' salaries accounted for fifty-six per cent of the operating budgets of American public schools. By 1989, the percentage had dropped to forty-point-four percent. Most of the decline is due to increased salaries for special personnel and administrators. Stevenson and Stigler call these statistics shocking.[19]

New York State is investigating the retirement packages of its school superintendents, which include low-interest loans, free life insurance, and buybacks not available to other employees. One is retiring a millionaire. That kind of money is used to attract administrators when teaching positions are lost for want of funds. According to the Governor's Task Force on Public Sector Compensation, a Westchester County school district paid its superintendent $148,000 and gave him a $60,000 mortgage loan at seven percent interest. "These are not ordinary benefits for rank-and-file employees, and their provision to certain administrators raises question worthy of public review," said state Budget Division Director Patrick Bulgaro.[20]

The lowest step of the Albany school district teacher salary scales is $31,621; the lowest of the administrator scale is $46,291. The highest step of the teachers' scale is $55,656; the highest step of the administrators' is $70,990.[21]

Not only are administrators better paid than teachers, but they enjoy better working conditions. They work surrounded by adult colleagues, sit at spacious desks in private offices, with secretarial teams, and have moments when they can relax. Teachers work amid children all day for five hours and often much longer, with no private space of their own, doing all their own paperwork. The only time they meet with colleagues is a thirty-minute, routinely interrupted lunch.

Susan Dichter's study of ex-teachers describes one who moved on to a "bigger career." What she remembered most about teaching is how tired she was. All the participants in the study stated that teaching was the toughest work they had ever done.[22] In her observations of teachers taking college courses, Rita Kramer remarks:

> All of these young people look tired.... They balance cardboard cups of Coke or coffee with some fast-food item—a bag of chips, half a sandwich—in this version of the business lunch. At four o'clock it's the first break they've had in their teaching day.[23]

Working at a desk or telephone, hours at a stretch, is tedious but it is not nearly as demanding as working with thirty or more children every minute for five hours. I could not interrupt my work to exchange words with a colleague, tie my shoe, or go the bathroom, amenities that most American workers take for granted. Any parent who has dreaded the invasion of an offspring's friends for an entire party or day's picnic understands the energy and patience required. A. S. Neill, who started Summerhill School in England to teach children in a place of love, freedom, and respect said, "The noise of children is ever varied and strident. It can get on one's nerves."[24]

Despite the fact that teachers have more difficult working conditions and are more crucial to children's education, they are paid less than administrators because in this country education of children has not been seen as important as administration of anything. It is argued that administrators are paid more because they have more responsibilities and work longer hours. The responsibilities would be better shared among teachers, thus providing them a career ladder without having to leave the classroom. The longer hours are only true if the work teachers do at home is discounted.

## Effects of Salary on the Teaching Profession

Even as he argues that salary does not affect teaching, Sowell claims that teachers come from the dregs of the college graduates, noting that the students who choose teaching as a career come from the lowest half of their classes and eighty-five percent of the top twenty percent leave after brief careers.[25] A meager teacher salary not only fails to attract high caliber candidates, it also weakens the professional standing of teaching itself.

"When one thinks of the hierarchy of a university," said Alexander W. Astin, professor of education at the University of California, Los Angeles, and one of the country's foremost education researchers, "there might be some dispute over what to put at the top: law, medicine, physics. But there is little dispute over what goes at the bottom: nursing and education."[26]

"Why," asked Derek Bok, president of Harvard University, are teacher training programs "relegated to the margins of the university, fighting for their existence at a time when they should occupy center stage in the national effort to improve our public schools?"[27] Bernard R. Gifford, former dean of education at the University of California at Berkeley, declares, "What's wrong with schools and departments of education today is very simple. Education suffers from congenital prestige deprivation."[28]

From the beginning, universities have disdained teacher education, claiming among other things that education does not have a specific body of knowledge as other fields do. But Bok says that fact alone is not enough to account for the disdain for education, because business schools also lack a specific body of knowledge and they have nonetheless attracted hordes of able students. "Schoolteachers in America have never earned much money and can hardly support their professional schools at a level resembling that of businessmen or lawyers. Nor has their status been high enough, at least in this century, to attract large numbers of able recruits to join their ranks. Unable to lure talented students, the teaching profession has lacked the strength to impose a model around which education could orient their efforts."[29]

Bok described the picture, but not the whole picture. For two centuries, teaching attracted talented women because women seeking to use their talents outside the home had few other options, but the women it attracted did not attain the status and financial recompense they would have if they were men; hence teaching never attained the status of male professions. Fields such as medicine, law, and architecture typify the success code of capitalism: money buys prestige and prestige breeds success.

Teaching never attracted money in the first place, because it was women's work, and in the second, because it is child care, which in this country is demeaning work. This also explains why university teachers, who are men working with adults, are better paid. As

Stevenson and Stigler note, American universities and colleges, which serve only a portion of the population, receive a high proportion of all educational funds, which has resulted in a system of higher education that is equal to or superior to that of any other country in the world, but it may also have contributed to weakening elementary and secondary education."[30]

## The Instability of Teachers' Salaries

The American school system is over 200 years old and its teachers didn't begin earning decent salaries until the last two decades. Even when they are equitable, teachers' salaries are ever in jeopardy. In recessions, one of the first ways taxpayers save money is by cutting teachers' salaries. At an 1843 school board meeting in Albany, New York, a letter was read from the Mayor requesting from the teachers a voluntary contribution of six percent of their salaries for five months. The superintendent presented the matter to the Albany Teachers Association salary committee, who responded overwhelmingly to acquiesce in the Mayor's request as their civic participation.[31]

Nancy Hoffman's *Woman's True Profession* cites the diary of a woman teacher who taught in the South immediately after the Civil War. "I will not take a salary any longer, but reserve it for the other teachers, so that the school may go on as it is for one or two years longer." Another states, "Ours is a free school—no tuition exacted—and we have no salary."[32] In June of 1993, the teachers in Los Angeles were asked to take a ten percent cut in salary. They have been forced to accept a six percent cut with no guarantee that the same sacrifice will not be asked next year. Pleasantville, New York, teachers negotiated in November a two percent cut for the next school year. In upstate New York, school districts like East Greenbush and Guilderland organized groups to elect school board members who will reduce teacher salaries. School board members campaign solely on this issue.[33]

The ignominy for teachers is not simply low salaries. It is the demeaning way in which teachers all over the country must beg for their wages like menials dependent on the good will of the lord of the manor. When they achieve equitable wages, teachers have to apologize for them and live with the reality that at the next election another politician will make his name in saving property owners money by taking it from the the teachers. Local control treats teacher salaries not as fair earnings but as allowances based on good behavior in the way fathers dole allowances to children. It will always be so as long as teacher salaries are paid by property owners whose homes are in jeopardy to school taxes.

## Teacher Salary in School Reform

While the military promises pensions, training, and travel to attract soldiers, school critics cite studies to show that teacher salaries have no effect on teaching. "Increasing teachers' salaries doesn't buy better schooling," says *The Wall Street Journal*.[34] *The New York Times* wrote that the Department of Education's annual statistics indicate that the amount spent per pupil, on higher teacher salaries, or on improving the teacher-student ratio, has almost no correlation with performance.[35]

These are remarkable studies and should inspire similar research in other fields. Surely it can be demonstrated that doctors' or attorneys' salaries and the number of their clients have no correlation to patient healing or court judgments. Undoubtedly it can be established that soldiers' wages had no effect on Operation Desert Storm.

Sowell declares that "one of the few rises in test scores occurred after one of the few declines in the real income of teachers."[36] Linking teacher salary to test scores without considering any other factor is as simplistic as considering salary the sole factor of achievement in other area. For example, despite the climbing salaries of the medical profession in the last decades, the number of people dying from AIDS rose. Despite the fact that American police are paid as well if not better than those of other nations, the rate of murders in this country is ten times that of Japan, Canada, and most European countries.

Sowell argues that private school teachers make less money and teach better, suggesting that the less we pay teachers, the more we improve teaching. Following that reasoning, if we paid teachers nothing at all, we would have the best schools in the world and a highly creative approach to reducing the national debt. Sowell's philosophy is that of the early school boards.[37] In 1899, school trustees whose pride, according to Diane Ravitch, was the economy of their system expected their low-paid teachers to be paragons of virtue and promised them that "while they might or might not receive their 'merited reward' from men, they would certainly receive 'what was infinitely more valuable—the approbation of Heaven'."[38] The scenario is traditional to the culture: men with power and money extol the underpaid labor of teachers, most of whom are women.

But private schools, despite their restricted enrollment, don't teach much better than public schools. Finn, former Assistant Secretary of Education, conceded that private schools also had a way to go to improve student achievement.[39] The eighty-five percent of private schools that are religiously affiliated have Scholastic Aptitude Test (SAT) scores not much different than those earned by public schools. A study by the *Los Angeles Times* demonstrated that only five percent of private schools do noticeably better than the average public school and that five percent spend three times as much money per pupil as the public school.[40]

The only definite advantage private schools have over public schools is that they cost less because the main item in school budgets is teachers and private school teachers are notoriously underpaid. Ronald Bazarini, in his delightful book *Boys: A Schoolmaster's Journal,* quotes his interview for a position in an exclusive private school in Manhattan:

"I hope you don't ask for much salary?"
"No. Enough to live on."
"Good."[41]

John Campbell, who has been portrayed in the film *Dead Poets Society*, complained often about teachers' fringe benefits at the prestigious coed school where he taught for twenty-eight years in a suburb of Detroit. The prestige of the prestigious private schools is subsidized by underpaid teachers.[42]

The majority of private schools in the nation are religion-affiliated and religion-affiliated schools have a long tradition of dependence on the labor of underpaid women. At the Logo workshops I gave in California, teachers from several Lutheran, Mormon, and Friends church schools told me that they tolerated the meager salaries because they had husbands who supported them and because they believed that the schools for their children were worth the sacrifice. The financial plight of Catholic schools is especially crucial today since the number of nuns has significantly decreased. For centuries, thousands of these remarkable women taught in parochial schools without pay.

It is not likely that tax dollars to religion-affiliated schools will raise the salaries of their teachers, because the mission of churches is to reach as many people as possible and to do that churches will always want to increase the number of their schools. The increase of the number of schools will be at the expense of teachers, as it always has been.

Advocates for them declare that private schools can hire whatever teachers they want without consulting unions or state regulations. That is precisely what the public schools did for two hundred years, and it explains why teachers were underpaid and lowly regarded.

As long as teaching does not meet the salaries of other fields, it will remain unattractive to men. The schools cannot afford to be a female domain, any more than Congress can be a male bastion. A blatant need of the schools is more African-American and Hispanic teachers, but African Americans and Hispanics have waited years for the chance to secure financial status. They are not going to find it in the schools.

In 1837, when he began his investigation of Massachusetts schools, one of the first observations Horace Mann made was that there were many unsatisfactory teachers.[43] He decided that the remedy was equitable salaries. The man was no dummy.

# Chapter 5

# Where Ignorance Was Cheaper

Like the Southern plantation owners, school boards understood that it was easier to exploit an uneducated labor force. How to keep teachers uneducated was a formidable challenge, but not beyond the scope of Yankee ingenuity. Districts simply hired women who were forbidden education by custom, religion, and local mandates. Ralph Waldo Emerson called the education of children women's "organic office in the world."[1] In fact, women's role in teaching stemmed not from organic but from financial considerations.

## Uneducation of Women

In Massachusetts, where Puritans believed reading and learning the *Bible* was essential to eternal salvation, girls were taught to read. But Puritans also believed that if a woman used her brain for advanced learning, it would explode. They may have also guessed that higher education would enable women to recognize exploitation when they saw it. But since they never recorded this fear for posterity, we can only surmise.

At any rate, in early Massachusetts education above the elementary level was not allowed girls. High schools were designed to prepare boys for the colleges and universities. Schools in the town of Deerfield excluded all girls over eighteen and the towns of Lynn and Medford allowed girls to attend their town schools only after the boys' afternoon dismissal. Some towns admitted girls only in the summer months.[2] One Ebenezer Bailey petitioned the Boston fathers for permission to open a girls' school. Expecting that only a few girls would be interested and thinking, perhaps, to humor Bailey, the benevolent fathers agreed. The school was so popular and had so many applicants that the city couldn't afford it and ordered it closed.[3] For all its leadership in education, by the eighteenth century only forty percent of the women in Massachusetts could write their own names.

Outside New England the situation was worse. Most girls were illiterate. Girls of wealthy families went to private schools to learn reading, writing, simple arithmetic, embroidery, music, painting, and French, although few Frenchmen lived in their neighborhoods. Advanced courses that stretched the mind and broadened the outlook were not taught in girls' schools, no matter how well endowed. The stepfather of one prominent Virginia girl found it merely amusing when she "thought it hard they would not teach me Greek and Latin because I was a girl—they laughed and said women ought not to know these things."[4]

Universities which depended on their own revenues realized at about the turn of the last century that money from women was also legal tender. To gain additional money, universities admitted women. Lest they rattle the ivory towers, however, women were permitted only in separate colleges: Barnard at Columbia in 1889 and Radcliffe at Harvard in 1893. Women were not admitted into Harvard itself until the twentieth century and then in limited numbers and proscribed courses. In the end, it was not the independent colleges but the state universities and land grant colleges, funded in part and regulated to a degree by the federal government, that opened their doors to women.

## Uneducation of Teachers

Although it must have been suspected that teachers ought to be erudite, little effort was made to procure educated teachers. As early as 1684, Massachusetts tried to license teachers, but the teacher shortage soon made licensing inexpedient and most people considered that if farming required little training, the education of small children should require much less. Newton Edwards holds that Americans believed "that the only necessary prerequisites of a good teacher were a knowledge of the subject matter to be taught and a will, backed up by physical strength and presence, to enforce rigorous discipline."[5]

The single stipulation for teaching on the elementary level was the ability to read and write. As late as 1911, only one state had made high school a prerequisite for elementary teaching certificates, only eleven had by 1919, and only thirty-three by 1928. When laws were passed demanding higher education for teachers, states saved money by putting an education department in the high schools. In Iowa, the primary purpose of the high schools was the preparation of teachers, and as late as 1900 two-fifths of its high schools were still preparing teachers.[6] The obvious advantage of keeping teacher training in the high schools was that the superintendents could mold their own staffs. Edwards points out that teacher education developed in America, particularly in the East, as an extension of elementary education and almost entirely outside the university.

## Normal Schools

At first women taught only on the elementary level. As more people went to high school and more teachers were needed, women were recruited for the secondary level. Obviously women teachers now had to be educated beyond high school. Instead of demanding university training for them, however, states initiated normal schools, which provided education only a little more advanced than high school. One can only guess as to why the schools were called normal. At best normal schools were stepping stones to more prestigious positions, or marriage, or missionary work; at worst they were a refuge for incompetents. They were funded by the states, which wanted both to politically control teachers and to provide the largest number of teachers for the lowest price. William H. Payne, professor of the Science and Art of Teaching at the University of Michigan, said the normal schools were not capable of educating superintendents, headmasters, principals, or even first assistants.[7]

Normal schools had more than their share of inferior teachers. The best teachers were at the universities, where the money and prestige was. Normal schools also had poor textbooks, but they did use paper and pencil instead of slate and chalk. Anyone who applied to a normal school was admitted, provided she could read and count to a hundred by twos. A high school diploma was not necessary. One reason given for not insisting on high school as an entrance requirement was that it would have eliminated many rural youth and filled the normal schools with city-bred girls. Local communities wanted control of their own schools at any price.

As inferior as normal schools were, many teachers never completed the entire course. Some obtained their licenses upon examination after attending for a short time. Even if normal schools had offered sound education, there were not enough of them to accommodate all the needed teachers. In 1865, there were twenty-two normal schools from Massachusetts to Kansas, far too few for a nation of 35,000,000 people with a growing population and rising mandates for compulsory education. At any rate, school officials thought teacher education a waste of resources. In 1850, the Committee on Education of the Massachusetts Legislature wanted to abolish normal schools, declaring that "academies and high schools cost the Commonwealth nothing and they are fully adequate to furnish a competent supply of teachers."[8]

## Men Teachers

In 1875, Payne, who directed schools in Michigan, found the increasing proportion of women in the teaching force a disturbing trend, relating it to the emancipation of women. He thought men were needed to render the staff more permanent, to make the science of teaching more effective, and to assure a healthy discipline. He was not in favor of a single salary schedule for men and women.[9]

Indeed, most school officials were not in favor of a single salary schedule. In fact, to attract men, schools offered them higher salaries for the same job women did. In 1872, the Albany School Board minutes listed twelve teachers, four men and eight women. The women were paid about one third the salary of the men. College degrees gave the men teachers not only more money but also more respect. The men were listed as "Professor," while the women were simply labeled "Miss."[10] Schools paid men more money not only because it was assumed they needed the money more than women, but also because they were better educated than women. They had, after all, gone to universities and colleges, whereas the majority of women were educated in the normal schools. The *Annual Report of the Board of Education for the City of Albany* shows that the elementary schools had no male teachers, but more than half of the high school teachers were men with university degrees, as opposed to the women who had mainly a normal or high school education.[11] An indication that males were expected to attend college while females attended normal schools was the Peabody Fund, which provided money to subsidize girls' normal schools and scholarships to colleges for men who would agree to teach in public schools.[12]

Because they were better educated, men taught mainly in the secondary schools, thus establishing the tradition in American education that secondary schools were superior to elementary and required better working conditions and more money. In the Anaheim district, high school teachers have a shorter day, teach fewer subjects, and have a lighter student load than the junior high teachers. In the staff directory of personnel, the high schools have a separate listing from the junior highs and they are listed first.

Since women teachers' training did not provide sound background in science or math, those subjects were taught on the secondary level mostly by men teachers. Word soon got out that women were incapable of teaching math and science.

## Teachers and the Universities

Demanding of teachers the stringent education required of doctors, lawyers, and other professions was never popular because education costs money and if the schools raised their requirements for teachers, they would have to raise their salaries. Nonetheless, the normal schools gradually became unnormal and provided studies that would enable teachers to secure a valid degree. In 1890, the Albany normal school was one of the first to confer degrees, but only in education—such as Bachelor of Pedagogy and Master of Pedagogy. The degrees led to the movement from normal schools to teacher colleges, which were still cheaper than university colleges and still inferior.

Teacher colleges disappeared as education departments developed at the universities. However, university schools of education raised neither the prestige nor the quality of teacher education because, while the universities recognized the value of other professions, they rated teaching as women's work, beneath their consideration. Faculties of higher education didn't believe that teaching required university training or education research, and contrived to keep teacher education out of the university altogether. Edwards claims that the problems the schools of education had in getting university recognition was that their faculties were so ill-prepared.[13] I believe the problem in getting prepared faculties was that the education of children was not considered professional work and paid little money.

Harvard especially considered pedagogy trivial. President Charles William Eliot insisted that teaching could only be learned by example.[14] It is incomprehensible that the universities, which could design education to enhance medicine, architecture, writing, business administration, even politics, all of which in fact is finally learned by example, could not advance teaching in the public schools. West Point and the other armed forces academies have improved defense from foot soldiers behind rocks to fox holes to tanks to scud missiles. Education progressed from one-room school houses to multi-room school houses. One of Lewis J. Perleman's criticisms of education is that it has never spent as much money in research as has the army.[15] Education never had a national academy either.

Paula Fass in her discussion of the education of African Americans relates that during the second world war, the army used the most advanced teaching and research to educate illiterate soldiers. She mentions that the army hired Dean William Russell of Columbia's Teachers College as a special consultant for the project.[16] William K. Kilpatrick writes that the "armed forces actually outshine the schools in doing things the schools are supposed to do best, such as teaching math, science, technological skills, history, languages, geography, and map reading."[17] I remember a sales representative at a Computer Using Educators (CUE) convention describing his reading instruction software: "The army uses it to teach hundreds of soldiers," he said, "It's the latest, most effective reading instruction software available."

I wondered then and I wonder now, how is it that the army has the best reading instruction tools when thousands of schools have only outdated workbooks? How is it that the universities can do for the army in months what they couldn't do for the public schools in two hundred years? Nothing can explain this phenomenon except the fact that the army attracts prestige and power, and therefore money; the schools do not.

## Schools of Education

Sixty years ago, when medical school standards were low, there was an oversupply of doctors, many of whom were poorly prepared and grossly underpaid. Conditions changed primarily through the power of the American Medical Association. When the Carnegie Foundation for the Advancement of Teaching reported the substandard level of schools of medicine, there were 160 such schools. Under the control of the AMA, the number of schools was reduced to eighty.[18]

By contrast, because of the need to put a teacher in front of every child in the nation at the lowest possible cost, schools of education grew without limit and under questionable standards. Moreover, the National Education Association was formed not by teachers but by administrators whose schools needed great numbers of teachers. It was not in the immediate interest of administrators to have well-educated teachers, who would cost more and conform less.

Cornell University and the University of Chicago established departments of education in 1901, and by 1904 fifty-two percent of American colleges and universities (250 out of 480) had schools of education. But teachers themselves recognized the limitations of ed school courses. For one thing, schools of education mandated extensive credit in methods.

❊    ❊    ❊    ❊    ❊

*In the 1950s, as part of my work towards a bachelor's in education at Fordham, I had to take nine courses in teaching methods. I learned the same thing in every course and I could have learned all of that in one rainy afternoon. Moreover, I never applied anything I was taught except what I learned about art from the indomitable Miss Gray, herself an artist, who, defying the catalog description, taught art, not methods. Every methods course taught the same Lancasterian discipline strategy. I know that because every teacher I ever knew had heard about it. The idea was not to smile until Christmas lest the students find you vulnerable—translate human—and take advantage. My first day in a class of fifteen third graders, the children were so funny, I wrote down their antics and remarks in my journal. When he saw me doing this, eight-year-old Henry demanded to know what I was doing.*

*"You writing reports on us to the principal?"*

*"No. I'm writing down the funny things that happen in this class so I can share them with my friends."*

*The next day when Eddy tripped over his chair, Henry called to me: "You better write that down, teacher. That's funny."*

*Maybe I should have waited until Christmas.*

*I'm not saying methods courses are a waste of time. I'm saying those taught in isolation from the classroom by instructors who have never been or have not recently been in a classroom are a waste of time.*

✻    ✻    ✻    ✻    ✻

Schools of education did not provide solid background in the arts and sciences, yet these areas were crucial to our own education and the substance of what we taught. For instance, all elementary teachers were expected to teach science, as I was. If my friend, Mary Hayes, a fellow sixth-grade teacher who minored in chemistry, hadn't taught science for me while I taught her class art, I think I would have skipped science altogether—which I suspect many teachers did. Nearly all American students do poorly in science. It is not surprising that American students show little achievement in science; it's surprising that they show any achievement at all in science.

Harold W. Stevenson and James W. Stigler contend that American math students do poorly because, while Asian teachers prefer to teach math, American teachers prefer to teach reading.[19] The same education bias that causes girls to do poorly in science and math bred women teachers weak in those subjects. Most elementary teachers are women. If they did not major in education, they majored in liberal arts and have precious little science and math background. Of course they prefer to teach reading. Because they themselves have received a biased education, women teachers not only teach a biased curriculum, but they also lack the background to combat such bias. Susan Rothenberg, widely recognized as one of the most innovative and authoritative painters of our time, says of her own school days, "And I was a failure at math."[20] Generations of women who went through America's schools could say the same thing.

## John Dewey and Ella Flagg Young

An illustration of men's place in the university and women educators' subordination is the story of John Dewey and Ella Flagg Young. Dewey was the first reformer of teacher education. Young was Dewey's student and superintendent of Chicago's schools. Dewey not only acknowledged her understanding of the principles of education, he sought it. Other students said that Dewey didn't teach classes when Young attended; he just held discussions with her.

"I have known," Dewey said, "but one other person—also a woman—who so consistently reflected upon her experiences, digested them, turned them into significance or meanings for future use.... I often think that [Eleanor] Roosevelt's knowledge of politics is the only analogue to Mrs. Young's knowledge of educational matters with which I am acquainted."[21]

With Dewey's support, Young became a professor while working for her degree and suggested that the department of **pedagogy** be changed to the department of education. If women had some stature on the university level, more Youngs might have emerged and changed the course of both teacher education and public school education. Unfortunately, there weren't enough Deweys to open doors.

## Teaching Credentials

When I left the parochial system to teach in a New York public high school, I had to take an English methods course for the secondary level, although I already had taken courses in teaching English

and reading for the elementary level and had taught high school
English in the parochial system for four years, preparing students
successfully for advanced placement credit in college. I thought then
and I do now that the fees for both the credentials and courses benefited the state coffers a whole lot more than they did my teaching.

✳     ✳     ✳     ✳     ✳

*On the other hand, in 1970 when I was hired to teach an Emotion-
ally Disturbed (ED) class in Anaheim, I was not required to get special
training. Later the class was renamed Educationally Handicapped
(EH) and I still did not need a credential. Although it wasn't required,
I took courses in special education at California State University,
Fullerton, thinking I could get help in reaching the youngsters in my
class. Most of what I learned was behavior modification with allusions
to Pavlov's dog. I don't believe the college professors who taught me had
ever been in a classroom. If I applied what they taught in my class, half
of my fifteen students would have walked out and the other half would
have cheered them on.*

*Eight years later, California mandated credentials for teachers of
EH classes. It mattered naught that by now I had been teaching for eight
years with success as judged by the administration, parents, and students. I could take advantage of a "grandfather" clause, but even that
required additional fees and courses for a special education credential.
More of Pavlov's dog.*

*About two years later, when I wanted to teach Learning Disabled
(LD) students, I had to qualify for still another credential with more
courses. The programs were so similar that I had students from the EH
program who were now LD. When the LD program was changed to a
Resource Program, I had to requalify again. In the meantime, I was
teaching the same kinds of children with the same kinds of learning
problems and learning far more on the job than I could learn in a
university seminar. The professors gave me lifeless statistics and ane-
mic psychological case studies, but I could have given them techniques
on how to get junior high students to read when they hated the printed
word and how to help them know they were as good as any kid in the
school when their own assessment was clearly the opposite.*

✳     ✳     ✳     ✳     ✳

*In the 1980s, when California moved to push technology in the* schools, the Anaheim District made computer literacy a district requirement for graduation. The problem was that few district schools had computer courses and none offered computer courses to all students. The district declared that students could fill the requirement by passing a computer literacy test. It was like granting a pilot's license to someone who never left the ground. Protesting such muddy maneuvers proved fruitless because in Anaheim, as in most districts, teachers had no input in education policy.

Fortunately at that time Jan Billings was principal at Walker. Billings, who knew nothing about computers and almost everything about teaching teenagers, determined to offer a computer course at Walker. Together we wrote a grant to fund Walker's first student computers. After that I wrote several other grants to build up the computer lab, joined the district committee to write a district course outline, set up the lab, and taught the course.

About two years later, at a CUE conference, the state technology implementation committees announced that the state was compiling requirements for computer teachers' credentials. For the fourth time in my career, it looked like I was going to have to take courses to learn how to teach what I had already successfully taught for years. When I left, California state education officials were still debating the issue.

## The Fight for Higher Standards

Despite credentialing horror stories, it is precisely the lack of standards for teaching that stifled the growth of excellence in education. Without credentialing, schools would be back to where they started: hiring the least educated person for the smallest amount of money. When in 1959 Kentucky demanded a certificate of competence for elementary teachers, two-thirds of the teachers didn't meet the grade.[22] When Georgia passed similar standards in 1960, 5,000 teachers couldn't meet the requirements.[23] In 1968, the University of North Dakota received a grant because fifty-nine percent of North Dakota's teachers lacked a college degree.[24] In the 1980s, states were still trying to establish standards for teacher education. President Bill Clinton proved himself an outstanding governor primarily because he raised the teaching standards of Arkansas.

Some critics have contended that a piece of paper does not a good teacher make, that good teachers are born, not made. But not enough good teachers may be born in any given year. To say that teachers are born, not made, implies that there is nothing new to learn in education, as if, like any other field, it isn't developing and growing all the time. For instance, gender and racial inequities have been built into the American school system. One of the foremost ways to change that is to mandate teacher training in these areas. The *AAUW Report* recommends that state certification for teachers require "course work on gender issues, including new research on women, bias in classroom interaction patterns, and the ways in which schools can develop and implement gender-fair multicultural curricula."[25]

First of all, credentialing boards should have representation from teachers who have at least five years experience in the classroom, the more the better. Secondly, when revising requirements, credentialing boards should consider monitored fieldwork equivalent to course work. Lastly, credentials should have national standards so that teachers in New York and California are of equal caliber to those in Louisiana and Georgia. The standards ought to be of high caliber, demanding more than high school competency. Stevenson and Stigler report that in Japan a candidate for a teacher's credential may take the test many times before she passes;[26] in this country, almost anyone who takes the test passes.

National standards of competency for teachers make it easier to implement national standards of compensation for teachers. In addition, standards of competency for teachers may be the only way to move to standards of competency for students. Suggestions of national standards or national testing for students mean little without similar standards for teachers.

## Teacher Training Today

All over the country colleges and universities are revising teacher education. Books have been written about the strengths and weaknesses of the present system. After thirty-five years in the classroom, evaluating what worked and what wasted my time, I devised my own list. First of all, since nothing prepares a teacher better than a solid foundation in the arts and sciences, the entry requirement to schools of education should be a bachelor's degree with equal background in science and math and liberal arts.

Second, every professor of education ought to have taught in the elementary and secondary schools at least five years, with recent teaching experience in the last seven years. For years, professors of education have been theorists who never taught in the schools or who taught a year or two while waiting for a university position. For years, their students have been women teachers who knew more about the classroom than they could learn from sixteen courses in a school of education.

Third, classroom teachers should be part of the teacher education process. James N. Johnson, in an article on teacher education, notes that while professions like medicine and law use case anecdotes in training, beginning teachers' accounts of their experience are not a source of teacher training.[27] The best methods courses I took were those in the writing process. My instructors in the writing process were classroom teachers who used their own experience to develop a writing program that works in the typical public school classroom.

Fourth, schools of education should be affiliated with specific public schools. Finally, no teacher should be allowed in the classroom without having served a year's paid internship in an approved school. The way the system is now, most new teachers suffer through an agonizing first year, waiting only for the semester to end so they can rectify serious errors in lesson planning, classroom management, or student assessment. A good number of promising teachers quit after the first year. In an intern program, mentors would reduce the likelihood of such errors and engineer remedies should they occur. Without mentors, new teachers have no clear idea of what should happen in a well-run classroom.

## Continuing Education of Teachers

School Improvement Programs (SIP) in California, and similar programs in New York, have made money available for continuing education or in-service training for teachers. During the four years I worked on the planning committee for such training at Walker, the main problem was time. SIP gave us five days scattered throughout the year, about the time given in workshops on how to make and double a fortune in real estate. The ratio of SIP participants who incorporated what they learned into their teaching was about equal to the number of real estate seminar participants who become millionaires.

\* \* \* \* \*

*About the only worthwhile program that was successfully learned in one SIP day turned out to be earthquake preparedness. All day long we sifted through reams of instructions on multi-colored handouts and listened to hours of dry directions about dismissal routines, emergency supplies, and communications setup. Every class received its emergency water, marked exit, and place to meet in the athletic field. One October morning before school started, during a faculty meeting in the library, we felt the earth move. As we fell to the floor, crouched under tables, and watched the bookstacks sway, we envisioned the turmoil outside in the schoolyard where students were just arriving. We needn't have worried. As instructed, every last one of them left the buildings, marched to the fields, and waited in the designated areas.*

\* \* \* \* \*

But implementing schoolwide curriculum or pedagogical changes requires more time. Teachers need a time and place to meet and learn, not only from visiting experts, but from each other. It took me years to master computer use and classroom management techniques that actually work with junior high students, but the only teacher I ever shared them with was Filomena because she was the only teacher I had time to talk to—and that was because we taught next door to each other. Fil and I scrounged minutes of our lunch half-hour, came in early or left late, to find time to share and evaluate projects. When we did find the time, we couldn't find a place without displacing our students. Unlike Asian teachers, American teachers are valued only for the time they are actually in front of a class. In Asia, teachers have time scheduled into their day for "teaching fairs" among themselves, where teachers appraise their own work.[28] They have large rooms for community sharing in which each teacher has a desk.

\* \* \* \* \*

*At Walker the teachers' room was a lounge filled with round tables that could accommodate three-fourths of the faculty for lunch. The only way to get from one end of the room to the other was to walk sideways between the tables, the steam wagons used to cart lunch from the cafeteria on the other side of the campus, and a wall of mailboxes. One side of the room opened to bathrooms and a room the size of a telephone booth, which harbored the phone and the one typewriter on campus allotted to teachers. The typewriter, obviously, could be used only when the phone was idle. On the other side was a workroom the size of three phone booths. It held the only dependable copying machine on campus and, as it was intended for the office, teachers could use it only in an emergency. It's hard to believe, but the principal's office at Walker was nearly the same size as the teachers' lounge. Indeed, we often used it for conference meetings.*

※　※　※　※　※

Education critics lament the constant succession of new programs in the schools. The reason new programs come and go is not, as Thomas Sowell would have it, that teachers are trying to avoid the hard work of teaching, but rather that programs are imposed upon the schools without the evaluation and support of teachers. If teachers had the time and opportunity to evaluate and implement change, frivolous programs would die for lack of sponsors and valid programs would have longer, healthier lives. Teachers ought never to stop looking for improvement in education. A. S. Neill of Summerhill was right when he remarked that teachers trying new ideas are less guilty than those who know exactly what is right for every child.[29]

# Chapter 6

# Acorns
# in the Schoolyard

I t is 1991. The school bell shrieks an end to the fifth period of the day at Walker Junior High. Nine hundred kids spill onto a designated blacktop area to devour lunch in the thirty minutes allotted. Students who buy a meal get to sit in the cafeteria at long wooden tables. Those who brown bag it or buy only snacks squat against stucco walls or spread out on sparse patches of grass. A lucky few find space at the dozen picnic tables under a corrugated metal overhang that provides some protection from the hot California sun most of the year and driving downpours during the infrequent rains.

Every other kid pokes another kid. Every other arm that stuffs a mouth jabs another arm that topples food, drink, or worse to the table, ground, clothes, or hair. Friends and enemies alike nudge elbows, tickle *necks, slap backs for the sheer delight of it or the sheer deviltry of playing "guess who." Paper plates, napkins, old fruit, and half-eaten sandwiches fall under tables, stick to cracks in the macadam, and collect along the stucco walls. Hungry, screeching sea gulls snatch unattended droppings. Carrying canes tipped with ice picks, the counselors, assistant principal, and the principal herself roam hither and yon among the crowd stabbing litter and depositing it in bulging trash cans.*

*Each cluster of chums has at least five more chums sitting clear across the yard and these must be paged no matter how. Acorns fly at unwary victims, who yell and fling revenge. The handy missiles which lie by the thousands within reach of restless feet and grasping fists come from the one tall oak that stands in a dusty corner of the lunch area, and others like it spaced strategically in brick planters around the school. Whether walking to class, the gym, or the office, no student is more than a few steps away from a shiny acorn.*

*Every kid in the school has been told not to throw acorns in the schoolyard. Not a kid in the school listens. Every teacher in the school has been told to tell kids not to throw acorns in the schoolyard. Not a teacher in the school expects them to listen. Teachers know that when acorns and kids come together, something has to hit the fan. No teacher worth her chalk would plant oaks in a schoolyard any more than she would pass out rubber bands in a classroom.*

*So who planted the trees? Some poetic administrator who envisioned the school, like Longfellow's smithy, "under the spreading chestnut tree?" Or a school board member who dreamed that from little acorns mighty oaks must grow? Most likely, a district director of purchasing, who got a steal on oak saplings.*

✳   ✳   ✳   ✳   ✳

Walker Junior High is in Anaheim, but the scenario is any public school in the country: school officials plant the trees, teachers cope with the acorns.

✳   ✳   ✳   ✳   ✳

*Last year a district administrator ordered a new bell system for the Walker campus. The sound was so harsh, we had to reduce the bells by seconds to ease the pain on the ears. A switch for the office intercom in the new system was installed in my class at elbow height, right next to a student computer station. The first morning after it was in place, the kids called the office fifteen times. The office called back to inform me that the calls were interruptive. I said to the class, "Please don't throw acorns in the schoolyard."*

✳    ✳    ✳    ✳    ✳

*In 1970, when I first came to Walker, the buildings were surrounded by grass, scrawny in places but luxuriously green in most areas, sweet smelling when newly mown, and easy on the errant children who fell when they dared to run through the schoolyard. About 1975, Walker got an administrator who, wanting to save money on grass mowers and lawn sprinklers, ordered the entire school yard paved in macadam. Thus it remains today, glaringly hot when the sun shines, dismally depressing all the rest of the time. There are ugly corners in the schoolyard from which one can see only stucco walls, black macadam, and chainlink fence.*

*Unhappy with the pea green walls inside, teachers all over the school used their own time and money to add color. When we moved from a portable classroom to the main building, my students and I painted all the cupboards a bright red. Filomena's son painted her classroom a robin's egg blue and Ric covered his room with the warm colors of Mexico, which the administrator said looked too much like a celebration of Cinco de Mayo. The math teachers, Joan Lewis and Linda Carter, not only had their classes painted but also installed new carpet because their floor tiles leaked tar.*

*At a faculty meeting, the administrator bemoaned the fact that we had ruined the woodwork. The woodwork looked like unadulterated plywood. To rectify matters, during the summer he ordered the entire school repainted in a color the shade of stale coffee with too much milk. Maybe he didn't choose that color. Maybe he had to use whatever paint came from the district director of purchasing. At any rate, the paint covered not only every cupboard in the school, effectively sealing the drawers forever, but also every wall, including one in the gym with a lifesize sports mural bought and designed by a graduating class two years before.*

✳    ✳    ✳    ✳    ✳

Most schools are painted in colors that look like they were chosen by camouflage experts. In fact, they were chosen by cost efficiency experts who look for the lowest priced, longest lasting paint wholesale, retail, or navy surplus.

✻   ✻   ✻   ✻   ✻

*On the outside, Walker Junior High is brown from the ground to about three feet up and tan from there to the roof. Its doors are a glaring color close to orange. On the inside, the school is tan and white. The paint is faded now, peeling and cracked in spots where the plaster shows. Newly painted, it was a clean ugly.*

*The day after cost efficiency experts had carpeting installed in the computer lab, the seams split. Although I never actually caught anyone at it, I suspect that students pulled the loose threads and unraveled the carpet in much the way one does an old sweater. In weeks, kids were tripping over the loose threads, which were surprisingly long and strong and gathered like dust balls in the aisles.*

*Every Walker classroom is illuminated by long fluorescent tubes that cast a sickening glare detrimental to hyperactive and other kinds of children. When they die, the tubes emit a sickening dead battery smell that burns the nostrils and upsets the stomach, and may also be detrimental to hyperactive and other kinds of children. It takes weeks to replace dead fluorescent tubes and months to fumigate the classroom.*

*Whenever it rains, which fortunately for the school is seldom, Walker's poorly drained yard has more lakes than Minnesota. Rain gutters start somewhere along the middle of the roof and end right outside the door of the home economics room.*

✻   ✻   ✻   ✻   ✻

*About five years ago the teachers at Walker were the first in the district to implement the SIT program. SIT required teachers to meet regularly with problem students, assessing situations, assigning interventions, and monitoring results. It also required biweekly meetings with parents and the district psychologist, keeping records, phone calls, and tutoring. Despite our best efforts, we found that this was an exorbitant amount of time to ask of a staff that already maintained regular extracurricular activities and carried six classes per day totaling about two hundred students.*

*After two years, the faculty voted to drop SIT. By that time, however, the district and, so they said, the state of California mandated SIT programs in all schools. As Superintendent Cynthia Grennan, put it, "You **will** have a SIT program." The mandate, of course, didn't provide* *any more time for teachers who worked in SIT. Grennan didn't consider the experience of the Walker faculty or seek their input as to whether or not such a program was feasible. The fact that schools have such a program makes good press and many an absentee educator, whether he was a legislator or district administrator, was proud to have thought of it.*

\* \* \* \* \*

*A district administrator in charge of special ed decided that the Individual Education Plan (IEP) paperwork mandated by the state was insufficient. She inaugurated her own system of daily logs on sensitized paper for triplicate storage. Into these logs the special ed teachers were to record daily the goals, progress, and activities of each student. At the end of each semester, when the district called for the logs, I took them out of my back cupboard, wrote a sample, and asked my aide to copy it on all the others. I sent the white copies to the parents, and stored the pink copies back in the cupboard. The yellow copies I dutifully sent to the district because I felt that, after all, district administrators had to make a living too. While I always regretted that I couldn't put the aide's time and all that paper to better use, I knew that the administrator had succeeded in adding yet another "innovative" program to her resume.*

\* \* \* \* \*

The point and tragedy is not that a principal macadamized and coffee-washed the school, or that a superintendent and state legislature mandated inane programs, but that these people have the legal right and revered tradition to macadamize schoolyards and dictate classroom strategy. The tragedy is not that Walker has a prison bell, but that the superintendent legally, with public approval, has the power of a warden.

## Political Control of the Schools

If the nation had deliberately planned to cripple public education, it could not have devised a more effective method than the present system in which citizens entrust the education of their children to teachers, then subjugate teachers to the vagaries of politicians.

From the beginning, school boards were either elected or appointed and frequently reflected not so much the hopes of parents as their own political aspirations. Teachers were political pawns. Diane Ravitch relates that often teachers whose sole qualification was knowing a trustee were hired as young as sixteen. Her history of New York City's schools recounts episode after episode of such questionable politics.

For example, in 1851 the president of the Board of Education expressed his regret that teachers had no established tenure of office but were subject to the whims of those who could remove them. In 1864, the entire board of trustees of one ward was suspended for collaborating in extorting payments from teachers. On a change of ward officers, all the teachers in a school were dismissed.[1] At one time, the Alabama legislature provided for the firing of teachers who advocated desegregation.[2] Such job insecurity was not only demoralizing to teachers, but also filled their ranks with unqualified candidates who were unwilling to question policy.

Political control of the schools led teachers to seek and gain tenure, not because they were more entitled to their jobs than any other workers, but because they were as worthy of jobs as any other workers and wanted their hiring and firing to be based on fair evaluation, not political favor. In 1864, a New York state law guaranteed that teachers could be dismissed only for cause related to morality or competency.[3]

As late as 1987, however, the state legislature removed from the California Education Code the stipulation that administrators give reason within ten days of notifying probationary teachers for "non re-election of hire." Gary Eagles, assistant superintendent of schools for Humboldt County, supports the ruling because teachers who were given reasons for their dismissals could demand hearings and hearings waste administrators' time. With hearings, many teachers were retained "because they taught kids well, even though other problems existed like repeatedly breaking the school rules, leaving too early every day, or not being a team player."[4]

## School Boards

Political corruption of school boards did not end in the nineteenth century. From his own experience, Joseph Fernandez describes district boards as those bastions of "'decentralization' that had become, for everybody to see, little more than throwbacks to the old political clubs where patronage and nepotism and out-and-out larceny ruled and the hell with what's right and what's responsible."[5] A teacher in New York City describes parties given by school board members to collect money. Anyone who wants a guarantee of a good evaluation goes to these affairs. Near the entrance is a table with a bowl for donations to which every guest is expected to contribute. Another teacher talks of people buying principalships for $10,000.[6] Nationwide, school boards are investigated for mismanagement of funds.

School boards, elected by about six percent of the voters, seldom represent the parents whose children fill the schools. For years in Albany, the way to get elected was to have a name high in the alphabet. The school board roll seldom contained a name that began with a letter past G. Voters just voted for the first six names. In 1980, the school board members were Callahan, Chicorelli, Christenson, Gibbons, Rosentock, and Touhey. In 1987, they were Abrookin, Amodeo, Cahill, Callahan, Chicorelli, Christenson, and Gibbons. Today they are Abrookin, Allen, Amodeo, DeWitt, Murray, and Swidorski. Even when school board members are deliberately elected, they sometimes have a narrow focus, because as Fernandez, who worked with school board members both in Florida and New York, observed, they get elected on one item. In bad economic times, the one item is teacher salary.

Board members communicate mostly with disgruntled assertive parents. They seldom hear from satisfied parents and almost never from parents who are intimidated by the school system, no matter how badly their children are treated.

There is no mechanism in the school system to guarantee communication between teachers and the school board. Indeed, board members often have little respect for teachers. Many of them campaign on the premise that they will make teachers toe the line, cut their salaries, or show them who's boss in some way or other. The Anaheim board reappointed a superintendent after ninety percent of the teachers gave her a vote of no confidence.

Board members speak to teachers as if they were their wards or wayward children. An Albany School Board member called the teachers "duds." Another publicly deplored the ignorance of a teacher, saying she didn't even know the Berlin Wall had come down because she gave his sixth-grade son an assignment of naming the countries of old Eastern Europe. It turned out that the teacher not only knew Eastern Europe but had her students communicating with school children in Eastern Europe. The assignment had been to show the changes before and after the Berlin Wall fell. Direct contact with his son's teacher might have uncovered that fact, but the board member chose to publicly humiliate the teacher.

✳    ✳    ✳    ✳    ✳

*Anaheim board members have often publicly reprimanded teachers, interrupted them, and refused to answer their questions. One school board member said she would attend to the important issues after the teachers left to go home to do "whatever it is that teachers do."[7] The only time I ever heard a board member talk to me without condescension was when the children of one of them attended Walker. Although we didn't always agree with him, Richard Lutz's gracious willingness to meet with Walker teachers gave both sides a much needed perspective.*

✳    ✳    ✳    ✳    ✳

Worst of all, since school board members do not have to be educators, school policy, curriculum, and discipline are regulated by bankers, farmers, lawyers, anyone but teachers. It is inconceivable that the male-dominated professions of law, medicine, and finance would tolerate such lay dictatorship, but school teachers have always been subjugated to it. In her observation of American schools, Elena Kovyazina, a teacher from Ukraine, found that the American school board system made it "impossible to regulate the process of teaching and the level of learning."[8]

## Absolute Power of Superintendents

Typically, the superintendent is appointed without input from either parents or teachers and answers only to the school board. When the board members want to know how good a job the superintendent is doing, they ask him. The superintendent's primary job, therefore, is to placate the school board. In one instance the superintendent's friend was a school board member whose husband was assigned a junior high principalship.

Speaking of his own years as superintendent, Fernandez says, "The worst thing a risk-taker can do is surround himself with yes-people."[9] But the system encourages yes-people. Administrators who are hired to implement the superintendent's program have no tenure in their positions, although they do have tenure in the district, and it is their greatest fear that they may be demoted to the classroom. Not too many principals are likely to question the superintendent. Renowned principals like Madeline Cartwright, Joe Clark, and "Doc" Litky describe the difficulties they had trying to pursue their programs under the dictates of the district.[10]

\* \* \* \* \*

*Every Wednesday the Anaheim principals left their campuses for most of the school day to meet at the district. One day a week, one-fifth of an administrator's time, was devoted to district business because on every issue—testing, drugs, in-service workshops, promotion, even fire drills—there is a district line that administrators must convey to their staffs.*

\* \* \* \* \*

*Henry Gradillas, the principal who supported Jaimie Escalante and called by some "probably the best high-school principal in the city," sharply reduced gang activity at Los Angeles' Garfield High School, cut back shop classes in favor of algebra, and extended the Advanced Placement program far beyond Escalante's calculus. The district assigned him to scheduling asbestos inspections, while regularly promoting other principals with much feebler records. A colleague heard a district administrator rule him out because he was "too confrontational." Gradillas has since left the schools for a state-level position.[11]*

\* \* \* \* \*

*In talks between teachers' unions and the district, the superintendent hired an expensive law firm to represent the district. It is a clear example of the power of the superintendent when money budgeted for education can be used for expensive lawyers to represent the superintendent in talking to teachers.*

\* \* \* \* \*

The adversarial relationship between superintendents and teachers is mutually demoralizing. Patricia Albjerg Graham relates that most superintendents are talented persons who simply do not want to put up with the con-stant attack and limited support that school superintendents get.[12]

## District Administrators

District administrators of curriculum exist to reinforce district policy. I can see little other reason. What does a director of curriculum do besides funnel information from the state to the teachers? District administrators in any field go to conventions to learn about the latest developments. Teachers need permission in triplicate before they can even consider attending such workshops. Administrators receive copies of the latest books and newest software. All that experience and materials fills some district office, when it really belongs in a classroom with a teacher. At conventions, vendors cater to administrators who can buy their wares in large numbers, but it is the teachers who use the material in the classrooms.

✳ ✳ ✳ ✳ ✳

*The Anaheim district office has a room full of software that teachers can examine. I have done it a couple of times, but what good is software to me when I can only look at it—and how much can I see in periodic visits? The software and books should be in some classroom. When I see it there, I at least have access to a teacher who has actually used the product and can show me how and if it works. When the district software, manuals, and books are out of date, they are passed on to the schools in mint condition.*

## Site Administrators

Just as superintendents should not be appointed without the approval of parents and teachers, so they should not be allowed to appoint other administrators without approval of parents and teachers. Fernandez relates how the Community School Board #24 sued him over his directive to give parents and teachers a say in the hiring of principals and assistant principals. They lost.[13] But the question remains: why would a board refuse to give teachers the right to hire principals? No one wants or needs successful principals more than teachers do. The reason districts deny teachers the right to choose principals can only be that districts do not trust teachers. Therein lies the crisis in education. Similarly, principals should be evaluated not by the superintendent, but by the teachers and parents. The superintendent's evaluation is based on how well the principal supports the bureaucracy of the district. Teachers' evaluation is based on how well the principal supports education on campus. For the past ten years or so, Anaheim teachers have been filling out questionnaires that include some items on the site administrator. Apparently, however, their evaluation means nothing, because administrators who have received excellent support from their staff have nevertheless received poor district evaluations. Furthermore, administrators who cannot relate to teachers are often promoted. Indeed, a teacher in New Rochelle tells about an administrator promoted to district administration precisely for that reason.[14]

✳    ✳    ✳    ✳    ✳

*In a similar situation before I arrived, Walker had an administrator with the build and manner of Marshall Dillon. He ran the school like a sheriff, intimidating the entire staff, regulating the length of women's dresses, and basing his evaluations on his appraisal of personalities. The gym teacher, for example, was told she didn't have the personality to coach. She has since spent twenty years doing a commendable job. On one occasion, Dillon brought a rifle to school and practiced shooting it on the schoolyard. It took the faculty two years to prepare protests and be heard at the district level. The marshal was transferred from Walker and became a district administrator. All the rest of his years in the district he remained an administrator.*

✳    ✳    ✳    ✳    ✳

The absolute rule of the superintendent in the district is reinforced by the absolute power of administrators in the schools. Clark told the teachers, "I'm the boss." When asked about a well-respected music teacher who complained that Clark, behind her back, nullified her contacts with the Metropolitan Opera so that her students lost an opportunity to work with the company, Clark said, "I canceled to get her out of here because she was doing things without my permission."[15]

James Herndon describes the principal in his school: "Mr. Grisson spoke quietly but in quite definite and commanding tones, like an actor or an officer."[16] James Nehring talks about the principal who had three assistant principals give speeches and teachers pick their own schools. "Some people said I was crazy, and my assistants bellyached to high heaven, but they did it—you know, 'cause I'm the principal."[17] In Tracy Kidder's book, the principal, Al, described himself: "One thing you're gonna learn about me, I'm not gonna change." Kidder notes that Al could be brusque, even with Chris, who was "one of his favorites."[18] Al pipes his music into the classrooms literally and figuratively.

It is not surprising, given their heritage, that teachers internalized the system and see themselves as beings owing homage to administrators. On a social trip to Puerto Rico, Chris calls the vice principal "Mr. Barrett," although he calls her simply "Chris."[19]

＊　＊　＊　＊　＊

*Weeks before my first Christmas at Walker, the social chairperson reminded us it was time to collect for Christmas presents for the administrator. The administrator happened to be a caring cheerful man, well-liked by probably everyone on the staff. I liked him, too, but I didn't see that as a reason to donate for his gift.*

*"Why should we give him a gift?" I asked. "Are we giving anyone else a gift?"*

*Nowadays, teachers at Walker give Christmas gifts as a token of friendship, not homage.*

## Serfs

While American democracy was always embarrassed by its denial of civil rights to all men, until a few decades ago it made no apologies for its similar treatment of women. The subjugation of teachers in the schools was never questioned, because the majority of teachers were always women. Just as society lauded submission in women, so school officials expected servile compliance from teachers.

＊　＊　＊　＊　＊

*When I taught at the high school in Dover Plains, New York, the principal required us to punch time clocks before and after school each day. When Alan Laughead interviewed me for a job in Anaheim Union High School District, he asked me why the principal in Dover didn't approve of me.*

*"I thought he did. Why?"*

*"His is the only negative reference in your file."*

*For twenty years I resented that man in Dover. I pondered a hundred reasons why he thought me less than an ideal candidate. Maybe it's because I quit in July, I thought, which gave him little time to hire a new teacher. Maybe it's because I refused to take the drama or journalism clubs, which are routinely dumped on any English teacher too meek to protest. Before I left Walker, I decided to find out for myself what the Dover principal considered negative about my work. When I called the personnel office in October, I was told I could not see my file unless I gave them at least an hour's notice.*

*"Why?"*

*"So we can remove all confidential papers."*

*"Why?"*

*"Because no employee is allowed to see them."*

*"Why?"*

*"District policy."*

*I realized this line of questioning was about as useful as keys inside a locked car.*

*In May, I tried again. Either I got a secretary ignorant of the law or the law changed. She gave me the folder thick with the paper account of my last twenty years. One batch of papers was sealed with a blue band marked in caps and underlined.* **THIS CONFIDENTIAL INFORMATION SHOULD NEVER BE RETURNED TO CANDIDATE.** *The band was printed by the Orange County Schools Teacher Advisory Service in Santa Ana, California.*

*The Dover principal had written that I had "remarkably few problems in either academic or pupil control area." Under weaknesses, he wrote that I had "assumed a little too much on part of the students in terms of their achievement." He was right, I have always assumed that the students could do at least a little better than they did. I still do. "As the year progressed," his letter said, "I felt that she began to become restless and to feel somewhat confined by the departmental regulations and curriculum." He said that I had problems with the department head and librarian, and was "strong willed." Ironically, he also said that I was "pretty much a follower." I guess I was a strong-willed follower, but not of department heads or librarians. Try as I might, I cannot recall the librarian, although I must have spoken to her or him. The department chair I do remember since, although I didn't think it was a problem, we did disagree on how we taught grammar and literature.*

*It was a revelation to me to discover that what the administrator considered my weaknesses, I had always considered strengths. When asked if he would reemploy the candidate, the man from Dover said: "Yes. I felt she would become a fine teacher if she had remained." Under his tutelage, no doubt.*

## Controlling the Serfs

Part of the way teachers are controlled is the cumbersome paperwork that is entailed in each assignment, field trip, workshop, curriculum development, pupil conference, every action involved in teaching. The paperwork requires more time than the work itself and is often the reason for not doing the work at all. Paperwork is assigned with subtle threats. A teacher in New Rochelle told an interviewer, "I gather there is a state law that a lesson plan must be in your desk drawer at all times."[20] State law justified every regulation from schoolyard supervision to the IQ level of students in an advanced program.

Not to be outdone, the district office publishes as many regulations as the state, maybe more. Most district regulations are founded on distrust of teachers and are designed to make teachers account for every minute of the day.

❊   ❊   ❊   ❊   ❊

*As a mentor teacher in technology, I worked with many teachers on campus, set up computer labs, gave workshops, wrote grants and course outlines. None of these were enough evidence, however, to prove I earned the mentor stipend. A district coordinator gave me, as he did all mentor teachers, a binder full of yellow, pink, green, and salmon sheets on which to keep a running account of dates, times, people, and descriptions to verify that I was indeed working as a mentor. I was to mark the amount of materials and time to the hour that I spent on mentor-related work according to specific goals and objectives. The day before it was due, I filled in the charts with fictitious dates and descriptions. I don't think anyone ever looked at that information, but if they wanted to know whether I earned my mentor money, they could have come out to the Walker campus, observed, and asked questions.*

*When the Walker planning team suggested giving two teachers free periods in which to plan school restructure for grants or meet with individual students, the district would not allow it, considering that a teacher wasn't educating unless she was in the classroom with a room full of students.*

✳    ✳    ✳    ✳    ✳

No one asks the superintendent what she does every minute; we assume she is doing her job. No one asks any administrator, counselor, or maintenance man. They are judged on the basis of the job done. But teachers must be teaching every minute. No time is allotted for anything else, not planning, not team evaluation, not student conferences. One recommendation of the *AAUW Report* was that schools "acknowledge that curricular design and revision are central—not peripheral—to teachers' work with students" so that teachers could participate in curriculum-change efforts.[21] The recommendation would not only result in equity for girls but also for teachers.

Control of teachers in the schools reduces their status to that of children. Like children, teachers are given minute instructions and are held accountable for them every minute. Administrators dole out supplies as if they were distributing candy. In a New York City school, thermostats were encased in plastic in order to prevent teachers from making individual adjustments in room temperature. Teachers had to wrap them in a cold wet cloth to get relief from the heat. Herndon recalls teachers hoarding material all year so as not to run out of it by June. All the educational materials he and other teachers used had to be approved by the principal. In his comments on technology in education, Perelman remarks, "The telephone is a century-old technology; yet hardly any schoolteachers in America have their own classroom or office telephone or even access to one."[22] This past year the one fax machine installed at Walker is in the principal's office.

Teachers are so inured to begging for supplies that they often feel obligated to subsidize the schools. A teacher writes of a partner-ship with Burger King. "The restaurant pays ten of its employees to tutor our students once a week. In return, once every six weeks, we teachers make popcorn, take it to the restaurant, and sell it for a nominal price.... The profits we make go for school playground equipment."[23]

## Teacher Evaluation

Nowhere do state and district regulations mandate more waste in time and energy than in teacher evaluations. Most administrators I had, although they didn't dare say so in words, gave me the distinct impression that they also knew the evaluations were a waste of time but had to be done because it was state law and district policy.

In the earliest schools, teachers were evaluated like children. They kept their positions "during good behavior." They were exam-ined not by peers but by members of the school board, regardless of the board members' profession. The examiners, furthermore, made every effort to catch teachers unaware as if, like children, they could be caught in naughty acts. "It shall be the duty of the sub-committees to visit their particular schools at least once a month, without giving any previous notice to the teacher, for the purpose of making a careful examination of their condition and progress, of the atten-dance, discipline, habits, and improvement of the pupils."[24]

While in other professions evaluation is made on a candidate's finest work, substantial effort was made to find teachers at their worst. For years, examiners visited classrooms unannounced. In many districts, they still do. Most pernicious of all is that teacher performance was rated primarily on "order and quiet" in the class-room, the same Lancasterian qualities administrators demanded from the teachers themselves, and the same qualities for which teachers are ridiculed in American culture.

The reports of the examiners, to use Diane Ravitch's phrase, "reeked of condescension." One committee endeavored "to suggest to the principals and teachers the various improvements which might be made in the methods of teaching, and to show with as much delicacy as possible wherein the instruction was deficient in the opinion of the committee. These hints and suggestions were gener-ally kindly received, and it is possible that they will be acted upon in cases where they were manifestly founded upon noticeable defects or failures."[25]

Early committee members did not recognize the absurdity of their role in the classrooms, but even they realized the stupidity of the amount of time devoted to it. "It is impossible that men of business, such as compose this Board, can give more of their time to these examinations than has been given this year, in all about twenty-five full days."[26]

Today administrators take the place of the old spying school committees. They come into a class once or twice a year for fifteen minutes and write an evaluation based on those visits. It's like observing a river from the shore to determine its power and depth. Herndon tells how, during his evaluation his administrator, Mr. Grisson, "opened the interview by stating that it was always painful to him to have to make judgments, but that evaluation was his job." Herndon believed the most important part of his evaluation would be classroom management, but he was evaluated on attributes like "Neat, Well-groomed, Friendly."[27]

Kidder observed that the administrator visited the classrooms of new teachers who needed help in keeping order and also observed one lesson taught by each of his veteran teachers.[28] Considering that the principal has little time to observe even one lesson, it is unsuitable and certainly unfair of him to make any judgments. But even if he had the time, why should he be making judgments at all on veteran teachers? At some point surely it must be conceded that the teacher knows her job and can do it without supervision. The first administrator I had in Anaheim wrote, "Outstanding. Runs a most successful EH program with confidence personally and compassion for her children." Unless they had reason to believe I changed, why should administrators waste their time and mine for yearly evaluations? Verification of teacher competency comes from parents, children, test scores, anything but a five-minute or even an hour-long observation.

The administrator evaluates according to his philosophy, often disregarding teacher expertise. For example, Perelman relates how the Houston Independent School District during the mid-1980s provided an intensive, three-hundred-hour teacher training course in the effective use of instructional technology. Yet when the teachers tried to use what they learned in the classroom, the most effective teachers got negative grades on the state-imposed teacher evaluation instrument, which judges teachers by their blackboard ability.[29]

Outstanding teachers are often appreciated by everyone but the administrators. John Campbell, the role model for the film, *Dead Poets Society*, was fired from the private academy where he taught because, as headmaster Gerald T. Hansen put it, Campbell did "not satisfactorily demonstrate a willingness to adhere to all the academic and professional standards of the school."[30] Not a word about his teaching prowess. Campbell himself says that his sin, metaphorically speaking, was failing to keep his classroom chairs in a row. People came from all over the world to learn from A. S. Neill's Summerhill school, yet one of the official English school inspectors recommended that he close it.

In California, teachers are evaluated according to the Stull Bill, which mandates a preliminary conference in which the teacher states "expected student progress." At the final evaluation, the evaluator asks whether the objectives have been met. I can't imagine any teacher responding in the negative. The entire process serves not a single purpose except paper proof that it happened. Nevertheless, the process is repeated year after stultifying year.

In all my years of teaching, only one administrator ever spent more than fifteen minutes observing my teaching. Some have taken fewer than five. In Dover, no administrator ever stepped inside my class, although one of them prepared the detailed evaluation in my personnel file. In Anaheim, one administrator wrote that the "room decor" could be improved because the "environment seems rather sterile." I consider that an astute observation and the only true one the administrator could have made in the five minutes he was in my room.

Neill said it for all teachers. "What puzzles me is why the teaching professions should tolerate inspection. The doctors and the lawyers, with their powerful trade unions, would not.... But the National Union of Teachers accepts its low, bus conductor status. I belong to a profession that has no guts. I am gutless myself; I should take a stand against inspection."[31]

## Rewarding the Serfs

Just as the hiring and evaluation of them is based on how well teachers submit to district control, so are teacher rewards. The most conforming teacher enjoys the highest district approval. Rewards such as teacher of the year often go to teachers who have little endorsement from their colleagues but a great deal from administrators. Alan Marks, who was a New Mexico teacher of the year, states that the people who chose him had nothing to do with education. They were "industry" people.[32]

\* \* \* \* \*

*In my first twenty years in Anaheim, teachers only once had the opportunity to vote for teacher of the year. Ironically, it was the administrator of the coffee-colored paint who insisted that teachers should choose the Chamber of Commerce teacher of the year award; other administrators doled out the title themselves. When the teacher vote was tied between Filomena and Joan Lewis, a gifted math teacher, the administrator asked the Chamber of Commerce to give the award to both teachers.*

\* \* \* \* \*

*One morning Elizabeth Jackman told me that I was teacher of the year at Walker.*

*"I like you a lot, Elizabeth," I said, "but I can't accept. It's a meaningless pat on the head. The only people who can recognize the teacher of the year are teachers."*

*I might have grumbled for a half hour, but Elizabeth interrupted to tell me that the teachers did vote.*

*"Didn't you get a ballot?"*

*"You know, I may have. I saw something about teacher of the year, but I threw it away."*

*Asking teachers to nominate the teacher of the year was typical of Jackman's teacher advocate philosophy. I don't know how all the schools in the district choose a teacher of the year, but when I left, in a number of schools the choice was still made by the principal. At any rate, the names of the teacher of the year for each school were sent to the district, where a district panel of administrators decided which candidate would represent the district at the county level. One can only guess what type of teacher was chosen.*

✳ ✳ ✳ ✳ ✳

In the first place, awards to teachers should be based on instructional competency as judged by other teachers. Teacher of the year awards as now delegated are political attempts to bolster teacher dignity in the public mind. But it can't be done. This kind of empty dignity has been bestowed on women in this country for centuries: men opened car doors for them and paid for their meals, but wouldn't allow them to vote or own property in their own names.

## Salute to the System

That American schools are run by a system that subjugates women is evident in most public tributes to the schools. Across from the capitol on the top of State Street Hill, bounded by Academy Park on the east and Washington Park on the south, the State Education Building in Albany looks like a page out of an ancient history textbook. It has the paraphernalia of a Parthenon—massive Greek pillars, wide shallow steps, and intricate bas relief. High above the broad entrance is a bronze circular plaque depicting a solemn woman holding an open book, her hair drawn back in a bun. Children stand at her sides. It is a touching emblem for an education building, depicting the teacher exactly in her place.

Inside the main lobby is a sculpture of Andrew Draper Sloan, New York's first Commissioner of Education. He stands erect with the stature of a leader. He wears the cowl and gown of an academic. The inscription at his feet says, "Erected by the school teachers of the State of New York." A long corridor off the lobby honors the other administrators of education. On its walls, as in a museum, hang the framed portraits of dignified superintendents, deans of education. Not one is a woman. I dare say not one office off the corridor belongs to a woman.

The plaque and the portraits reflect the system under which public education developed: the women worked, teaching the children; the men ruled.

The last page of *Standing Tall,* that bicentennial tribute to public education in Albany, is a photo depicting Mrs. Alvania Hill and her elementary class during American Education Week, visiting David Bray, Superintendent of Schools. He stands proudly before the camera as she ushers the children through his office for the world to acknowledge.[33] The scene is representative of American education: the female adult surrounded by the children in official obeisance to the male reign.

The image of the American teacher stems from the traditional image of the American woman. In Bennington, Vermont, outside a museum dedicated to the work of Grandma Moses, stands a monument that epitomizes the Puritan ethic that shaped the New England philosophy which in turn shaped the American schools. The monument is a sculpture of Abraham Lincoln, who in a suit and top hat stands erect with one hand on the head of a woman crouched at his feet, draped in a sarong that bares her breasts and legs. At Lincoln's other side stands an erect naked child. Both males in the monument stand erect while the woman kneels. Lincoln is fully dressed, clear to his tall top hat. The woman is half naked, to show both her vulnerability and to establish that her sole purpose on this planet is physical. The monument bears the words, "Faith, Charity, Hope." Lincoln as a fitting father of the nation represents Charity. The child is Hope. Faith, of course, is represented by the woman, servile, vulnerable, and dependent. Great men lead and from their leadership comes the hope of children. Women follow.

Albany's Academy Park, which surrounds the city's public school district offices, has four monuments. Not one of them honors women. Two are dedicated to men who fought in wars, one to a local economist. The other honors a teacher, a male scientist who was the founder of the Albany Academy for Boys.

# Chapter 7

# Team Spirit

To be fair, the current education debate should evaluate secondary schools on achievement in sports. Based on sports, American schools are an unqualified success. No national or international tests document poor sports performance by American schools. No one denies that American schools produce more than their share of successful athletes. There are few sports dropouts. In deprived areas, American schools shine in sports and the poorest schools boast teams which are the pride of their communities. Furthermore, American athletes excel in world competition. If schools did half as well academically as they do in sports, we would be reading about the triumph, not the crisis, in American education. And no wonder. Sports are the schools' sturdiest investment and richest inheritance.

## Sports Legacy of School Administrators

From the beginning and throughout most of school history, teachers were subjected to male school boards and administrators who acted as spiritual vicars and paternal leaders. In the last few decades, the paternal administrator was replaced by the coach.

For the past fifty years, the majority of school administrators were teachers of physical education, industrial arts, or business—men hardly distinguished in the academic fields in which the schools now seem to be weak. *One to Twenty-Eight,* a history of the Anaheim School District, includes early career information on twenty-nine principals from the founding of the district until 1991. Of the twenty-nine, nine were coaches; six taught business, agriculture, industrial arts or cadet corps; one taught art; one taught health. Only forty-one percent taught academic subjects. Those who taught in academic fields were part-time coaches; the most popular combination was math/coach. One national study shows that most school administrators have a social studies background, not physical education, but the study didn't note that most male social studies teachers, in fact most male teachers, are part-time coaches. Many an administrator owes his advancement to coaching. The second superintendent of the Anaheim School District, Paul Demaree, had the longest term, sixteen years. He was hired as a coach and one of his most acknowledged achievements was saving the athletics program in 1926.[1]

Enthusiasm for sports gave male principals instant rapport with men on the staff, who habitually huddled to savor the latest scores and plays in a congenial male coterie seldom invaded by the women on the staff, except for the women coaches and mothers of jocks who also understood the sacredness of sports. In all the years we had male principals at Walker, it was not uncommon to see men teachers gather in the principal's office to discuss the latest world series or super bowl or cotton bowl or salad bowl or whatever. Coach administrators cultivated team spirit in the schools, but it was all too clear who on campus was varsity and who second-string.

Administrators talked like coaches. During a faculty meeting, Tracy Kidder observed the principal: "Al formed a T with lifted hands, emitted a quick referee's whistle and said, 'Time out...About the new institution of the two-day-a-week 'late bus' he told his teachers, 'this is a home run for us, it really is.'"[2]

Precisely why so many coaches became administrators is debatable. One reason is that when the state mandated administration degrees rather than teaching experience for principals, physical ed and industrial arts teachers who had little paperwork to take home were in a better position to enroll in evening administration classes. Another reason is that administrators who were coaches hired administrators who were coaches. Still another reason is that few women were encouraged to seek administrative positions. Anaheim had no women principals until 1969 and no woman in a second level administrative position until ten years later.

The most likely reason why so many coaches became administrators is that communities had high regard for sports and saw coaches as educational leaders. Not only in Anaheim, but in school districts across the country, local communities gave strong support to sports even when they evinced little enthusiasm for academics. For instance, when remedial reading classes were cut at Anaheim schools, about fifteen people showed up to voice their concern to the school board. But when a coach was transferred from one of the high schools, parents filled the board room in protest.

## Prestige of Scholastic Sports

The tradition of sports in secondary schools is an honored one stemming from collegiate sports. Early in the century, some educators foresaw the damaging effect of sports in colleges and many wanted them taken off campus, but college presidents and President Theodore Roosevelt wanted them to remain. As were most decisions in the schools, so this one was decided by parsimony. Colleges wanted the money and prestige sports offered. The rationalization for the emphasis on sports in the schools was that sports kept kids (boys, of course) in school. Theodore Sizer's treatise on education reform repeats this theory: "The fact remains that you'll lose a lot of kids if you cut out voc ed and athletics."[3] Jim Stuart, counselor at Walker, himself a high school basketball star, could list any number of boys who would have been dropouts but for sports.

Sizer and Stuart, and those who agree with them, are correct. Sports is the only part of schooling not considered effeminate, which is why it used to attract boys to school. What the boys stayed for, they got. The schools developed sports rituals probably unmatched anywhere in the world. School spirit became team spirit. Open House or any other evening event could not be scheduled during the world series or one of those bowls. During one Open House, I remember a teacher sports enthusiast who spent the evening within inches of his pocket radio lest he miss the action on the field. The miracle of the Walkman has not gone unappreciated in the schools. Don Clapp, a Texas seventh grade coach, told Morley Safer of *Sixty Minutes*, "One thing is certain, football in these parts is much more than football. It ranks up there with academics and is really much closer to a kind of theology."[4] In *Catcher in the Rye*, Holden Caulfield speaks for any school in the land: "It was the last game of the year, and you were supposed to commit suicide or something if old Pencey didn't win."[5]

## Sports Funding

The lion's share of school funds has always gone to athletics. If the school could not provide enough money for sports, booster clubs did. Even during the depression, high schools collected money for sports. Donald R. Bahret in his history of the Anaheim school district relates the woes of a teacher: "Hedstrom almost lost his desire for football during the depression years [because he was assigned to collect money and most people didn't have it].... He simply collected from those who could donate a few coins and had to let it go at that."[6] When Texas schools were among the worst in the country with test scores falling and the dropout rate rising and the state spending the least amount of money on education than any state in the union, it still spent generously on high school football teams.[7] An Anaheim school that was squeezing the budget for money to buy new textbooks and computer hardware was buying new helmets for the football team at ninety dollars a head and outfitting each football player at three hundred dollars a kid. The money that was spent on football could have furnished half a computer lab. In at least two Anaheim high schools, the teachers wanted input to the budget precisely because they believed the sports department got more than it share.

A goodly amount of sports money pays the salaries of coaches, who are mostly men. In Florida, Joseph Fernandez, who was Dade County superintendent in the 1980s, appointed the district's first female athletic business manager.[8] Female coaches were always paid less than men until Title IX was passed in 1972, prohibiting sex discrimination by schools receiving federal funds.

While it is preposterous to suggest that teachers need assistants, it is unwritten law that every coach needs a staff of assistant coaches. *One to Twenty-Eight* includes a photo of the eleven men on the coaching staff of a junior high school.[9] Guaranteed, the school did not have eleven English or math teachers.

## Sports and Academics

Although coaches in Anaheim always received stipends for after-school time, it was years before moderators of journalism and foreign language clubs received stipends. Many other after-school academic activities still are not compensated. At Walker, Morrie Aborne spent every day after school and many weekends, coaching students for a program called *Odyssey of the Mind* in which students competed by solving problems through invention and the arts. He wasn't paid a dime for his time. Moreover, students involved in sports have very little time for other activities. One reason that Fil held foreign language club meetings before school or during lunch was that after school, the meetings would conflict with sports practice and students would be dropped from the team.

*One to Twenty-Eight* includes 163 photos depicting school life from 1908 until 1980. Eighty, or one-half of the photos, are of sports events.[10] A count of photos in any yearbook will yield similar results. The only department that competes with sports for money and prestige is the school band, which is often featured at sports events. Just about every band instructor in the Anaheim secondary schools is a man.

For years many secondary teachers were hired on the basis of their willingness to coach. At an interview for an English teaching job at Golden West Junior College in Orange County, California, the personnel director told me that although my teaching experience and credentials were what he was looking for, they were not enough because he also wanted a coach. Schools often advertised for coaches with an accompanying teaching positions. "Available: coach basketball, teach ninth grade history." Such positions not only automatically excluded women but also guaranteed the schools coaching skills, not teaching skills. Today such ads are not promulgated, but many administrators still seek coaches by word of mouth and entice them with suitable assignments. When schools are told to reduce their staffs, coaches are seldom surplused (sent to another school). Teachers are surplused according to a point system established by both the union and the district, but there are ways to manipulate the point system, and it is often done for coaches because administrators have the know-how and motivation to do it.

❋　❋　❋　❋　❋

*When I first started teaching special ed at Anaheim, at least one-fourth of the special ed teachers were coaches who chose that field because it gave them an extra conference period, which they used for coaching, although it was intended for parent and student conferences. The last physical ed class of the day was reserved for athletes. No other students, certainly not special ed students, could be assigned to that class. Special ed teachers who were coaches often took their entire class out to the sports field as a substitute for an academic class. All coaches were excused from the special ed monthly department meetings because they either had games or practices for games. As department chair one year, I asked that a special ed teacher be transferred to the Physical Education department because he spent more time there than he did in class. The principal told me that while I had good rapport with the children in class, this teacher had good rapport with them on the athletic field and that was just as important.*

## Community Support for Sports

Communities continue to show more enthusiasm for sports than academics. The people of San Francisco were concerned when lack of funds caused their schools to curtail remedial reading classes and drama clubs. When lack of funds caused the schools to curtail the sports program, the mayor and the business community hosted a fundraiser to keep it intact. In June 1993, voters in the Guilderland, New York, school district defeated the school budget but voted for a proposal securing the funding to guarantee interscholastic sports for the next school year. I know next to nothing about the city of Rensselaer, but I know it is the "Home of the Rams Basketball/ Baseball N.Y.S. Class C Champions 1990," because that information is proudly posted at every entrance to the city. Many cities post similar sports awards in that fashion. If schools received community support for academic affairs the way they do for sports events, academic achievers would be heroes, not nerds.

It was once done. Early in the century, communities supported spelling bees. Each school had it spelling champion, whose name was known throughout the area. Weeks before the contest, people speculated on its outcome. On the day of the event, families wore their finest apparel. Teenagers brought their dates, parents their children. Spectators brought picnic baskets to enjoy while they watched their favorite spell down the opposition. The entire community honored the winner. Every child in the school strived to spell well. America had excellent spellers in those days and might have today if the same interest were there. Given that kind of support, American students might yearn to be math champions, or science wizards, instead of halfbacks or forwards, and school trophy cases might not be the exclusive domains of jocks.

In his book on the schools, Lewis J. Perelman writes, "I've noticed that highlearning families I know often are avid sports fans—especially for baseball, which demands constant study of history and statistics to be fully enjoyed."[11] Using sports to study history is like buying *Playboy* for its articles. Furthermore, sports might be great history and statistics for the boys, but it doesn't do a whole lot for girls. I remember teachers using sports to teach math in my own school days. I think they did it to get the boys' attention. I had little idea what was going on and was too bored to say so. I am more inclined to agree with Louis L'Amour, author and dropout at age fifteen, who said, "Education depends on the quality of the teacher, not...the winning record of the football team, and I like football."[12]

In their effort to get equal funding for girls' sports, feminists cite studies which show that athletes are more apt than non-athletes to improve their academic standing. But I suspect it is not the sport that helps the athletes grow academically, it is the attention and nurturing the community and the rest of the school shower upon them. Imprinted on all school literature, book covers, and notebooks, the school logo includes the name of the school team and its mascot. At least one-half of all announcements over the school intercoms are for sports. Star athletes are honored at awards banquets; star scholars receive awards in much simpler ceremonies. Walker always had sports awards ceremonies outside school hours. It started scholastic awards nights about six years ago. If schools did for mathematicians what they do for jocks, the reading and history and other marks of the mathematician would improve too.

School sports promote physical fitness mostly in jocks, who already have it, and discourage it in others who feel excluded. Boys who are weak in sports are ridiculed and even bullied by school jocks.

✵ ✵ ✵ ✵ ✵

*I had boys in special education who would ditch school every afternoon rather than go to physical education, where most of the program for boys was sports. When I complained to a coach about the bullying, he made it clear how little I knew:*

*"You can't follow your students around like a mother hen. The kid has to learn to take care of himself."*

*"How many kids ever learn to take care of themselves in a gang of bullies?" I wondered.*

✵ ✵ ✵ ✵ ✵

Holden Caulfield, that dropout from Pencey, put it this way: "In every school I've gone to, all the athletic bastards stick together."

## Sports Exploitation of Girls

In their struggle for girls' rights, women's groups are nevertheless wise to fight for equity in sports because the coach mentality has made sports the hub of American public schools. The fight for equity has been strenuous, however, because sports gave the schools a focus that staunchly resists any change threatening established male eminence. Although Title IX was supposed to equalize participation in sports for boys and girls, as of 1987 girls' participation rose from four percent to only twenty-six percent; boys' participation is still twice that of girls. Moreover, the percentage of women coaches has decreased, not increased.[13] Critics who minimize the importance of Title IX underestimate the power of the scholastic sports culture.

The big three sports on campus have been basketball, football, and soccer. Girls sometimes have a basketball or soccer team, but mostly they have softball and volleyball teams, which any fool knows can't compare in skill or money to real sports.

In the 1980s, amid much parental and coach protest, the junior high schools in Anaheim eliminated varsity football and cheerleading, which removed a good portion of the jock syndrome in the seventh and eighth grades. At Walker, both boys and girls have intramural teams in volleyball, tennis, and track, with a district playoff at the end of each season. Walker coaches make every effort to publicize girls' games as well as boys.

But on the senior high level, cheerleading and drill team are still the girls' outstanding sport. Cheerleaders are chosen, first of all, for their looks. Cheerleader advocates staunchly deny this, but let anyone who doubts it check the girls who make the team.

The adulation given to boys because of their sports prowess is given to girls for their physical beauty, and cheerleading is the best way for girls to get it. The old story of the football captain marrying the most popular cheerleader is not a lost legacy. Its effect is seen as early as junior high, where girls considered attractive bask in the attention and girls considered unattractive try not to notice.

The emphasis on boys' sports and girls' cheerleading reinforces the passive role of girls in the schools and unquestionably establishes their second-rate status. Worse than the fact that cheerleading is professional training for ignoring personal talent to call attention to someone else's is the fact that cheerleading supports the image of a sports hero surrounded by adoring females. The most popular students in the schools are the male jocks and the girls who can get their attention. The retarded girl who was raped and mutilated by four high school boys became their victim because she was originally flattered to attract the attention of school athletes.

The more scholastic sports ape professional sports, the more schoolboys emulate professional jocks who thrive on the conquest of women. Magic Johnson, that darling of professional sports, proudly asserted that he made love to more than a 1,000 women. Even the language of exploiting women is the language of sports. Jocks "score" when they have sex and only get to "first base" if they don't. The high school jocks in Long Beach who tally the number of girls with whom they had sex, even if the girls were coerced, exemplify the worst tragedies encouraged by sports worship in the schools. The incident publicly manifested what many of us privately suspected: the sports hero is not the clean-cut all-American boy the schools profess him to be. A recent issue of the *Journal of the American Medical Association* reports studies that indicate that jocks more than other students engage in excessive drinking and casual sex.[14]

If Magic Johnson's boast is not sufficient evidence of how jocks use women, *Sports Illustrated* is. Its celebrated swimsuit issue not only sells millions of magazines but sells millions of boys the concept that sports conquest leads to sexual conquest.

✳   ✳   ✳   ✳   ✳

*The day I took a copy from Michael who was passing it around, he came back for it after school highly indignant: "It's a sports magazine," he protested. "There's nothing wrong with it."*

*But Lisa and her friends had a different opinion.*

*"Ms. Walsh, did you see Norman's sketch? It's awful."*

*"No."*

*"The boys show it around, Ms. Walsh, and laugh and say dirty things to us," said Lisa, watching my face for signs of indignation.*

*"She's telling the truth, Ms. Walsh," said Kelly, nodding her head.*

*"And we don't appreciate their filthy mouths," said Brandee, a tall girl who walked the campus like a queen. Nobody pushed Brandee around. Lyn Mikel Brown and Carol Gilligan would have been proud of her.*

*"It's his art picture. He's doing it for the contest," added Kelly.*

*"Whatcha you gonna do about it, Ms. Walsh?" demanded Brandee.*

*What I did was ask Norman to show me the drawing, a painstakingly detailed sketch of a female Viking perched on a motorcycle wearing not much more than a vest Madonna would covet.*

*"There's nothing wrong with it. I didn't get it from a dirty magazine," protested Norman, sounding exactly like Michael. "If it was bad, it wouldn't be in* Sports Illustrated. *Anyway it's an assignment for my art class."*

*"Look, may I have the picture, I want to check it out with the art teacher."*

*La Palma is not south central Los Angeles. Norman gave me the picture without a murmur of protest. By the time I got to the art teacher, he knew my concern before I said a word.*

*"I don't think that picture should be in the contest either. I told Norman it was poorly done."*

*"That's not the point. Should seventh grade boys be drawing pictures of near-naked women for school assignments?"*

*"No. I agree with you. I told Norman he couldn't use it."*

*Norman came the next morning and politely asked for his picture. I just as politely returned it, telling him I didn't want to see it in my class again. During lunch Fil and Fran listened to my tirade and agreed with me, let's face it, much more heartily than did the art teacher. Fran was another regular at our lunch table, an English teacher, the wife of an English teacher who also coaches, and the mother of two sons who have worn some kind of sports uniform since they were six. Norman's mother called while we were at the height of our indignation.*

*"How dare you take my son's drawing? You have no right to interfere with his art class. He's been drawing since he's eight years old and his teachers have always thought him very talented."*

*"I think so, too." I was remembering the elaborate Halloween banner he put up outside our class, the laughing scarecrows and pumpkins in space helmets. "I just think a drawing of a near-naked woman is inappropriate in a junior high class."*

*"There's nothing wrong with that drawing."*

*"It doesn't belong in a computer class. Some of the girls resented it."*

*"My son has great respect for women. I always taught him that."*

*Norman liked girls and they liked him. Everybody liked him. He was one of the easiest boys in the class to talk to. Unlike many popular junior high boys, Norman never bullied or ridiculed people for a laugh. And he didn't understand what the girls found offensive.*

*"Listen, I haven't time, now. The bell just rang for my next class. Can we talk about this later?"*

*"I don't want to talk about this later. I want to talk to the principal now."*

*Norman's mother and I never did get together, but it would have been better if we had. She simply wanted to defend Norman and develop his talent. We could have come to terms.*

## Sports and Sexual Harassment by Boys

The *AAUW Report* states that "rather than viewing sexual harassment as serious misconduct, school authorities too often treat it as a joke."[15] The baneful effect of *Sports Illustrated* and its ilk makes it more and more difficult to be serious about sexual harassment. In the decades I spent in the classroom, boys of every generation brought such pictures to school, but they passed them around surreptitiously, not daring to flaunt them in front of girls and certainly not in front of teachers. While *Playboy* and *Hustler* are still not overt in the schools, at least not Walker, *Sports Illustrated* may be gradually eroding their unacceptance.

✳   ✳   ✳   ✳   ✳

*During my last year at Walker, I observed that a growing number of boys covered their notebooks with vivid pictures of near-naked women. As I walked by students' desks checking assignments, girls signaled my attention and pointed covertly toward the pictures. Even before several told me that they were offended, I quietly asked the boys to find more suitable notebook covers. But like Norman, other boys believed the pictures perfectly suitable.*

*"What's wrong with it?" they asked.*

*"It's offensive."*

*"We don't mind if the girls carry pictures of men like that."*

✳   ✳   ✳   ✳   ✳

But the pictures of men aren't like that. Men in nude photos are posed standing tall, feet flat on the ground with a look in their eyes that defies the world. Women slither, slouch, kneel, and beckon. That *Sports Illustrated* exploits women, not simply photographs attractive bodies, is demonstrated in their rejection of an Adidas ad depicting males wearing nothing but cleated shoes, covering their private parts with their hands, or a ball, or a trophy.[16] That women appear in the magazine wearing little more, and that these women have nothing to do with sports, clearly reveals the callous exploitation of women by sports promoters.

Schoolboys into sports model themselves on professional sports, and well they would since becoming a pro is every young athlete's dream and training him to do it is every coach's dream. But the overall benefits of scholastic sports to boys must also be evaluated in view of what sports does to girls.

## Verbal Degradation of Girls

"Locker room talk" derived its label from athletics which traditionally excluded women, giving athletes the opportunity to degrade females without interference. That such talk has been around for centuries doesn't lessen its impact. Furthermore, two factors have changed. First, the popularizing of such language by rap, graffiti, and the mass media has destroyed the inhibitions about using it outside the locker room. Secondly, in the name of equity, women have claimed the right to such language. But equity is not possible. The most contemptuous American invectives like "bitch" or "whore" are aimed at females. There are no such degrading terms for males.

As early as the year 1405, women wondered why men "are so inclined to express so many wicked insults about women."[17] Women today continue to wonder. When he calls her a "ho," the teen-age girl in *Boyz N the Hood* asks her boyfriend why he always speaks that way of girls. "Because that's how girls are," he says. In a faculty discussion of this kind of language, a male teacher commented that girls' use of these terms is worse than the boys. That is one more indication of girls' low self-esteem.

Edgar Gregerson, a linguist at Queens College in New York, has completed a study of insults and dirty works in over 175 different languages.[18] He says American insults come from different cultures and, in all the cultures he studied, the insults are either political, religious, or sexual; and when they are sexual or religious, they are directed against women. In northern Italy, religious swearing is directed at the Virgin Mary. In India among Hindus, "son of a widow" is one of the worst insults because widows who do not commit suicide after their husband's death are socially stigmatized.

Few people are unaware of the popularity of "fuck you" and "son of a bitch" in American culture. Although they pride themselves on their originality, their designation of woman as a "ho" and their venomous attacks on women by rappers is a modern manifestation of the centuries-old degradation of women. Consciously or otherwise, rappers demonstrate their attempt to emulate the culture of the empowered society. White men in power, as is evident from movies, television, and literature, find masculinity in subjugating women.

Laura M. Towne noted similar behavior in African-American men in 1867. Her diary describes the burning desire and struggle for education in her classroom for freed slaves. At first, the men made no distinctions between the sexes, but gradually they developed the typical historical attitude. She cites African-American leaders who urged men to get women into their proper place. "It is too funny," she wrote, "to see how much more jealous the men are of one kind of liberty they have achieved than of the other. Political freedom they are rather shy of, and ignorant of; but domestic freedom—the right, just found, to have their own way in their families and rule their wives—that is an inestimable privilege!"[19] Politically subjugated men have historically found power in subjugation of women. Rappers repeat history.

※    ※    ※    ※    ※

*Conversations of the students in my class led me to believe that male coaches are inclined to accept or at least ignore foul language. As a matter of fact, I heard a coach tell a student to "get your ass in here."*

*At the risk of being called prudes, classroom teachers at Walker refused to tolerate such language. I remember Danny, the soccer player who swaggered about campus surrounded by admirers. He would saunter into class, pull out a chair with his foot and slide into it slowly, his hands on the desk, his eyes scanning the room for approval. The morning I found that Danny hadn't copied the day's notes from the board, I told him he couldn't go the computers until he did.*

*That was all, not a word more, but as I walked to the front of the room, Danny whispered, "whore."*

*Whether I was more stunned than furious I couldn't tell. I spun on my heel and faced him.*

*"She heard you, you fool," said his buddy.*

*Danny sobered. The grin with which he awaited class endorsement disappeared. No one said a word. I could have heard the old pin drop.*

*"Out," I said.*

*I knew I wasn't allowed to send a student out of my room without some kind of form in triplicate but I wasn't in the mood for procedure. At first Danny didn't move.*

*"I didn't mean you," he said. I was supposed to be relieved that he meant someone else.*

*"Out."*

*Although they might have extolled his language out of class, at that moment not one student gave Danny encouragement. Not one laughed. One girl, it might have been Brandee, said, "Yeah, get out of here." Danny went to the office. Before the day was out I phoned his mother. For the rest of the term Danny's eyes smoldered with resentment, but aloud he spoke with the politeness of Lancelot and did his work as if he were sworn to it.*

## Silence of Girls

The need of girls to be liked by boys is not going to change, for which we can all be thankful. But that need does not explain girls' adulation of jocks, their willingness to accept abuse from boyfriends, and their silence in the face of degradation.

✳    ✳    ✳    ✳    ✳

*"The girls don't mind these pictures," Norman insisted. "They like them."*

*"Trust me, they mind."*

*"Hey, Rita, you don't mind, do you?"*

*Rita shook her head and smiled weakly.*

*Like Rita, other girls in my class resented the pictures boys displayed, but they didn't tell them so. Girls seldom object aloud to boys' sexually harassing comments. In the first place, if they object, they will no doubt invite further harassment. Secondly, if girls object to pictures of attractive females no matter how scantily clothed, they are accused of being jealous, prudish, or worst of all, not wanting boys' attention. The same applies to a girl who takes umbrage when boys whistle at an attractive female. Sometimes, maybe many times, girls who are whistled at are flattered, but all the time girls who are not whistled at are put down by the omission. When an attractive girl walked into the room and some boy whistled, most of the other girls pretended not to hear it. The more confident a girl was about her physical appearance, the easier it was for her to ignore such behavior. But the junior high age is hardly the age when youth is confident about its physical appearance.*

\*    \*    \*    \*    \*

*Kim yelled and jumped up from her seat.*
*"He pinched my butt," she screamed.*
*But when I called the offender to my desk, Kim withdrew her accusation.*

\*    \*    \*    \*    \*

Girls are intimidated by the constant rating of their bodies by the mass media, society in general, and boys in particular. Such scrutiny makes them continually vulnerable. Even when they are devastated by derogatory remarks on their physical appearance, girls have absolutely no defense against the sneering boy who whispers to his laughing comrades, "dog." What humiliation girls endure to which boys, even those as ugly as sin, are not subjected can only be guessed.

Most of the girls interviewed who listened to him shrugged off the antics of Howard Stern, who creates and promulgates his TV show based in large part on the humiliation of women. But one 14-year old girl had the courage to speak out. "I think it has a negative effect on the guys I know. They act more powerful and they look at girls differently. They just, like, tear us apart. When a girls walks by, they'll say things like, 'Look, she's got ugly legs.' Stern may not cause it, but I know he doesn't help it at all."[20]

Because they don't overtly protest, boys believe that girls find sexual harassment funny or flirtatious. But AAUW research found that when asked to describe their ideal school, young women responded: "Boys would treat us with respect.... If they run by and grab your tits, they would get into trouble."[21] A second grader in suburban Minneapolis filed a sexual harassment complaint against the U.S. Department of Education because boys on the school bus teased her with four-letter words and lewd body language.[22] Since Anita Hill, American men may be becoming aware of the ugliness of sexual harassment, but that awareness has escaped American schoolboys and school jocks.

## Subjugation of Girls

School sports' denigration of girls is supported by entertainment based on the subjugation of women which grows stronger and more vivid with each generation. Fonzy of *Happy Days* was idolized by every boy in town because every attractive girl adored him. To the awe of his fellow males, he gloated in triumph when admiring girls jumped like dogs to do his bidding at the snap of his fingers. The girls were portrayed as attractive and happy. Films like *Animal House* and *Porky's* trivialized the sexual humiliation of girls. Today's rap lyrics and MTV thrive on the abasement of women and adoring girls. Girls learn quickly what makes them attractive to boys.

✳    ✳    ✳    ✳    ✳

*At Walker, as in many schools in the district, Hispanic students secretly circulated the underground pen pal periodical* Teen Angels, *a collection of mimeographed black and white photos, drawings, graffiti, and hand-written letters. School and civic authorities wanted copies to trace gang members and their tags (gang nicknames). Students bought it to see their photos and letters in print. Almost every page is adorned with naked or near-naked women, slinking and crawling among cars, and powerfully garbed men, often armed with guns. The letters written by young men, some in or just out of prison, some in their twenties, seek loyal pen pals to love. Teenage girls write to express their undying love: "Mijo chulo, Everyday when I wake up, I thank the Lord for having you and every night I pray that you never leave me." "I really love you & want to be yours forever." The letters are frequently self-effacing. "I want to thank you for putting up with me for the last years. I love you."*

✳    ✳    ✳    ✳    ✳

William K. Kilpatrick cites two recent studies conducted in the Northeast that revealed that one-third of high school girls in a relationship are regularly abused by their boyfriends and that one-half of the girls accepted the violence as a sign of love.[23] He asserts that such thinking stems from the influence of the romanticism of Jean-Jacques Rousseau and the progressivism of John Dewey in the schools. He does not consider at all the development of the male paragon of strength, master of his universe, unweakened by female influence, whose greatest insult is to be designated a "sissy," and whose contemporary ideal is the jock.

\*    \*    \*    \*    \*

*During the last junior high dance of the year, Carla and her friends chattered and giggled on their way to the cafetorium. Carla kept turning around, searching for her boyfriend Alonso, one of the handsomest, most popular boys on campus. Finally sighting him, she ran and called his name, clapping her hands with glee the way only junior high girls can. Alonso strode to her, held her face in his hands, looked into her eyes, and spoke softly. They were a delight to behold, equally tall, she with her chin held high, he smiling. Her friends cooed with delight. Suddenly, still smiling, he slapped her across the face so hard her head rocked to the side and he ran into the crowd. From my position in the doorway, I saw Carla's shock. Her smile froze. She rubbed her cheek and looked indignant; yet when Alonso turned from across the room to wave, she waved back.*

\*    \*    \*    \*    \*

While it is true that sports cannot be blamed for the portrayal of women in the media, it is time for the schools to admit it is not an antidote either.

## Sports and School Discipline

One of the reasons given for the emphasis on sports in the schools is that sports teach sportsmanship and team spirit. Yet more and more, team spirit simply means destroying the other side. Several high schools in high violence areas do not allow audiences at varsity games because, no matter who wins, violence erupts as students fight for their teams.

Professional players pride themselves on their exhibition of toughness. Along with the skills of their game, hockey players learn to inflict pain on their opponents. There was a time when boxing was considered too brutal a sport. Now no sport is complete without some kind of fistfighting. Baseball teams rush to television cameras to pound opposing teams in view of the world. The first tennis player to dramatize his temper tantrums has since become a role model for others. Professional baseball player Vince Coleman threw a cherry bomb from a Jeep at a group of fans in Los Angeles, then laughed as he and his buddies drove away. Three fans were burned, including a two-year-old girl whose face, eye, and hand were burned. That he should be immediately suspended from the game was considered too severe a punishment, yet baseball consistently advertises itself as an ennobling sport. What matter that it is played by less than noble men.

Sports commentators have long since declared violence integral to the game. I heard one say that foul language is a particular player's trademark and that it should not reflect on his athletic prowess. Sports builds character about as much as street brawls do.

## Removing Sports from the Schools

That sports dominate American culture may be credited entirely to the schools that have been fostering it for the past fifty years. For the last decade, there has been a battle between the schools and sports to maintain academic standards. The schools lost. Anaheim district policy and California law mandates that students not be allowed to participate in school sports unless they maintain a passing average. Jocks have learned how to outmaneuver the mandate. They take no courses that are academically challenging. A math teacher at Albany High reports that athletes drop math courses, especially higher math courses, if the work interferes with their practice time. All jocks drop courses if it looks like they are going to fail them.

In his battle to help students succeed in calculus, Jaime Escalante complained that many dropped out in order to pursue sports. On the January 9, 1994, *Sixty Minutes* report about a teacher fired because she failed too many students, the district involved could provide only three students who would speak against the teacher. Only one chose to be interviewed on television. The boy told Mike Wallace that although the teacher offered tutoring before and after school, he could not attend because he was too involved in sports at that time.[24]

Teachers are pressured to make allowances for jocks. Parents call and request less homework and retests for children who stand to be dropped from the team. Students develop cunning cheating strategies for copying assignments and passing tests. It is true that jocks are not the only students who resort to cheating, but no students have more pressure to do so than the jocks.

The best solution is to remove sports from the schools. First of all, with sports outside the school, teachers will not be allowed to cripple athletes with academic requirements. Jocks will be able to devote their whole time to sports unimpeded. Secondly, the school will be free to devote its time and adulation on academic and artistic achievement, which purportedly is the school's prime mission. Third, at a time when financial considerations are critical, the schools will not have to spend any of their budget on sports. It would save the schools millions of dollars.

As I argued earlier, schools should not be supported by property taxes because such support is not equitable to all students. But if sports were supported by property taxes, the inequity would exist only in sports, which are not yet compulsory for all children. Besides, sports have always attracted more money than academics and would continue to do so. Sports arenas would be town parks or school gymnasiums used by the town. Coaches would be city employees paid by the town and sports spectators. Let communities provide the sports. The jocks will come.

If, as Sizer and others predict, dropping sports would cause many students to drop out of school, perhaps it is time to consider whether it is wise to retain dropouts who cannot be motivated by scholastic achievement.

# Chapter 8

# My Student Myself

In 1626, Marie de Gournay argued that all differences between the sexes were due to unequal education.[1] Three hundred years later, feminists charged that schools socialized female students to accept an inferior status. In 1992, the *AAUW Report* found that the schools still shortchange girls. The report, moreover, indicated that not only the schools in general, but women teachers in particular, shortchange girls. Lyn Mikel Brown and Carol Gilligan, authors of *Meeting at the Crossroads*, "were shocked to discover the complicity of women teachers...in the muting of female vigor and trenchancy that occurs at adolescence."[2] The shock of cognizant feminists at women teachers' role in the second-class education of girls indicates that even they underestimate the predicament and legacy of women teachers. More than any other group of women, teachers have always been defined by the very stereotypes that have limited women for centuries.

## Teachers as Mothers

The reason that women were allowed, even encouraged, to work outside the home as teachers is that teaching was a surrogate motherhood. Every aspect of the teacher's job was designed not to make schooling more effective but to make teachers effective mothers. Like the old woman (mother) in the shoe, they were given so many children they didn't know what to do. They were expected to spend every moment with the children. They endured abbreviated lunch breaks, sometimes no lunch breaks at all, for the sake of the children. They subsidized children's school supplies and supervised children's play without compensation.

For years, organizers could not get teachers to strike for better labor conditions because of what might happen to the children. When teachers finally did strike, the nation was shocked at their callousness toward the children. For the past two decades, there has been talk of the guilt mothers lay upon their children. It couldn't begin to compare with that laid upon the nation's schoolteachers.

School officials expected teachers, like mothers, to donate their work. When teachers demanded to be paid for summer and evening teaching, they were denounced for their lack of dedication. On July 31, 1942, the superintendent's annual report congratulated the public school system of Albany "for the fine spirit shown by the vast majority of the various school faculty in their willingness to perform many added duties."[3]

In *For the Children*, Madeline Cartwright describes how she renewed education and hope at Blain School in a Philadelphia ghetto. Barefooted, she scrubbed a foul-smelling school bathroom. She and her staff bathed children and washed their clothes They spent a month scrubbing classrooms. She took children home with her, fed them, gave them a safe place to sleep.[4] Mother Theresa could not have done more.

Dennie Litky, the principal immortalized in the docudrama *A Town Torn Apart*, assigns a severely troubled student to a teacher's class:

"I know you can do this because you're such a great teacher."
She responds, "That kid will kill somebody."
He appeals to her maternal concern. "Do you want to give him up?"[5]

The *AAUW Report* criticizes Western culture for honoring "the role of mothers above all others for women."[6] William K. Kilpatrick finds such criticism a rejection of motherhood. He makes no comment, however, on Western culture's emphasis on males' roles as artists, political leaders, economic entrepreneurs, with little stress on fatherhood. He does not consider that such emphasis is a denial of fatherhood. Kilpatrick is especially incensed at Elizabeth Cady Stanton's advice to women: "Put it down in capital letters: SELF-DEVELOPMENT IS A HIGHER DUTY THAN SELF SACRIFICE."[7] Kilpatrick does not seem to understand how self-development would stem the rising number of teenage pregnancies far more effectively than emphasis on motherhood.

American schools have always imposed upon teachers the dedication and self-effacement of motherhood. Consciously or otherwise, teachers expect or accept self-effacement as part of their motherly role, and that attitude has a direct impact on their teaching of girls.

## Motherhood in American Culture

In America, motherhood is celebrated with a national holiday, sports heroes wave first to their mothers on national television, the favorite national maxim is "as American as motherhood and apple pie." On the other hand, America's basest insults are directed at mothers. Generations ago, it was the seemingly innocuous, "Your mother wears army boots." But, true to the law that says each generation must surpass its predecessor, the insult has evolved into "you mother," or, more specifically, "you mother-fucking son of a bitch." The recent *AAUW Report* noted the popularity of such invectives against mothers, but back in 1968 James Herndon observed "it was fatal to ever mention your mother at GW."[8]

Edgar Gregerson's study of insults shows that not only is sexual slander directed at women, but most particularly at mothers. Latin American and other Spanish-speaking cultures use "tu madre," translated "your mother," as an abbreviation for mother-related insults. In Puerto Rico, "son of the biggest one," meaning "son of the biggest whore," is a common insult. In Romany and Eastern Europe, "I [fuck]...your mother's grave" is a common insult. In West Africa, Gergerson says, the most common invective is "mother ——[fuck-er]."[9] It is curious that fathers suffer no such indignity.

## Teachers as Virgins

Paradoxically, while school teachers were historically esteemed as mothers to the nation's children, they were also expected to be virgins. School boards and administrators directed not only the school work of teachers but also their morals, and morals for women meant chastity. Teachers were not allowed to socialize with men. In most districts, married women were fired; hence the image of the spinster schoolmarm. Until the 1930s, the school board yearly report for the Albany School District lists almost every women teacher as "miss." A friend of mine who began teaching in the 1940s recalls how she had to marry secretly to keep from being fired. In the 1960s, pregnant teachers were not allowed on campus. Not only did school regulations forbid marriage, they also forbade drinking, smoking, and dating, and specified which public places teachers could frequent, if any.

Rome had its vestal virgins, who tended the hearth fire; America had those who tended the schoolhouse. Vestal virgins vowed to serve in complete chastity for thirty years. They enjoyed great prestige throughout the land, but were punished severely for break-ing their vows. Similarly, schoolmarms were respected by the community but punished if they violated the strict mores assigned them. In his review of the book, *Good Morning Miss Dove*, Kilpatrick writes that she is "an older single woman, satisfied with her life...a Teacher, first and foremost."[10]

The epitome of virgin women dedicated to the education of children were nuns. American nuns staffed the Catholic schools which educated thousands of immigrants. Critics of contemporary schools compare the problems of today's immigrants to the ease in which yesterday's immigrants were assimilated into society. They forget that the early immigrants, such as the Irish, Polish, Italians, Germans, and many others, had schools of their own where nuns from their own country understood not only their language but also validated their heritage and culture. If the nuns didn't teach the immigrant children during the day, they taught them after school or in Sunday schools. The nuns worked for nothing, devoting their entire lives, not for thirty years, but from adolescence until death.

## Effeminization of Morality

Just as schooling in this country became effeminate because it was the realm of schoolmarms, so the strict mores imposed upon them made schoolmarms the guardians of morality as well as literacy. Both in the home and certainly in the school, women were expected to be the epitome of virtue themselves and responsible for virtue in everyone else.

This attitude was nurtured especially during the Victorian era. Predictably, Kilpatrick rues the passing of Victorian culture. He argues that people in the Victorian age valued the Christian virtues of charity and duty, and then proceeds to describe the Victorian women—not the men—who cared about creating homes and schools with a moral tone. He lauds the Victorian customs of the Philippines, where girls are chaperoned and boys are expected to court a girl in her home under a parent's watchful eye, where most girls are virgins at marriage, where traditional ideas about sex roles prevail. He does not declare that young men are virgins at marriage, nor does he consider that the traditional man's role as master in the house and head of the family taught thousands of Christian women to tolerate abuse by their husbands in the name of holy matrimony. Submission to violence by girls may well have been exacerbated by Victorian thinking, which extolled submissiveness as a feminine virtue.

Their traditional Victorian upbringing did not protect Filipino women and girls against the prostitution condoned by the U.S. Navy, which left hundreds of women and their babies abandoned by sailors at American naval bases in that country.

Ironically, women were expected to cultivate virtue but had no power to effect policy for themselves or anyone else. Nuns did all their charitable works and still do for a church that denies them membership in its priesthood or any part of its clerical hierarchy. Similar custom prevails in most church-run schools.

## Morality of Girls

Critics of the schools like Kilpatrick insinuate that the solution to today's sexual problems, such as rape and teenage pregnancy, are girls' responsibility. He laments that "at one time modesty, not a condom, was a young woman's protection against any hasty indulgence,"[11] but he says nothing about a boy's protection against hasty indulgence. William Bennett also declares that girls ought to learn modesty.[12] What boys should learn is not clear. Kilpatrick says that in Japan, where the general level of educational achievement is much higher than ours, only seventeen percent of unmarried girls below the age of twenty have lost their virginity, compared to sixty-five percent of American girls. He does not give the statistics on male virginity.[13] At Eastside High, Joe Clark exults in his initiation of a Virgins' Club, a support group for young women who are, says Clark, under constant intense pressure to "give it up."[14] He does not seem to understand how much more effective it would be if boys belonged to a virgins' club.

Kilpatrick explains that virtue is more natural to girls because they are more easily socialized, whereas a boy's natural inclinations are "aggressive, irresponsible." He remarks that boys like heroes who are not tied down to commitments like spouse or family. Kilpatrick declares that in her study of primative societies, Margaret Mead observed more concern that boys would not grow up to be men than that girls would not grow up to be women. But that concern was not universal and depended upon what society considered the male role. For instance, Mead remarks that, among the Dakota Indians, "the importance of an ability to stand any degree of danger or hardship was frantically insisted upon as a masculine characteristic."[15] If the same ability were professed for women, the society would have equal concern that girls wouldn't grow up to be women.

Additionally, in her introduction to *Sex and Temperament*, Mead is more in agreement with Marie de Gournay when she declares that the discussion of women's character and temperament should not obscure the basic issue: "The recognition that the cultural plot behind human relations is the way in which the roles of the two sexes are conceived, and that the growing boy is shaped to a local and special emphasis as inexorably as is the growing girl."[16]

Mead admits that **before** her studies, she "was innocent of any suspicion" that "the temperaments which we regard as native to one sex might instead be mere variations of human temperament, to which the members of either or both sexes may, with more or less success in the case of different individuals, be educated to approximate."[17]

The aggressiveness assigned to males comes not from nature but from the male rites of passage. Western literature is stamped with the concept of the virtuous restricted woman and the unencumbered male. In her book, *Good Boys and Dead Girls*, Mary Gordon discusses the protagonists of William Faulkner, Theodore Drieser, and Herman Melville.[18] They are men who need to be moving and not tied down to women. It is the hero inherited by today's television and film: the Indiana Jones and every western cowboy who left his errant wild days for a virtuous woman. The demand that only girls be chaste or virgins or chaperoned says loudly and clearly that real men are promiscuous and free.

Julie Hatfield calls their preoccupation with makeup girls' "rite of passage."[19] She is right. The sports culture with its role models cultivates jocks and the sports aspirations of boys; the beauty culture with its fashion models cultivates anorexia and the beauty goddess dreams of girls. And the cosmetic industry is not the only force of such socialization. Girls' toys, including the illustrious Barbie, girls' magazines, and the mass media all play a part. The AAUW reports that girls in grades six and seven rate being popular and well-liked as more important than being perceived as competent or independent, whereas boys rank independence and competence as important.[20] It's no mystery.

## The Media and the Male Rite of Passage

Television, music, and video games establish role models for the young as effectively as tribal rites ever did. Media gender roles that reflect the belief that girls are more easily socialized and have a natural tendency to love while boys are difficult to socialize and have a natural tendency to aggression have led to an emphasis on submission in girls and aggression in boys. The ultimate manifestation of such roles is boys' violence and, conversely, girls' acceptance of violence as a sign of manliness.

Media moguls have decided that the only sure way to grab the Nielsen ratings and box office is through sex and violence. Violence is enhanced by fear and fear is easily aroused by aggressive males preying upon submissive women. A representative for the video games manufacturer Sega of America testified that "Night Trap," in which holes are bored into a scantily-clad woman's body, may not be fit for thirteen-year-olds, but was legitimate entertainment for those seventeen or older.

Pick a movie at random, or a television show. Guaranteed, if the woman in it isn't running from danger partially clad with shirt unbuttoned to the waist, barefoot or in high heels, clutching the hand of a fully dressed man in sturdy shoes, she is all alone on a country road out of gas, in a dark alley, or a deserted warehouse. It doesn't matter how she got there, the fool. It doesn't matter how old she is. She could be an eight-year-old who left her wiser younger brother playing in safer environments. She could be a giddy teenager looking for her lost lipstick, or a fully grown woman blindly facing peril in search of her child, money, or respect. Who cares, the idiot will be beaten, or raped, or murdered and cut to a thousand pieces lest we find the episode dreadfully dull.

Not only does this titillating entertainment make women more vulnerable to violence by men, but it also makes girls more scorned by boys who are planning to become men.

## Women Teachers

Many of the first women to struggle for women's rights, like Susan B. Anthony and Anna Julia Cooper, came from the ranks of teachers because that was the only career open to them. But even today the roster of those in the forefront of the struggle for feminine equity includes a large number of women teachers. Their struggle in the classroom is formidable.

Twenty years ago women teachers who worked for equity in girls' education were considered lethal.

✳   ✳   ✳   ✳   ✳

*In 1970, as president of Orange Country NOW, I was interviewed by a radio talk-show host about sexism in textbooks. Although he had never met me before and had talked to me for about three minutes, he declared that I was a foul-mouthed, bike-riding, leather-booted radical who had no right to teach the innocent children in our schools. His bilious description was so far afield that the one teacher at Walker who heard the broadcast asked me if I knew that someone else in the county had my name. Not very likely. She could not link me with his diatribe because he wasn't talking about me. He was raving about some mad woman who hated men, smacked babies, and smoked in church.*

✳  ✳  ✳  ✳  ✳

Such treatment by the media made any women who protested sexist practices a radical, and radicals are not tolerated by the schools. In the 1970s, school boards and parent groups quoted the scriptures to denounce the feminist movement and teachers who promoted feminist ideas. In all fields, women met such opposition, but it was especially fierce for teachers who were expected to be the epitome of morality based on traditional gender roles. Years later, several teachers told me that my association with the women's movement led others to believe I was a lesbian. Lesbian teachers could not hold teaching jobs. In the late 1970s, California even tried to pass an initiative forbidding lesbians or gay men to teach in the schools.

When they are not considered lesbians, women who object to the culture that exploits them are often considered prudes devoid of sexuality. The label is even more threatening to women teachers who inherit the cultural image of spinster.

In their struggle to gain equity for girls, women teachers need the support that comes from studies like the AAUW's, which says loudly and clearly that lewd drawings, offensive comments, and objectionable behavior are not the natural manifestation of school-boys' puberty, but rather of the humiliation of women destructive to the growth and education of girls.

But the *AAUW Report* itself is castigated by some who profess school reform. Discussing Gilligan, whose work is cited in the *Report*, Kilpatrick declares that it would be unfair to lump her with all feminists thinkers, then proceeds to do exactly that. "A good deal of feminist thought, Gilligan's included," he says, "can be traced to Nietzsche. Simone de Beauvoir was also influenced by Nietzsche and she prefigured all the curious contradictions that make up feminist psychology."[21] Similarly, he claims not to link feminism with Nazism. "It is a big jump from Nazism to current feminist philosophies of education and is not a connection I intend to make."[22] Still, he argues that Hitler was influenced by Nietzsche as were Gilligan and De Beauvoir. By innuendo, Kilpatrick links feminism to Nazism as surely as does another writer who speaks of "feminazis." A cunning word from a cunning little buddha.

Those who claim that the women's movement has caused a breakdown in society are right. The breakdown stems from women's rejection of the notion that morality is a woman's issue, and womanhood an issue of morality. For two centuries, the relegation of morality to women seemed to work because women who, like the vestal virgins, were both victimized and esteemed fulfilled their role. Men sowed their oats, married virgins, developed their life and talents, and with some of the profits supported children. Women remained virgins or pretended to until marriage, then became mothers and sacrificed their lives for their children. It took two hundred years for women to demand not only equal rights but also equity in the responsibility for morality. Determination to bring back the old days is, as nostalgia always is, a fantasy. Instead, both men and women need to find ways to accept the new role of women in the family and in society, and then to find ways to teach it in the schools.

Any attempt to stem promiscuity among teenagers will fail unless it addresses morality, virtue, and chastity as the responsibility of both sexes. From the demand for equity, girls have learned that illicit behavior and talk doesn't destroy womanhood; boys have yet to be told that chastity does not imperil manhood.

## Men Teachers

The idea that virtue was woman's responsibility explains why for years teachers, especially men teachers, believed that sexual harassment of girls by boys was caused by girls' short skirts and revealing clothes against which boys had no defense. Until dress codes became impossible to enforce, and in some cases illegal, schools tried to dictate sexual behavior by regulating the dress of girls. It was a losing battle at best, because what the schools said meant little in comparison to Barbie, who was becoming more voluptuous with every new doll model, or to Miss America, whose swimsuit figure was winning scholarships.

The schools, like any other arena, reflect the society, and there, like anywhere else, sexist practices went unnoticed or at least unprotested for years.

✳ ✳ ✳ ✳ ✳

*On an errand to his class, I once heard an art teacher teach an eighth grade class how to make designs from numbers. He drew a 3 on the board and asked the class what shapes came to mind. "No, not boobs," he said, grinning at his own joke.*

✳ ✳ ✳ ✳ ✳

Men teachers, like American men elsewhere, pride themselves on their open and frank discussion of nudity. James Herndon speaks of the coach, Skates, who got a good evaluation from his principal even though "several teachers had taken offense at his heedless remarks and that female teachers especially thought him overly frank in matters relating to sex."[23] It's one of history's little mysteries that the female anatomy for centuries has been almost totally ignored in medicine, yet almost exclusively represented in nude art. An art teacher once told me it is because the female shape is round and sensuous, more artistic, while the male form is not. Women object to talk about sex and nudity because it is usually not just about sex and nudity, it is about female sex and nudity and how to exploit it. Women who object are considered prudes, and worse, uninterested in sex, an accusation that from girlhood intimidates them to silence.

✳ ✳ ✳ ✳ ✳

*At a faculty meeting, the male administrator introduced a new female faculty member. "Meet our very attractive new English teacher." He thought she would be flattered. He thought his observation made him debonair.*

*Then he introduced the new male history teacher. "Jim has taught two years in junior high. He will be a great asset to the social studies department."*

*While several of us women teachers exchanged knowing looks, none of us protested aloud.*

✳ ✳ ✳ ✳ ✳

*Because she was full breasted, an attractive woman on campus made even more attractive by her clothes and makeup, she was often the subject of lewd remarks by men on the staff. At faculty meetings the remarks were sometimes made in fun and evoked some laughter. Although all of us expressed our umbrage at our lunch summit, none of us spoke out at the meetings.*

※     ※     ※     ※     ※

*The year I came to Walker, the band teacher described for Mordie, a counselor, a funny experience he had recruiting band members in the local elementary school.*

*"As usual, as each kid signs up for band, I asked him which instrument he wants to play. This kid in jeans, sweatshirt, blue eyes and long blond hair, chooses the drum. I can't tell if it's a boy or a girl. I don't want to ask and embarrass the kid so I say, 'What's your name?' The kid says 'Chris.'"*

*Mordie appreciates the anecdote and enjoys a laugh over it. I see the humor, too, but I'm a bit perplexed.*

*"Why is it important to know whether it's a boy or girl?"*

*It turns out my question is funnier than the band teacher's anecdote. Both he and Mordie laugh even harder.*

*"Because I can't have girls playing the drums, now can I?"*

*My consternation must have been visible.*

*"Can you picture a girl carrying that big drum in a parade?"*

※     ※     ※     ※     ※

*A couple of years ago a male teacher told me he noticed that I was less uptight about women's issues than I was when I first came to Walker. But I didn't change; Walker did. Today girls carry drums. Women teachers protest sexist insults and male principals do not introduce women teachers as if they were in a beauty pageant lineup.*

※     ※     ※     ※     ※

Still, there's much to be done. The AAUW's latest report, *Hostile Hallways,* demonstrates that sexual harassment of students, both female and male, is prevalent in most schools.[24]

More than most men, male teachers are in a position to support women's equity. First of all, men teachers work in a field that has been defined by the low status of women. Instead of validation for ambition, creativity, leadership, and assertiveness, male teachers, like female teachers, are expected to be dedicated, loyal, and self-effacing. They suffer the same indignity and subordination as women teachers.

Secondly, men teachers have long recognized the equal competence of women because they have long worked with them in equal status on committees, workshops, and seminars. They have shared responsibility with women in and out of the classroom. Two male Walker social studies teachers and I spent one July at the University of California, Santa Barbara, with fifty other teachers in training for the use of technology in the classroom. As it happened, as many if not more women teachers than men had technological expertise, but neither women nor men were intimidated or embarrassed to get help from the experts. On the other hand, of course, the program was led by a male university professor, assisted by women.

Finally, men teachers have always recognized the diginity of working with children.

## Biased Curriculum

Although the *AAUW Report* is thoroughly documented, Kilpatrick denys that girls are shortchanged in the schools, citing the *Report*'s observations that girls get better grades, are less likely to drop out of school, and are more likely to go on to college.[25] But he ignores the *Report*'s findings that even though more girls than boys graduate and get higher grades in schools, scholarships based on test scores are twice as likely to go to boys. While more women earn bachelor's and master's degrees than men, more men are awarded doctorates and first-professional degrees. Girls choose majors in fields that are less well paid. The fact that girls do better in school and still fail to achieve equity in both career placement and compensation indicates that schools are indeed shortchanging girls.

Kilpatrick further suggests that schools cannot be shortchanging girls when seventy-two percent of all teachers are female. At the same time, he acknowledges that the agenda for the schools is set in university schools of education, where most professors are men.[26] Not only are most university professors men, but most school administrators are as well, especially superintendents. Since professors and administrators mandate, research, and establish curriculum, it is not surprising that even though the majority of teachers are women, the curriculum is nevertheless biased in favor of men. Every reading course or workshop I took on both the elementary and secondary level recommended that teachers find books and literature suitable to boys because, while girls will be interested in any selection, boys will read only boys' books. In his discussion of reading for children, Kilpatrick, a professor of education at Boston College, stresses the importance of heroes in children's lives. His list of heroes include: Galahad, Saint George, the Lone Ranger, Jim Hawkins, Luke Skywalker, Bilbo Baggins, Wonder Woman, Indiana Jones, Ulysses, Sinbad the Sailor, and the Knights of the Round Table.[27] That the list of recommended reading at the back of Kilpatrick's book is evenly balanced among books with male and female protagonists is, I believe, a result of the influence of the feminist movement he scorns. If he had written his book in 1972, or even 1982, the list would probably have included two feminine protagonists, which was typical of reading lists at that time. Furthermore, although he declares them the best source of reading material, Kilpatrick makes no comment on the dominance of male protagonists in the *Bible*, myths, and fairy tales, nor on the fact that in these works women are presented as passive and weak, serving as foils to glorify the strength and virtue of men. It is an issue seldom discussed by professors of education. It is a discussion they owe to women teachers and girls.

## Biased Classroom Management

Since teacher evaluations are based primarily on classroom control, teachers seek compliance of all students but, specifically, girls, because they comply more easily than boys. It is another vicious circle: teachers expect girls to comply because girls comply more readily, and girls comply more readily because they are expected to. Especially when they have large classes, which has been true throughout most of the history of the schools, teachers are apt to cultivate submission in girls.

Women teachers aid and abet in the acquiescence of girls because, as women, they themselves have been socialized to acquiesce and to expect girls to be acquiescent. The cartoon section of any newspaper offers an illustration of the way girls are socialized to be passive and acquiescent. Except when the protagonist is female, like Luann and Little Orphan Annie, every cartoon strip shows girls in the passive role. Every original idea in "Hi and Lois," "The Family Circus," and "Fox Trot" comes from the boys; girls, poor things, wander through the strips looking for love, loss of weight, and a brain. The genius in "Fox Trot" is Jason, who torments his idiot sister Paige. A typical "Family Circus" has one of the boys engineering original play while his passive sister either follows him or tattletales to Mom.

The AAUW research indicates that boys receive disproportionately more attention from teachers than girls do.[28] In *Among Schoolchildren,* Tracy Kidder notes that the first time that Chris got to talk to the girls in her class was during a field trip near the end of the year.[29] Teachers give more attention to boys because teachers expect boys to be disruptive and arrange their teaching to circumvent it. On the other hand, teachers expect girls to be supportive and teach as if girls do not have to be encouraged to learn.

In the one-room schoolhouses, teachers found girls "as a rule more tractable, and caused the teacher beastly less trouble than the boys."[30] But although through the ages teachers have found girls more tractable, they have also found untractable girls more formidable than untractable boys. At Summerhill, A. S. Neill found small boys "more easy to live with than small girls."[31]

Most secondary teachers avow that rebellious girls are much more difficult to reach than rebellious boys.

❊   ❊   ❊   ❊   ❊

*Because they couldn't deal with untractable girls, Walker coaches separated boys and girls by using one class list and sending the boys to the male and the girls to the female coaches. Even female coaches declared that they would rather deal with boys' disruptive behavior than girls. Female teachers of reading, math, almost any subject, will admit that they would rather have a boy angry at them than a girl.*

*"Girls are catty."*

*"They're sneaky. They get into secret groups and gossip and spread tales about you. You have no way to defend yourself."*

*"At least boys are open. If they don't like something, they tell you to your face."*

*I taught boys for over fifteen years in special ed and no matter what*

*the situation, no matter how angry either I or the boys were, I never felt
uncomfortable discussing the problem and finding solutions together.
Girls, if they agreed with me, were my mainstay. They not only coop-
erated but they spread cooperation as if it were contagious. If, on the
other hand, they disagreed with me, the disagreements became personal. While they seldom said anything aloud, they whispered insults
about my personal appearance, ridiculed everything about the class,
wrote hateful notes, and spread vicious rumors. It took days, maybe
weeks or months, to build their trust.*

✳    ✳    ✳    ✳    ✳

I believe that the same socialization that makes girls conform-
ists makes the rebellious among them insidious. Because they are
not expected to express rage or resentment aloud, girls express it
covertly. They attack the personal appearance of their adversaries
because they believe that is a person's most important quality. Sadly,
the difficult behavior of angry girls is another reason why teachers
do not confront girls as often as they do boys.

## Gender Segregated Schools

Joseph Fernandez, who was school superintendent of Dade
County, favors all-boy schools because boys have more problems in
the schools than girls. He suggests that feminist leaders who object
might be persuaded to consider all-girls schools.[32]

He misses the point. Feminists don't believe that an education
program for girls should be derived from a program developed for
boys or that because the boys have a program, then for legal reasons,
girls ought to have one also. Any feminist who has the slightest
inkling of history mistrusts all-boys' schools. They know what
separate but equal education has done for African Americans and
what 2,000 years of such schooling has wrought upon womankind.
Gerda Lerner cites women's outrage at education injustice since the
Middle Ages and quotes Mary Astell's *Serious Proposal of 1730*:
"Boys have much Time and Pains, Care and Cost bestowed on their
Education, Girls have little or none. The former are early initiated
in the Sciences, are made acquainted with ancient and modern
Discoveries, they study Books and Men have all imaginable Encour-
agement."[33]

No reform should look at the problems of the schools as boys' problem. It is not just semantics. As has been noted earlier, some education reformers recommend African-American male schools because Black boys need Black male teachers. I submit that Black boys need girls to have more Black male teachers in the schools. Male African-American teachers are not simply a role model for Black boys; they provide an image of African-American men for Black girls, all girls, and, in fact, all boys, because children now get their images from the media. Solutions in education must be child-centered, not boy-centered.

In her arguments against boys' schools for African-American males, Sharon Knox, a teacher and psychologist in the Baltimore City Schools, notes that females have historically faced discrimination. With segregated schools, they would face it an even earlier age as they watch boys attend special schools and receive special privileges. She also disputes the argument that inner-city Black male children consciously or unconsciously reject females (and females teachers) as role models because women cannot provide appropriate examples of survival outside of home and school. "That's ridiculous," she says. "What about Fannie Lou James, Rosa Parks, Sojourner Truth, and Harriet Tubman?"[34]

In the same article, Clarice Herberts, a Spanish teacher at Frederick Douglass High School in Baltimore, argues the other side of the debate. She says, "For centuries, institutions isolated or separated White males as a way of producing a so-called superior product."[35] The epitome of male academies in this country have been the military academies for officers and incidents like Tailhook indicate what such training does for women of the nation.

Kilpatrick says that the education of boys by men is an ancient, honorable tradition.[36] Like most honorable educational traditions, that tradition thrived while women were denied any education at all. Traditionally, segregated boys' schools have been for sons of the powerful at well-endowed academies with superior resources. The power and endowments raised achievement, not the segregation.

A new study released by the National Coalition of Girls Schools indicates that girls at all-girl high schools are more likely to take and succeed in math and science than both boys and girls at coed schools.[37] The *AAUW Report* cites research that girls often learn and perform better in same-sex work groups than they do in mixed-sex groupings.[38]

Since 1991, applications to women's colleges rose fourteen percent.[39]

*During the four years I taught at an all-girls school, girls starred on debate teams, excelled in basketball, walked off with the science fair trophies. On fieldtrips, girls went where they chose and apologized to no one for their choices. Students packed the busses to support girls' teams. Smart girls were proud, no one thought dumb was cute, and coyness was thought to be silly. What a letdown it was for me to teach girls in a coed junior high, to learn that only the boldest girls spoke in class, that the brightest girls were the most often silent.*

\* \* \* \* \*

My disappointment did not convince me that public schools should be gender segregated, but that all schools should afford girls the respect, attention, and opportunity they enjoy in all-girls' schools. What girls need is non-segregated schools where they major in science and math and where their bodies are no more subject to scrutiny than those of boys. Girls also need the freedom to make their own choices about segregated schools. The supreme court decision to allow Shannon Faulkner a Citadel education is yet another victory in the ongoing battle for girls' right to choose.

\* \* \* \* \*

*"We like to get help from you, after school, Ms. Walsh. There's less confusion," said Parisa.*

*Parisa was from Pakistan; her cousin Irene spent most of her life in California.*

*"It's better for me, too, because I don't have to answer so many questions from so many students," I told her.*

*"It's terrible how some of the kids don't listen, Ms. Walsh. They have no respect," said Irene. "You know what else? That boy with the long ponytail, whenever he's on the GS doing graphics, he draws pornography. Things so bad I can't tell you, but I'm embarrassed when I see it."*

*I know the boy, Nicholas. I watched him grow from a shy seventh-grader in neat clothes into a rebellious eighth-grader in seedy shirts, torn jeans, and the long ponytail. I'm not shocked that he draws pornog-*

raphy, but I'm surprised that he draws it to embarrass the girls.

"Some boys are mean," said Irene.

"Some aren't," I said, "but I'll talk to Nicholas. I don't think he's really mean."

"He's mean."

"Some kids have no respect for anyone," said Parisa, pulling her long black silky hair away from her face.

"Well, you certainly do. I'd like a class full of Parisas and Irenes."

"It is because our parents teach us this way. Our parents are very strict. They want us to show respect to teachers and learn."

"Yes," agreed Irene, whose fair complexion looked more European than Pakistani. "Did you know we're not supposed to talk to boys?"

"No, I didn't."

"Yes, we have to cover our bodies all the time. You notice we always wear long sleeves and pants."

"I practically live in this sweater," said Parisa laughing.

"You know Amir?" Irene asks me. I nod. I do know Amir, a dark handsome young man and one of the best students in the class.

"He is not supposed to wear shorts either, but he does anyway."

"Yeah," said Parisa.

"Remember when you told him to show me the work I missed when I first transferred to this class? It was hard because we're not supposed to talk to each other. We can't date either."

"How will you get to know men, if you can't talk to them."

"Our parents will pick one for us," explained Parisa.

"What if you don't like him?"

"Other people marry for love, that's why the divorce rate is so high. Our marriages last for ever."

"You know," said Irene, "boys are allowed to talk to girls, but girls can't talk to boys. I think it's because, on a date, boys can force girls to do things, but girls can't force boys."

I thought of Golda Meir. Describing the assaults on women by men, one of her advisors suggested that there be a curfew for women after dark. She replied that there should rather be a curfew for men.

When I assigned Amir as partner to Irene because they were both Pakistani, I didn't know about her cultural objection to working with boys. After a few weeks, Irene accepted his help without discomfort and discovered there were times when she could help him.

❊   ❊   ❊   ❊   ❊

In an interview, an Indian professional woman said she didn't mind wearing a chador because the robe allowed her to concentrate on her work and gave her freedom from unwelcomed attention of men.[40] Segregated schools give girls the security of a chador. In public schools, garbed from toes to fingertips, Irene and Parisa have the security of a chador. Amir, on the other hand, is as secure in his shorts.

# Chapter 9

# Schoolhouse Keepers

Through the years, teachers were paid as if they considered teaching its own reward, and were regulated as if they hated work. While teacher salaries have improved, the subjugation of teachers remains the same. But until teachers run the schools with the same authority that doctors run clinics and lawyers run law firms, education reform will continue to be meaningless.

## Dominant Principals

A popular panacea of reformers for the problems of the schools is powerful principals. Joseph Fernandez writes that "An exceptionally strong principal can turn a school around almost single-handedly."[1] Principal Joe Clark tells how he redeemed Eastside

High in Patterson, New Jersey. *A Town Torn Apart* is the film account of principal Dennie "Doc" Litky's reformation of a wild New Hampshire high school.[2] Madeline Cartwright writes the moving story of how she saved Blain Elementary School in Philadelphia.[3]

William Bennett asserts that a good principal can make a good school out of a bad school and offers Mara Clisby as an example. "Mara Clisby moved her desk into the girls' bathroom, and she held her meetings and counseling there, just to stay visible."[4]

Chester Finn praises "a crackerjack principal who takes no guff from anyone, who infuses the entire staff with team spirit, a strong sense of purpose, and an ethos of achievement and sound character."[5] And the Knights of the Round Table thought King Arthur couldn't be topped.

Dependence upon principals to redeem schools is a revered tradition, but it has three major flaws. In the first place, an individual responsible for the health of an entire school has a herculean task. When Elizabeth Jackman and Jan Billings were principals at Walker, they arrived before sunup and often left long after sundown. They were at the beck and call of the entire campus, taking telephone calls at home when the school day wasn't long enough. They arbitrated most disagreements among staff and students, directed every school innovation, and attended almost every school event. Since my sister Dianne became administrator at her school, she spends almost every evening at meetings and half her weekends on school work. Clark writes that the "love of a few thousand kids can be a very tiring commodity. Sometimes, I simply go home and straight to bed."[6] On the other hand, Cartwright says she had plenty of time for her personal life, but she also repeatedly states that she had exceptionally high energy.[7]

It is wishful thinking to expect that all principals will have the energy and opportunity to devote that kind of time to the schools. Administration of a school must be such that less than heroic but honest, capable people interested in children can accomplish it without sacrificing their personal lives. The sooner this is done the greater the likelihood that good education will happen in all schools, not just a miraculous few.

In the second place, success based on personalities disappears as soon as the person does. Clark said, "I hope the school blows up when I leave, goes back to what it was."[8] Schools cannot afford ephemeral solutions.

Finally, the so-called strong principal considers the school his personal domain. But if the school is the principal's domain, no one else has a vested interest in its success. All the eggs in one basket is no better for schools than it is for the farmer in the dell.

Dominant principals talk with enthusiasm about "my" school. Tracy Kidder observed this trait in Alphonse Laudato. Al belonged to Kelly School, he noted, and Kelly School belonged to Al.[9] When asked why he scolded teachers in front of students, Clark explained, "Because I want these kids to know they can come to me and only to me." Clark wrote, "I am the school's benevolent dictator," or "benevolent Big Brother."[10] When told that he sounded like the Wizard of Oz, Clark said, "Good." Now the Wizard of Oz is not a bad choice for school administrator if he could, as Clark claims to have done, provide "close, constant, affectionate, and perceptive contact with the student body."[11] And if every kid in the school wore emerald glasses.

Clark is the epitome of dominant principals. His story was national news and the subject of the film, *Lean on Me.* Clark, so esteemed by Bennett, is the paragon of dominant principals who save schools. He tells his story in *Laying Down the Law,* which in title and context offers a vivid illustration of the humiliation teachers endure in the schools. "If a teacher was incompetent," says Bennett, "Clark told him so to his face. Twenty transferred out."[12] Bennett continues: "I like Joe Clark's philosophy: accept no incompetence. Period. He told teachers that if they were incompetent they would leave in one of two ways, voluntarily or in a straitjacket (Joe pulls no punches), but that he would not let them ruin the education of those children.... Clark now has no bad teachers. Instead, for the first time in twenty years, teachers are lining up to teach at Eastside High."[13] Seven pages later, Bennett declares that we ought to give teachers our trust, our confidence. He descries the fact that teachers have too little autonomy. Go figure.

Explaining his relationship to teachers, Clark said: "I admit there has to be a crucifixion just to build up morale—to let them know someone is tending to the store, know I'm the boss doing my job in a flawless manner."[14] Of one teacher he says, "it was nice to see him blush, nice to know he was feeling some shame for his foolishness"[15] Later he conceded, "I don't yell at teachers in front of students anymore. I don't persecute teachers. We have a synergetic relationship."[16] Yet he says another teacher had better watch his step. "He's precariously perched. I have some good friends in Westside Orange.... He better watch his step or he's gonna be among the missing."[17]

His advice to all teachers: "If you follow the rules, if you go by the book, you don't have no problem. If you're hard working, dedicated, committed, pull your share, you have no problem with me, only one who is not pulling his or her load."[18] Of course, Clark determines who is hard working, dedicated, committed, and carrying the load.

This is the same Joe Clark of whom, when he was a teacher, his principal said he was a talented man but would "slip and slide when I asked him to use his talents for education."[19] And this is the same Joe Clark who, according to district appraisal, has not improved the school that marvelously after all. Joel Bloom, Assistant New Jersey Education Commissioner, says the scores at Eastside High are not good. Ninth-grade reading is up but math is the same and tenth-grade reading scores dropped twenty percent. The high turnover of teachers has led to the demoralization of the staff and the school still has a high dropout rate.[20]

Of the teachers who supposedly stood in line to get into his school, few would talk to reporters. One teacher confessed, "I'm afraid of losing my job." Another admitted that Clark often embarrassed him, saying things like "You can go. We don't need you."[21]

This is the same Joe Clark who brags about his war on teachers, on his ability to turn the screws, "upbraiding them before their students, and in the teeming corridors."[22]

If the crackerjack administrators of Bennett and Finn and others like them were a solution to the problems of education, excellence would be a hallmark of the schools, because the subjection of teachers to the absolute rule of the principal was the rule of the schools for two centuries. It started because women teachers were less educated than their male administrators and had few options besides teaching as a career. In fact, even today, dominant principals prefer female subordinates. Clark writes, "I believe that, on the whole, women are more likely to see the sense in complete loyalty to me and my program. Men seem more worried about losing their identity in obedience, are more likely to covet the catbird seat, and to oppose me on some point or other solely for political reasons."[23] Joe Clark needs teachers who "lean on" him.

## Subjugated Teachers

The philosophy of those who believe that schools should be run by dominant principals is based on the belief that teachers are inept, cannot be trusted, and if left unsupervised will do as little work as possible. As Clark put it, "You cannot afford to accept nonsense from teachers."[24] While Clark boasts that he does his job "in a flawless manner," he believes that there are few teachers "so excellent as to need no improvement in certain areas."[25] Developing a central intelligence agency of his own, he checked up on teachers by interrogating the students. If a teacher made a slip-up, he put it in her folder. Clark dictated what kind of assignments should be given, when teachers should give quizzes, term papers, and long-term projects.

In the tradition of dominant principals, Clark believed that teachers will prepare for class only if they are forced to. He imposed routine humiliation of teachers by weekly lesson plan inspection. Lesson plan inspection is a power tactic to assert a principal's authority, not to improve teaching. Indeed, the poorest teachers have been known to turn in the most impressive lesson plans. Inspection of lesson plans is implemented more on the elementary level than on the secondary level because there are more women teachers on the elementary level. On the college level, which has always been male-dominated, the practice is considered ludicrous and insulting.

I thought that inspection of lesson plans, like mandated virginity for teachers, was relinquished years ago, but a friend of mine in Watervliet, New York, tells me that a principal there not only checks lesson plans—he also collects them at the end of the year and keeps them. How he gets away with confiscating other people's property can only be explained by the intimidation of his teachers. In all my years teaching, I had to submit lesson plans about three times, in each case to the same principal. The hours I spent preparing for class could not be accommodated in plan-book grids, so I simply wrote the accepted buzz words and arranged them in the assigned boxes. Few principals have time to actually read lesson plans anyway. Of course, Clark may have been an exception, because anyone who can relate perceptively daily to a thousand students may be able to scrutinize four hundred and eighty lesson plans weekly. The only lesson plans that should be checked are those of beginning teachers, and then they should be checked by a colleague who is mentor to the novice.

Clark was not satisfied with peering through lesson plans, dictating class assignments, and checking on teachers through students; he also published a substantial volume with about one hundred and twenty headings, listing every detail of school procedure. Even the wording is written to abase teachers: "You will note that my name is the only one appearing with a title (Mr.). This holds true throughout the list and is no accident. The point must be made that one individual is the chief of the entire operation, others are subordinates: one chief, one operation, one purpose."[26]

A dominant principal who is sole redeemer of the school exerts absolute authority. Clark's vice principal claimed that if Clark, in his official capacity of principal, "declared that four was five, and you were foolish enough to correct him, you would receive a full blast of his wrath. Some people never understood this, and mistook his belief in this style of leadership for a show of arrogance."[27] How dare they?

Principals in full charge have little need to consult teachers. A teacher interviewed by Susan Dichter said that although he had a Ph.D. degree and had taught in college and schools in several parts of the country, he was never consulted on any issue and contributed only after he made several attempts to be heard.[28] Without asking them, Litky decided every teacher would have an extra period, called advisory. He told the teachers that he was going to throw the kids at them.[29] Whether they wanted an advisory period and knew what to do with it was inconsequential. When teachers complained that Clark told them nothing about his plans for the school, his only response was to remind them that he was the principal.[30]

Faculty meetings in the schools typically demonstrate the total charge of the principal and the mechanical compliance instilled in the staff.

❋     ❋     ❋     ❋     ❋

*Like all teachers, each September I was required to passively absorb reams of information at faculty meetings whose format and content were decided by the administration identically year after year, school after school.*

*First, the principal gave the latest pitch of the district, how we have no money, or why the drug problem is worse, vandalism up, and test scores down.*

*Nothing was definite as to what could be done about the problems, but the message was that whatever we were doing was not right, and whatever we could do better would be found in our mailboxes in the coming weeks.*

*Next the assistant principal presented his annual spiel on school discipline, which hadn't changed in fifty years, except that swatting was outlawed in 1975 and computerized forms for disciplinary action were initiated in 1990.*

*Then the counselor described all the forms that pass and have passed for twenty years between counselor and student, teacher and counselor, counselor and parent, counselor and the world. He also listed the dates of every standard test students were required to take until the end of the year. The counselor was followed by the librarian, who painstakingly outlined library procedures, textbook distribution, and overdue notices. The school nurse or her representative explained the procedures for sending a student to the health office and the first-aid emergency kit—which consisted of three band-aids, a small card of emergency numbers, and two safety pins.*

※   ※   ※   ※   ※

*One year I asked the assistant principal, "Isn't this just a little waste of time? It's not like we haven't heard it all before."*

*"What about the new teachers?" he replied.* This is a man with some kind of degree in administration.

*"Hold an orientation for the new teachers."*

*"You'd be surprised how many veteran teachers don't follow proper procedures."*

※   ※   ※   ※   ※

It doesn't take a degree in administration to learn that if veteran teachers don't follow procedures, it's not because they haven't heard them.

Kidder noted similar meetings at the school he observed for a year. The principal dragged out faculty meetings, sometimes distributing printed handouts and then reading the contents to the teachers.[31]

✳ ✳ ✳ ✳ ✳

*The last day of school the process was reversed. While I wanted to finish reports, file information, store equipment, and talk at leisure to lingering students and colleagues, I had to run about the campus collecting signatures to assure the principal that I had obediently finished the year the way a good teacher should.*

✳ ✳ ✳ ✳ ✳

James Nehring remarks on such an experience: "Thus reminded, in our terminal last day of the school year, of our lowly position in the great hierarchy of public education, we teachers dutifully obtain the needed signatures and, with heads bowed low, are granted our last paycheck for the next two and a half months."[32]

Because they know they have little to say about the school in general, teachers remain isolated in their classrooms, which explains why even strong, creative teachers have little effect on the teaching methods of their colleagues. Madeline Cartwright tried to encourage teachers to share ideas and work. "It's sometimes amazing," she wrote, "how insular, isolated, and autonomous a classroom can become, in a place as crowded as a school."[33] By January, James Herndon, the first-year teacher in *The Way It Spoz to Be*, admits that he didn't give a damn about what happened outside his class.[34]

## Female Principals

Patricia Albjerg Graham notes that although nearly all administrators were formerly teachers, the gap separating the two groups is immense.[35] Fernandez says we need to break down the barrier between teachers and principals, yet he admits that when he wanted to get all the students on his side he called an assembly and asked the teachers to leave the room.[36] One reason for the gap between administrators and teachers is that the requirement for administrators is degrees, not teaching experience. In many districts, moreover, the teachers who become principals are chosen for their loyalty to district norms. Often they are those who are least effective in the classroom and least respected among their colleagues. Cartwright admits that she saw many people become principals to get away from the children,[37] and I've seen a good number myself. The gap between administrators and teachers has a long history. For two centuries, administrators were powerful males and teachers were powerless females. What may change the relationship between them is the rise in the number of female administrators. In the *Second Stage*, Betty Friedan analyzes what she terms masculine and female methods of governance.[38] She explains that the masculine style, alpha, which seeks to control, originated from the need of our primitive ancestors to control and manipulate the environment. Beta deals with small groups and developed with family life. That beta traits are evident in women school administrators is demonstrated by studies which indicate that they govern collaboratively, working together with the whole group or small parts of the group, instead of controlling the group through dictation.

Whenever I worked under male administrators, I believed that the school was pretty much their domain. I knew that, outside my classroom, I was of little consequence. I did my job; they did theirs, and the twain never met. Except for predominantly informative faculty meetings and half-hour lunches, there were no group discussions among teachers.

❋ ❋ ❋ ❋ ❋

*During my first year at Walker, I taught the only special education class on campus and later chaired the department as several classes were added through the years. I knew that my high evaluations came because I kept the students happily in class, out of trouble, and out of the office. It was an assumption rather common in the schools.*

❋ ❋ ❋ ❋ ❋

Cartwright noticed the same phenomenon. She declares that teachers who kept students quiet and brought no attention to their classes were often the most rewarded.[39]

Alpha-style administrators needed to contact teachers only when they broke the rules, and they never needed teachers to contact each other.

✳ ✳ ✳ ✳ ✳

*One of my most difficult tasks as a special ed teacher was trying to contact regular class teachers. When we did meet, it was at 7:30 in the morning, for the benefit of working parents. Classes started at eight and teachers wanted to be in class at least five minutes before time. In the time between 7:30 and 7:50, I had to get input from six teachers. The rest of the time we communicated through notes in mailboxes.*

✳ ✳ ✳ ✳ ✳

*In 1982, when Walker got its first female principal, Jan Billings, I worked for the first time on a schoolwide project, gathering observations, statistics, and plans for a grant application. For the first time, I saw my class and my work as part of the whole. Billings garnered such help from teachers throughout the school. She called faculty-designed staff meetings, in which we discussed school concerns as a group, having the time and opportunity to compare notes, ideas, and objectives. In a kind of renaissance, teachers began meeting all over campus, submitting ideas to the entire faculty, displaying interest in what happened beyond the classroom door, and believing in school renewal. It wasn't that we hadn't worked as hard before, it was that for the first time we believed that not only our work, but also our suggestions, had meaning. That was the year Walker won the California Distinguished School Award.*

✳ ✳ ✳ ✳ ✳

*Elizabeth Jackman, our administrator after Billings, not only continued to seek input from teachers, but she also inaugurated committees in which teachers designed the daily schedule, yearly budget, and staff development. At that time, Jackman was the only principal in the district to allow teachers to plan the budget. The committees gave Walker teachers opportunity to affect the course of the school, to voice objection and support. They did more for morale than any awards had ever done.*

## Shared Decision-Making

Although school reformers have called for "shared decision-making" management, in which the principal shares decisive power with the staff, studies show that few teachers believe systemic change has occurred to make such management happen. In 1989, the teachers in Jefferson High School in South Central Los Angeles initiated a special program in which they wrote the curriculum, chose their own textbooks, and directly controlled the budget. They found that the greatest obstacles were the site administrators who felt that they would lose control and power and become gofers.[40] But administrators should lose power. Schools are much too important and complex to remain one person's personal domain.

✳ ✳ ✳ ✳ ✳

*The first step Walker took toward shared decision-making was the daily schedule, the most revered document on campus. The schedule determines what subjects will be taught, who will teach them, in what room, and to how many students. The schedule establishes who will be assigned the recalcitrant troublemakers and who the eager achievers; who will get first-period study hall, last-period conference, and second lunch shift; what English teacher will teach American literature, or world literature, or remedial writing.*

✳ ✳ ✳ ✳ ✳

Traditionally the schedule has been designed by the people it least affected: the principal, the assistant principal (AP), and the counselors. The more dominant the principal, the more secretly the schedule is made. Typically, the AP meets with department heads behind closed doors to discuss department needs. After that, behind closed doors, he and the counselors devise the schedule. Teachers who are savvy to the system arrange to meet privately with the AP. All discussions are confidential, so that teachers can't question or evaluate anyone else's assignment. Only strong, assertive, schedule-wise teachers can influence changes. The completed schedule is displayed in the office, where teachers could see it but not amend it. No document causes more ill feelings, distrust, and divisiveness.

This method of creating a school schedule explains why new teachers get the troublemakers, nonconforming teachers get the toughest assignments, and why some teachers have five different classes to prepare while others have two.

✳ ✳ ✳ ✳ ✳

*It explains why Walker initiated a scheduling committee. When a committee of teachers and administrators designed it, the Walker schedule came out from behind closed doors. Any teacher who wished could volunteer to serve on the committee, which announced the dates, time, and place it would be working and encouraged teachers' suggestions and criticisms. We publicized all requests and honored as many as we could. We didn't please everybody every year, but at least everybody knew why. Marlene Lipps requested that her home economics classes be scheduled back to back so that she could more easily have the food ready for cooking lessons. When we couldn't arrange it, we asked her to try. When she couldn't, she was disappointed, but at least she understood why it couldn't be done that year.*

*The principal forwarded all questions or complaints about the schedule to the committee. It was the first time teachers confronted each other openly on issues that had formerly bred secret rancor. I had my first disagreement and frankest discussion with a science teacher, a friend I had admired for years. It did nothing to mar our relationship and may have enhanced it.*

## Changing the Power Structure

While school reformers extol the tradition of powerful top-down management, industries whose similar power structure has remained unchanged for decades are now reevaluating worker/management policy. Business observers like Jane Bryant Quinn claim big-name companies that for years were the backbone of American industry have grown inefficient and complacent primarily because of their power structure.[41] Mark S. Handler and Myron E. Ullman, co-chief executives of Macy's, that symbol of American Christmas, talk about empowering employees to give them a chance to make decisions and carry them out.[42] Because of the recent violence of its workers, the Post Office has mandated a study of its management techniques. The main finding has been that workers are treated like robots, not given any role in the decisions that affect the workplace.[43]

The centralized power that thrived at IBM for years is now considered the reason for its downfall. Calling IBM's bureaucracy the "big gray cloud," Carla Lazzareschi describes how it was the cause of IBM's falling profits and rising layoffs.[44] She says IBM's corporate culture was once the model of American business for its strength, efficiency, depth, and commitment, but today its work force has become stultified with yes-men and middle management so devoted to the dictates of the machine that new life and creativity and awareness of the competition was impossible. Today, the first aim of the company is make its divisions more autonomous.[45] Lazzareschi could be talking about the public school system.

Schools have to rethink their entire power structure from the superintendent to the students. Superintendents have their own gray cloud of district and site administrators whose first alliance is to the district machine, not the school, and whose work force has largely become yes-men through years of enforced conformity. This is what has stymied reform. The first step for the schools is to cultivate autonomy at the school sites and erode the controlling power of the district. District offices ought to perform only those services that will assist the schools. Districts should not dictate local policy, design site budget, or determine site staff. The district school board should be composed of locally elected representatives from each school area. In this way, parents and local community members would dictate district policy, not politicians.

David Perkins says that almost all educational innovations fail in the long run because they are imposed rather than cultivated. He recommends that teachers be "allowed a role" in the reform.[46] Teachers should not be allowed a role, teachers should write the script and allow administrators a role. As successful as Jackman's shared decision-making was, it is not the final answer for the schools—schools without principals are the answer. If decentralization and sharing power with the workers is good, making the workers administrators is better. Shared decision-making still ultimately depends upon the principal. No matter how effective, a system that depends upon the final word of a single person will not save the schools.

## Schools without Principals

*One morning I shared with Elizabeth my thoughts on a student workshop.*

*"You know what I would like?" I said.*

*"Yes, I know. You would like my job."*

*Elizabeth has a sense of humor. Moreover, she was partly right: I didn't want her job; I wanted all the teachers to have her job. Six years earlier, when Walker's last male principal planned to retire, he jokingly asked me if I wanted to interview for the job. When I said no, he placed a notice in the faculty bulletin declaring that I applied for the job but failed the interview.*

*I responded with a notice declaring that a committee of teachers had conducted our own interviews for a new principal and, after serious consideration, decided that no one could do the job our principal did and that's exactly who should follow him.*

\* \* \* \* \*

As schools have grown, so have the responsibilities of the administrator, who must be the instructional leader, cafeteria manager, transportation coordinator, purchasing executive, building manager, and staff evaluator. To make the job more manageable, some schools have a vice principal in charge of curriculum, a vice principal in charge of discipline, a vice principal in charge of activities. The list continues, increasing the big gray cloud. Graham notes that typically the administrative cadre grows while the number of teachers remains static or shrinks. In 1991, when Los Angles schools had more than 16,000 new students, the district eliminated 2,000 teachers but none of over one hundred administrators, all of whom earned over $90,000 a year and thirty-three of whom earned over $100,000 a year.[47]

In a school without principals, the staff would be in charge and as a group delegate responsibility for tasks. There would be no hierarchy, no power pockets, and fairer salaries. Teachers would come together and devise their school policy, pooling resources in much the same way that lawyers form partnerships and doctors form health centers. The group would have time outside the classroom to plan curriculum, devise and evaluate pilot programs, plan innovations for grant proposals, study and evaluate textbooks, and meet with clients, both parents and students.

If need be, the group would hire someone to do administrative tasks like keep financial accounts or perform checks for conformity with state and federal regulations. All school operations might be done by the committees in much the same way it was at Walker, but each school would find its own way to operate. If the school chose to retain a principal, he or she would be chosen by the group, not the district, and would operate as part of the group and answer to it. Instead of being imposed, leadership would emerge from the dynamics of the group. Moreover, the more obligations a teacher assumed in running the school, the greater would be her compensation, thus establishing a type of career ladder now sadly missing in the schools.

One obstacle to schools without principals is principals who don't wish to relinquish power, but another is teachers who don't wish to assume it. Administrators who have used shared decision-making have found that many teachers do not want to serve on committees and prefer to have the principal make all decisions. The *Encyclopedia of Education* says that teachers have never had a great desire to obtain control over the school system.[48] It is not surprising, since they have been trained to subjugation for 200 years. The stories of outstanding teachers, however, demonstrate how their best efforts are thwarted by the absolute authority in the schools, from Jaimie Escalante, to Malva Collins, to the young teacher in *The River Runs Wide*. That teachers are apprehensive about assuming shared responsibility for the schools is precisely why they should.

The main obstacle to schools without principals is teachers without time. Teachers do not want to assume administrative tasks because they do not have the time. When Fil and I served on the scheduling and budget committee at Walker, we were at meetings three or four days a week for two or three hours before or after school. To give teachers the necessary time, schools without principals would designate administrative tasks as part of teachers' job descriptions, not added to their teaching assignments.

Money to buy time for teachers to run their own schools would come from the salaries now paid to administrators. Since money for schools is tax money, which is always limited, it should at least be more equitably divided among those who do the work of the schools. While substitute teachers are hired at little more than minimum wage, administrators in some districts are retiring as millionaires.

Teachers would also get time from assistant teachers who would assume many of the tasks now done by teachers: monitoring, testing, drill exercises, research, correcting papers, and recording marks. Assistant teachers would not be as qualified as teachers, nor as highly paid. The just concern of unions is that assistant teachers would be hired to do the job of teachers, thus jeopardizing the salary of teachers and leading to the hiring of unqualified teachers. Regulations would have to be devised in which teaching assistants would help teachers in much the same way that medical assistants help doctors.

As it is now, teachers are assisted by aides who are usually women and the most exploited workers in the system. Aides are not only underpaid, but they are also usually hired part-time so the district does not have to provide health benefits. Much of the achievement of special ed teachers would be impossible without the hard work aides do for a pittance.

✳   ✳   ✳   ✳   ✳

*The aides I worked with over the years were unfailingly generous, dependable, and creative. Joan Johnson worked with the students in class and accompanied us on field trips, including overnight ones, giving many extra hours and endless patience. Pat Wells not only worked with the students, but she also managed reams of special ed paperwork for me and all the teachers in our department. Celia Chen taught in Taiwan before she came to Walker. Through her and her family, I experienced firsthand the Asian devotion to education.*

## Unions

Bennett and columnists like Thomas Sowell contend that unions are the biggest barrier to reform in the schools.[49] Clark claims that the only way he could improve learning at Eastside High was to circumvent the union,[50] but Theodore Sizer's study of secondary schools demonstrates that many of the same problems Clark faced are apparent in districts that never had unions. Sizer believes that unions are the result of bad conditions, not the cause.[51]

School history validates Sizer's claim. Until unions, teachers barely earned the minimum wage, had no right to protest administrative decisions and evaluations, no limit to duty assignments, no appeal in firing or transfer decisions, no health or retirement benefits. In fact, before unions, teachers could not afford to retire.

Nehring, a teacher himself, declares that the unions should have no part in curricular issues but, as it is now, the unions afford teachers their only input in curricular issues.[52] If teachers ran the schools, they would not need the unions for curriculum issues, but only for labor issues.

Schools without principals will not eliminate the need for unions, but they will offer the best circumstances for negotiations for two reasons. First of all, teachers would gain an understanding of both administration and labor. Fernandez noticed that, in Dade County, when he gave the teachers more voice in managing the schools, teachers were more inclined to listen. When teachers are equal architects of the budget, they are less likely to strike for monetary issues.[53] During the Anaheim strike, superintendent Cynthia Grennan wrote an open letter to the teachers, assuring us that she was looking for a salary increase that was "fiscally prudent." If the budget were an open issue, both sides could find a "fiscally prudent" solution.

Secondly, in schools without principals, teachers would represent all the concerns of the school at the negotiating table; therefore, they could accept full responsibility for negotiated commitment. As it is now, negotiations must be held with principals and teachers in separate bargaining sessions, often pitting one group against the other.

## Teacher Accountability

School reformers recite horror stories of teachers who come to school unprepared, waste students' time with meaningless busy work, and return home without having enlightened a single mind. Terry Frith wrote a book on the secrets parents should know about the schools and spent six pages of it describing teachers who sullied the school by their presence.[54] To hear Clark tell it, one would think that Eastside had no good teachers until he got there and that there wouldn't likely be any when he leaves.

The traditional school system was designed on the premise that most teachers are unconscientious and will be conscientious only under the watchful eye of the principal. But just as students rise to the level of teacher expectations, so teachers rise to the level of competence expected of them. Schools will be improved if reform is based on what gifted teachers do right, not on what rotten teachers do wrong.

For all the publicity they get, strong principals in traditional schools have been able to do little about poor teachers. Frith, who describes the menace of poor teachers, was apparently unable to change them in her own role as school administrator. Administrators argue that it is the unions that won't let them deal properly with ineffective teachers, but in schools without unions, principals do no better in addressing the problem of poor teachers.

On the other hand, schools without principals provide a technique for remedying ineffective teaching that has never been used in the schools: peer pressure. No one resents a bad teacher more than a good teacher does. Bad teachers not only give all teachers a poor name, but they also give all teachers more work.

✳ ✳ ✳ ✳ ✳

*For example, at school assemblies, Walker teachers were to remain with their classes to help maintain order. With nine hundred students crowding into the cafetorium or gym, it was easy for a teacher to slip away, leaving a class unsupervised, no matter how strong the principal was. Those of us who remained resented having a larger group to supervise; those who left considered it a trivial matter.*

✳ ✳ ✳ ✳ ✳

If administration of the school were everyone's job and teachers held routine meetings to discuss school affairs, they would share their concerns. It would be routine also for teachers who were doing the job to set straight those who weren't. If teachers ran the school together and knew that they were responsible for everybody's success, they would not tolerate ineffective teachers. Moreover, ineffective teachers would find it easier to solicit and receive help in improving teaching skills because they could ask for help without risking administrative censor.

## The Risk of Schools without Principals

The risk of a school without a principal is that the teachers who are responsible for school administration might not do their jobs. But a principal might not do the job either. A school without a principal, therefore, constitutes less a risk because its administration is in the hands of several people; if one fails, only some damage is done. In a traditional school, on the other hand, the risk is greater because its administration depends upon only one person; if that person fails, the whole system fails. The more dominant the principal, the greater the risk. Clark declared that the single cause for a school's failure is the failure of its principal.[55] Schools must be designed so that their success is in the hands of more than one person.

## Advantages of Schools without Principals

The first advantage of a school without a principal is that it puts the money and prestige in the classroom where it belongs. Instead of offering advancement to one or two administrators at a school, administrative tasks would offer most teachers a career ladder without taking them from the classroom. As it is now in the school system, the farther away one gets from the children, the more one gains in prestige and money.

Secondly, in a school without a principal the people running the school are those who know what it is like to teach in a classroom, the main business of the schools. Today, decisions are made by principals who forget or never knew what it's like to teach children all day.

Third, in schools without principals, the school, not the district, is the first concern of educators, because those who make the administrative decisions have to answer to the school, not the district. The principal in *Among Schoolchildren* admits he does not consider himself an expert in instructional practices. He believes, as many administrators do, that principals do not need expertise in instructional practices. But schools should be managed by those with instructional expertise because instruction is the school's main objective.

The most important advantage of schools without principals is that it affords teachers dignity and autonomy. In this country, the teaching profession cannot compete with others for the best and brightest candidates because while doctors, lawyers, and engineers, for example, are respected and autonomous, teachers are powerless underlings. For years, the schools were staffed by the best and brightest of the nation's women because they had few other options. Today, however, unless the teaching profession develops professional opportunities, it will not only cease to attract these women, but it will continue to remain unattractive to men. Furthermore, the present lack of minority teachers will continue because minority youth who achieve success against great odds are not likely to choose a career that offers little power or prestige.

Ernest Boyer writes that in the schools he observed, when achievement was high, the principal made the difference.[56] But Boyer didn't observe schools without principals.

# Chapter 10

# Beyond the PTA

All the analyses, all the new programs, all the government summits, and all the big-name posturing will not change the fact that the only people who can effect lasting school reform are the teachers, and they can't do it without the parents. Parents need to monitor their children's education as carefully as they do their children's health. To do this, they need to respect teachers as they do doctors, and teachers need to operate the schools with the same authority that doctors do clinics.

## Traditional Role of Parents in the Schools

Traditionally, just as teachers had no input into school policy, so parent involvement in the schools was through the Parent Teacher Association (PTA), which was primarily a booster club. The PTAs provided much-needed financial and moral support, but they did not constitute a teacher-parent partnership. Although they were welcomed, even sought, in most schools, some schools did not want them on campus. For the first fifteen years I was at Walker, there was no PTA, although I heard the school had one when it was founded in 1959. One administrator refused to resurrect the organization even though parents requested it.

Until the last few decades, neither parents nor teachers felt the need for parents to do more than support booster clubs because parents gave the schools the right to act in their behalf, *in loco parentis*, and expected the schools to do their job without interference. The 1645 Dorchester, Massachusetts, school instructions reflect the spirit of the schools for centuries: "The schoolmaster shall have full power to punish all or any of his scholars, no matter who they are. No parent or other person shall go about to hinder the master in this...if any parent or others shall think there is just cause for complaint against the master for too much severity, they shall have liberty to tell him so in friendly and loving way."[1]

This kind of authority almost guaranteed a safe, distraction-free learning environment in the schools. But society has grown less tolerant of the absolute authority not only of the schools, but of all social institutions. Generations ago parents seldom questioned school policy, never questioned church authority, and accepted whatever financial terms banks proffered. Today parents debate church teachings, investigate bank procedures, and evaluate school practices. However much we may wish it, blind acceptance of revered institutions is not part of today's culture, which is moving not only toward democracy worldwide but also toward individual empowerment.

Other institutions have altered their way of dealing with clients. Years ago, for instance, the doctor's word was sacred. Patients did as they were told and hoped for the best. Today, not only do patients demand to know more about doctor's prescriptions, they also assume more responsibility for their own health through exercise, balanced diet, and stress control. Medicine has become holistic, considering the whole person, not just her physical needs. Similarly, education must consider a child holistically, an impossible task without an active teacher-parent partnership.

Critics who demand that schools exert the same authority they did thirty or even twenty years ago are craving a rumble seat ride. Those who would recall the strict schools of their youth need to remember that in their youth, parents were also more strict. The government had unquestioned power. Whole segments of the population had no rights.

## Changing the Parent-Teacher Relationship

Since schools can no longer depend on unquestioned *in loco parentis* to maintain order and foster learning, they need parental presence. Madeline Cartwright believes that the main reason for her success at Blain School was that she involved the parents. She considered her initial victory at Blain the overwhelming response to her first parent meeting. She encouraged the parents to help out in every capacity, even using them to administer standardized tests. Most of all, she encouraged them to become teachers themselves or to qualify as substitute teachers.[2]

When the Voorheesville, New York, school district took national honors, the district claimed it was community participation more than anything else that made their schools the best. They had ninety-five percent turnout for parents' night and thirty parents helped to present programs in an after-school science club, which drew a thousand students to participate.

\* \* \* \* \*

*Every year Fil and Ric held a foreign language potluck dinner. Students prepared songs, skits, and jokes using Spanish, French, and Latin. Parents prepared dishes representing world cultures. It was the most parent-involved event of the year, and the only one where student behavior was never a problem.*

\* \* \* \* \*

While such parent participation results in overall school improvement, it is not enough. Parents must also play a part in designing school policy, because people support best that which they helped to create. Across the nation, schools are implementing school councils in an attempt to include parent input to school policy. California's School Improvement Program (SIP) demands such a council as a condition of SIP funding.

For two years I served on Walker's SIP council, and while I see such councils as a step in the direction of real parent participation, I also see that the councils embrace the traditional power structure. Teachers and parents exchange dialog, but the central power still lies with the administration. In many schools, because he has the time and opportunity, the principal determines the election process for selection of parent representatives. He is in a position to influence the nomination of parents.

No matter how much principals support teachers and parents, they must answer first to the district; therefore, school site council agendas tend to center around programs that make the district bureaucracy look good. Before school site councils can have real meaning, district and local jurisdiction must be reorganized to give local sites more autonomy. The role of the district should be to help local sites implement their programs, not to dictate policy.

## Parent-Teacher Partnerships

Ultimately, site councils must involve teachers, parents, and the local community. In the first place, schools ought to have national standards so obvious and clear that teachers, parents, and the community have norms with which to evaluate their schools. Secondly, the partnership between parents and teachers must be based on mutual respect. Teachers have the responsibility of educating students to the national standards while accommodating the concerns and mores of parents and the local community. Parents and the local community ought to recognize the professional competency of teachers and respect their need for autonomy in designing and implementing education in the schools.

It is a difficult task for both sides, primarily because such partnerships are new and untested in American education. Traditionally, teachers have been expected to do their job, consulting parents only when children are delinquent. Parents have been accustomed to directing their concerns, not to teachers, but to higher officials, such as local or district administrators.

## Obstacles to Parent-Teacher Partnerships

One of the main obstacles to teacher-parent partnerships is principals. By job description, principals do not foster teacher-parent partnerships because their task is to act as a buffer between teachers and parents. Teachers interviewed by Susan Dichter tell of administrators who would prefer that teachers not discuss any disagreement with parents without the principal's mediation.[3]

All the administrators I have known encouraged teachers to contact parents directly. At the same time, however, they played interference whenever they thought it necessary. Having principals as a buffer makes it easier for teachers, but when they know that principals have the final word, neither teachers nor parents feel the need to come to terms. In his comparison of American and Japanese schools, for example, Harold W. Stevenson and James W. Stigler note that when disagreements arise between parents and teachers, American parents, rather than working with the teacher to resolve the difficulty, would be likely to try to have their children transferred to another classroom—a solution that could never occur in a Japanese school."[4]

Transferring a student to a different class is a common occurrence in American schools, because teachers have no say in students' transfers either in or out of their classes, but it is a poor strategy because it teaches students to evade difficult situations rather than resolve them. Moreover, it erodes the respect and authority teachers need to educate students and to work with parents.

Jesse Jackson tells parents to get to know teachers because teachers treat kids differently when they know their parents.[5] Jackson is right. Through thirty years of teaching, my most successful students were those whose parents I talked to or met in person, even when I disagreed with them, as I did the day I took Tommy's radio.

\* \* \* \* \*

*It was one of those New York wintry days when the sun sets too soon. I worked in my deserted classroom, trying to finish before dark. Just as I picked up the last report my sixth graders had written on why the Tigris-Euphrates Valley was a good place to live, a man's face appeared in the little glass square of the classroom door. Before I could move, he stomped into the room. Despite the cold, he wore no coat or jacket over his sweatshirt, which seemed too tight for his bulging biceps.*

*"Are you Miss Walsh?" he bawled.*

"Yes," I said, wondering if I should admit it.

"You took my son's radio."

So that's why he looked familiar. He was Tommy's father. In a few years and a lot more pounds, Tommy would look exactly like him.

"Yes," I said again

"Well, I want it back."

Now he didn't look like the kind of man anyone with a thirst for life and limb would refuse, but when I remembered how boldly Tommy twice turned on the radio in class after I told him to put it away, I lost my perspective.

"If you return this radio to Tommy, I will not teach him the rest of the year," I said, not as forcefully as I would have liked.

"You gonna throw him out of class?"

"No, I don't think I can do that. I will give him a seat in the back of the room and I'll just ignore him. I won't read his work or give him assignments. I'll pretend he's not there."

It was an empty threat and no way to talk to a parent. I could see him marching down the hall to the principal, or, if that didn't work, calling the school board and the superintendent.

"You can't do that."

"I can't teach him either, if he knows that he doesn't have to listen to me."

"He said some kid played the radio when he wasn't looking."

"Tommy had the radio in his desk the whole time."

When he didn't answer, I pressed my case, describing how Tommy and his radio disrupted the class, how unless Tommy did his part I couldn't teach him a thing, how lucky Tommy was to have a father to stick up for him.

"He's not really a bad boy, you know."

"I know."

Tommy's father and I talked for about fifteen minutes. I came to see that he thought his son was singled out unfairly; he realized that if Tommy didn't have to listen to me about the radio, he wasn't likely to listen to me about anything else. I kept the radio for a week. Tommy not only learned history, but he and I also became good friends. Years later, he told me I was one of his favorite teachers.

Tommy's father could have gone to the principal, not only because I took his son's radio, but also because I told him I wouldn't teach the boy for the rest of the year. He settled the matter with me because we had the *opportunity to meet and speak together. If Tommy's father had gone to the principal, we might have settled the radio dispute on the same terms, but our relationship would have been weakened because both of us would have known that our differences were settled by the principal's mediation, not our own mutual understanding.*

✳   ✳   ✳   ✳   ✳

If parents and teachers cannot come to terms, mediation must be available, but it doesn't have to come from the principal or any other authority figure. Ideally, the solution should be a conference in which the disputants confer in the presence of a parent advocate and a teacher advocate.

Another obstacle to parent-teacher partnerships is parents' fear of teachers. Cartwright says that parents are especially afraid that disagreement will lead to retaliation on their children.[6] Fears between parents and teachers have been cultivated by the system for years, and the only way to dissipate them is through meaningful and constant dialog, which would have to happen if teachers were responsible for the school and had to answer directly to the parents.

## Teacher Obstacles to Parent-Teacher Partnerships

Terry Frith, a former school administrator, claims that most teachers aren't trained to deal with parents.[7] Most of the teachers I worked with knew how to meet with parents, but if Frith is right, than the situation must be corrected. The fact that most teachers do not know how to work with parents doesn't mean that they shouldn't.

School officials and teachers themselves argue that teachers don't want to have to contend with parents, that they have enough to do in class, and want to give lesson preparation their full attention. But that is precisely the philosophy that for years has bred the isolated classroom.

The main obstacle to teachers forming partnerships with parents is that teachers have not enough time to meet with parents. In the first place, teachers often have too many students. In the second place, the time teachers now spend in secretarial tasks should be spent in parent contact. The secretarial tasks should be either eliminated or done by secretaries or teaching assistants.

Probably the biggest obstacle teachers present to partnership with parents is their fear of interference. Cartwright says teachers do not want parents snooping about like "unwanted mothers-in-law" who know they can do things better.[8] They are also afraid that failures will be publicized. As long as teachers are servile subordinates who have no control of their schools, who look to administrators to direct and defend them, they will be intimidated by parents instead of collaborating with them.

✳   ✳   ✳   ✳   ✳

*When the Walker teachers believed that the district was misinforming parents about our position on the contract, we called a teacher-parent meeting in the school library. Although we informed the principal, we did not ask her permission or direction. I considered the meeting an unqualified success because, for the first time, teachers were talking directly to parents in a friendly forum. Such meetings should be held on drugs in the schools, or violence, or school improvement, or any school program needing parent support.*

## Undermining Parents

Since the beginning of schools, parents have claimed that schools undermine them. They do. Schools have always undermined parents and always will, because education is meant to both enforce old skills and open the mind to new ideas. New ideas inevitably undermine some customs and beliefs of some parents. Novels have been written about the crisis that occurs when educated children reject the beliefs of their parents or when educated children are ashamed of uneducated parents. William K. Kilpatrick declares that both Plato and Socrates were justly accused of turning the young away from their parents.[9]

In earlier times, parents believed that schools should use more physical punishment. Colonial parents wanted more whipping. Farming parents wanted no schooling at all. In the early New York schools, Mariana Griswold van Rensselaer was not only a wealthy parent and heiress, but a member of the Public Education Association (PEA) and a tireless worker for school reform. She was also against women's suffrage and certainly found teachers who worked for the nineteenth amendment undermining her philosophy and tainting her children with their views.[10] In many schools today, parents think there should be more drill, more memorization than there is. They reject the American Council of Mathematics Teachers' recommendations that calculators be used in class and with tests.

The point is that while some parents believe the schools are undermining their values, other parents believe the school are reinforcing them. For that reason more than any other, parents and teachers need to meet as equals on the local level and come to terms. If schools had national standards, both parents and teachers would have a practical tool to use in such discussions.

## Need for Teacher-Parent Partnerships

Thomas Sowell repeatedly accuses the schools of not teaching essential curriculum in order to promote esoteric programs like death education, witchcraft, and hugging trees.[11] I don't know where these schools are. I have taught in public schools in farm towns, in an inner city, in the suburbs of upstate New York, and Orange County, California. I met with teachers from all over the country in technology workshops and education conventions. I never met a teacher who was into witchcraft. The only students I saw hugging trees were those in the schoolyard dodging acorns. But if such bizarre teachings do exist in the schools, they are only one more argument for parent-teacher partnerships. When teachers have to answer directly to parents, they are more apt to stand by accepted curriculum. In addition, they will be forced to justify, and explain, new programs and methods to parents.

Parents need parent-teacher partnerships in order to better understand and support the education of their children. Teachers need such partnerships to buttress their relationship with both parents and students. Without his mother's support, it would have been much more difficult for me to deal with Danny's unflattering invectives. Without their parents' ovation, my students would not have worked hours after school on tedious projects. Without parent support and recognition, I could not have had the tremendous satisfaction I did have in teaching.

## Parent Evaluation of Teachers

Chester Finn cites a study in which seventy-two percent of American parents rated their children's schools A or B. Nineteen percent of the rest rated them C. Ninety percent of American mothers judge their children's school "excellent."[12] Stevenson and Stigler say that although the scores of American children are lower than that of Asian children, American parents are more satisfied with their schools than Asian parents are.[13] Both Stevenson and Stigler and Finn declare that American parents are more satisfied with their schools because they do not have the national standards by which to judge them.

Creating national standards for this country is a little more complex than imposing standards on countries the size and with the homogeneous culture of Japan, but if schools are to become a national priority they ought to have some kind of national standards. National standards would equalize the academic norms across the land and increase national support for the schools. Some national standards are already used. Students in my advanced placement English class had to compete in a national test. National math standards were established four years ago by the National Council of Teachers of Mathematics. Recently the American Association for the Advancement of Science(AAAS) established national benchmarks for what students should know after the second, fifth, eighth and twelfth grades.

On the other hand, when they criticize American parents' high evaluation of their schools, Finn and Stevenson and Stigler may be seeing only half the picture. It is quite possible that American parents rate their schools higher than Asian parents do because American parents want more from their schools than higher test scores. Stevenson and Stigler acknowledge that American parents expect their children to be successful in non-academic skills, including social acceptance, appearance, sports prowess, and thinking skills. Sports, marching bands, field trips, and similar events are part of the American school picture. Parents judge schools by these events as much as by test scores. For example, one of the main things the parents on the Walker SIP council wanted most was a drama class.

Parent-teacher discussions need to address the effect of the programs they want on the school's achievement of national standards. They also need to communicate about what it is parents want and what teachers are prepared to give. If the schools, as Cartwright contends, are to provide social services as well as education, teachers' jobs either have to be redefined or other personnel in the school will have to work together with teachers. But teachers' jobs ought not be redefined; teachers ought to remain responsible exclusively for the scholarship of the next generation. Where necessary, social services ought to be provided by a supporting staff. Perhaps this is an area that ought to be privatized. In any case, a partnership of parents and teachers ought to decide how a school will provide, first of all, an education up to national standards, and, secondly, what other responsibilities a school shall undertake.

## Testing

National standards are not the same as national testing. Testing, as it exists in American public schools, is used primarily to intimidate teachers. For all their higher standards, Japanese schools do not teach for national testing. In her study of Japanese primary and intermediate education, Merry White writes that the first role of the schools is to teach virtues: sharing, respect for elders and country, perseverance in problem solving, and dedication to duty. So busy are they teaching and nurturing children in these virtues, notes White, that Japanese teachers do not have time to teach for tests. In fact, the Japanese teachers' unions contend that cramming for the examinations is a poor substitute for learning.[14]

Teaching for tests is not done in the Japanese schools but in the *juku,* a private after-school class whose job is to get students to cram for tests. Since only those students who do well on the tests are accepted into higher education, the tests are highly competitive. Between public school, *juku,* and private lessons, Japanese students spend almost all of every day from seven to seven studying. In fact, the Japanese people are currently reconsidering their emphasis on tests. It does not appear to be healthy for their young people, who have very little time for anything but school. Furthermore, by the time students get to college, they are burned out, and college has become a place to relax and have fun.

The AAAS criticized science teachers for covering too much material and demanding too much memorization, which is exactly what teachers do when they prepare students for the typical standard tests.

*  *  *  *  *

*When I taught in New York, where my students had to pass the state regents exam, I used the last three weeks of school as a* juku *session. I would pass out old copies of the regents test or regents study guides published by the state and private publishers. Everyday we would cram for the tests. Students hated the process, but no more than I. I never believed they were learning anything except how to pass a test, but given the school system, perhaps that was enough.*

*On the other hand, when I taught advanced placement English, I never concentrated on content but on the research, writing, and evaluation skills; yet all my students did well on the tests.*

*  *  *  *  *

The first reason for their success was that they were self-motivated and avid readers. The second was that the test itself was geared not to memorized facts, but to basic skills of writing, reading, and research. Students were given a sufficient choice of literature which required only that they were well-read, not that they had covered every selection in an era. National tests need to be designed in that fashion. New York State is considering revising its regents requirements to supplement tests with portfolios of student achievement.

That kind of national assessment would enable schools to concentrate on non-rote learning and the development of learning habits. Such a system would raise the educational level of all students and raise standard test scores as well.

## The Role of Mothers in Education

Originally, teaching was considered an extension of motherhood for American female teachers. Today, the role of mothers is integral to the discussion of education. For instance, the comparison of American and Japanese education and the higher scores of Japanese students cannot be seen in valid perspective without acknowledging the responsibility of Japanese mothers. Japanese mothers dedicate their lives to the education of their offspring and are personally shamed when children fail in school. Stevenson and Stigler note that Asian mothers buy extra textbooks so they can help students at home and also save money to send their children to private tutoring after school.[15] White tells of a Japanese mother who quit her job when her son began doing poorly in school.[16] The pressure for the cramming that Japanese children do for tests comes not from the schools but from Japanese mothers who cultivate what White calls "examination hysteria."

Their devotion to their offspring's education does not win Japanese mothers sentimental regard. On the contrary, they are considered nags. Even the male school teachers with whom Bruce Feiler worked considered their wives shrewish about school.[17]

There was a time when American mothers devoted more of their time to children's education. Douglas MacArthur was one of the few cadets at West Point to graduate first in his class, taking not only the top academic awards but also those in physical fitness, sports, and military training. It is said that he did so because his mother lived at the West Point hotel and watched him study through a telescope from her window.[18] Now every American mother was not a Ms. MacArthur, but most had time to devote to their children's education and had a strong identification with their success.

I believe that the crisis in education in this country can be explained in large measure by the fact that women today are seeking fulfillment not only in motherhood but also in achievements outside the home. I believe further that the real crisis in Japanese education will come when Japanese women are respected for their work both in and outside the home and cease to live their lives primarily for the education of their children. Moreover, there will be criticism of Japanese women for causing the moral breakdown of society just as there is of American women.

Feiler and White observed that Japanese men spend little time with their children.[19] I believe that because Japanese mothers concentrate so strongly on their children's scholastic success, the absence of fathers has no significant effect on Japanese education. For years, American mothers took full responsibility for supervising children's education. Few self-respecting fathers, for example, would be caught dead or alive at a PTA meeting. The system seemed to work here then as it does now in Japan. But today, as American women are taking on more work and challenges outside the home, they need the help of fathers. The fact that they're not getting it is greatly responsible for the education crisis. A recent Harvard University study declared that the majority of fathers interact meaningfully with their children about 37 seconds a day.[20]

## Tax-Supported Private Schools

Some school critics contend that the way to improve public schools is to take money from them and give it to private schools, by giving parents who choose private schools a tax subsidy. They claim that if tax dollars supported private schools, public schools would improve by competition with them. But public schools already compete with private schools.

No doubt more tax dollars will improve private schools, just as they would public schools, but money for education is already inequitable under the school property tax. To assign tax dollars to private education would exacerbate the inequities, because while public schools must educate every child, private schools are not required to do so. If public schools could relinquish their responsibilities, even as they relinquish their dollars, the proposition would be more just. If the public schools lose tax dollars, they should be allowed to deny education to the handicapped and delinquent children who are a major part of the schools' budgets. But such a situation would set the schools back fifty years, when they were allowed to do precisely that.

William Bennett says that all parents should be able to enjoy the advantages of private school.[21] The best way do that is to determine what it is about private schools that attracts parents and implement it in public schools.

First of all, private schools have less bureaucracy than do public schools. If public school teachers were locally autonomous, the district bureaucracy would shrink. Schools run by teacher-parent partnerships would have their own school boards. The district-wide school board would be composed of representatives from local school sites, not politicians.

Secondly, private schools enjoy a greater commitment from parents than do public schools. When parents invest a small fortune in their children's education, they are likely to monitor both the school and the child. Parents of children in church-supported schools are also more likely to monitor the school and support its teachers. Since public schools can depend on neither financial investment nor religious belief to foster parent support, they have an imperative need to cultivate teacher-parent partnerships. If parents and teachers ran their own schools, parents would have a greater investment in the schools and, hence, a greater commitment.

Third, private schools provide a safer learning environment, especially in the cities. This is explained partly by their right to exclude students whose behavior threatens that environment. It is due also to the fact that private schools can exert their own disciplinary codes, because parents give private schools more leeway in doing this than they do in public schools. Some private schools have the rights of *in loco parentis* in much the way all schools did years ago. If public schools were run by parent-teacher partnerships, parents would be able to design their own disciplinary codes and the means to enforce them.

Another advantage of private schools is prestige. Just as in England, where private schools offer prestige for the wealthy, so do the wealthy private schools in this country provide prestige to their graduates. Public subsidies to parents will not get children into these prestigious schools, because the prestigious need to keep their schools elite. If tax dollars enabled the poor to pay the tuition of these prestigious schools, the school would raise its tuition. In fact, requirement for acceptance at prestigious private schools is based not only on what you can pay, but also on who you know. Many private schools guarantee acceptance to children of alumni. Private schools are often the only way academically mediocre offspring of the wealthy can pave their way into prestigious colleges.

The argument as to whether public schools should be affiliated with religion has been alive since education in this country started through church schools, which were often funded by tax dollars. One reason for the argument was that although most Americans were people of strong religious belief, they all believed their children ought not be subjected to the teachings of other religions. It took over a hundred years for the schools to accept the doctrine of separation of church and state. Although it evolved for political reasons, its ultimate result has been to provide all religions equal access to the public schools.

Sowell remarks that Chicago teachers in overwhelming numbers send their children to private or parochial schools.[22] Chicago's teachers use the private schools because they know better than anyone how unsafe and poorly operated public schools are. That is not an argument to give tax money to private schools; it demonstrates a reason to reform Chicago's public schools. Fil sent both her sons to public schools, as did Fran Thimgan. Every teacher at Walker had children in public schools, as did most of the teachers in the Anaheim district.

## Schools for Profit

Another suggested way to improve public schools is privatization. The move to privatize schools is especially ironic at a time when the country is moving to nationalize health care. Moreover, privatization of major industries has not had a stunning record of success. After years of effort to transfer government work to private companies, the White House acknowledged that contractors are squandering vast sums because federal agencies fail to supervise how hundreds of billions of dollars are spent each year. Federal auditors found that private companies spent money on lavish expenses, including tickets to sporting events, cruises, and excessive salaries for executives. The public is still reeling from the deregulation of the airlines and the saving and loans industry. The *New York Times* reports that private industries like Borden, Pet, and Dean Foods have reaped millions of dollars of artificially inflated profits in selling milk to the public schools.[23] One can only guess what profits they would reap if they had full control of the schools. Recently, television's *Sixty Minutes* reported that over fifty percent of the emergency clinics in the country are staffed by incompetent doctors because the company that hires them cuts costs and makes profit by hiring cheaper, unqualified doctors. That similar profit-making strategies would occur in privatized education is highly probable. It bears noting that no matter what the cost of defense or the race to space, the nation has not been willing to relegate these services to the private sector.

The primary goal of private enterprise is profit, which is often more important than integrity, as is evidenced by the dairy industry.

What happens when profit is the first goal can be seen in the television industry? Eighty percent of Americans believe that there is too much violence on television, but the television industry says its first aim is to produce profit and violence sells. When business controls the schools, they will cater to the market just as television does. Regulation of business is a threat to free enterprise and it will be a threat to those in the business of making profit in the schools

Christopher Whittle is already making money in the schools by giving schools free television film in exchange for accompanying advertisement. When Whittle gets tax dollars to support his school, how will such advertisements be regulated without interfering with business operations and freedom from censorship? How many other business schemes will Whittle be free to implement? In speaking of the effect of television on children, Marilyn Miedzian is adamant: "I argue that if we want to stop our national bloodbath, we cannot continue to leave the enculturation of our children, without regulation, in the hands of people whose major concern is financial profit."[24] But if schools are privatized, they, too, will be in the hands of those whose major concern is financial gain.

In the last analysis, private and parochial schools subordinate the compensation and autonomy of teachers to either profit or the promulgation of God's message. Schools that exist for profit traditionally achieve profit by paring the main budget item: teachers. Schools that exist to uphold religious ideals sacrifice teacher status to the need to build more schools in order to reach more people.

## No Schools

The most radical plan to relieve the public of the burden of the schools comes from Lewis J. Perelman, who declares that hyperlearning is the end of the schools.[25] In his vision, the power of virtual reality and other video computer technologies enables parents and children to learn at home together at any age in any field. Perelman claims that modern technology makes education in the home so powerful, effective, constant, and fast that it makes schools obsolete.

Parent education of children at home is not news. Parents have been educating children at home with remarkable success for thirty years. Despite Perelman's enthusiasm, however, home schooling is not possible everywhere. While the parents in Perelman's scenario may eagerly embrace the opportunity to direct their children's education, many of today's parents find it difficult to direct their offsprings' television viewing, much less their laser technological education.

Parents now have difficulty finding day care for preschool children. If the schools did not educate older children during the day, parents would have to find some kind of supervision for them as well. Furthermore, if child care in Perelman's projection does not include academic learning, child custodians will not have to be educated. Care of children from preschool through secondary school age will again become menial underpaid labor.

While hyperlearning may be ideal for parents who have the time, will, and ability to educate their children, public education must always be available for those who don't.

## Commitment of Parents to Teacher-Parent Partnership

Teacher-parent partnership requires much more of a commitment from parents than the old PTA booster clubs, and there are parents who cannot or will not give it. But, just as assuredly, there are parents who can and will. Just as the schools cannot be regulated according to needs of the worst teachers, so partnerships cannot be designed for the least responsive parents. All parents will not participate in their children's education, but if the schools capitalized on just those who are willing and able, they would reap the benefit of tremendous parent power on campus. Teachers all over the country benefit from parent commitment to Girl Scouts, Boy Scouts, Little League, and similar for-children enterprises. As the word gets out that parents are as welcome and wanted as they were in at Blain School in Philadelphia, teacher-parent partnerships will thrive.

# Chapter 11

# Children Should Be Seen and Not Hushed

The gap between teachers and students is wider than the one between teachers and administrators and is directly related to it. Nowhere has the subjugation of teachers had more dismal effect than on school discipline, because teachers were not only subjected to stringent rules themselves but were also evaluated on the rigid order of their classes.

Generations passed through the schools, exchanging war stories of the harsh discipline they endured, considering it testimony to their rigorous education. The only reason that schools were happier than prisons was that many teachers evaded the rules and many students ignored them.

## Corporal Punishment

For centuries, teachers did not need to cultivate cooperation among students; they coerced them to it. Corporal punishment was the trademark of the schools. It is not difficult to see why. Healthy children are active, noisy, disruptive. Teachers were expected to keep them still, quiet, on task. Corporal punishment was used in the schools during the era when it was commonplace in the home, and it served the schools so well that it became ingrained. Because they themselves were treated with little respect, many teachers accepted the denigration of children through corporal punishment. In fact, what many teachers hated most about the school reforms of Horace Mann was his rejection of corporal punishment.[1]

Corporal punishment is outlawed in most states today, but until the 1970s it was highly regarded in many districts, including Anaheim, and used pretty much the way it was used with Billy.

※   ※   ※   ※   ※

*Billy was an eighth-grader in my educationally disabled (ED) class. The first year I had the class ED, stood for emotionally disturbed. But the boys in the class—there were seldom any girls—were neither disabled nor disturbed. They were a group of about fifteen who couldn't cope in regular classes because they couldn't read or adjust their behavior to the regular class regime. In special education, most students behaved well simply because the classes were small and they got more attention. Billy was an exception.*

*Billy stole from other children, poked, ridiculed, mimicked, and bullied them. I tried preaching, coaxing, bribery, threats. Nothing helped. When I talked to his mother, she told me that compared to what he did at home, Billy's school behavior was worthy of commendation. She and Billy's father didn't know what to do with him either. I developed patience in that class and tolerated much more than regular class teachers, but when Billy poured glue on a classmate's hair, I referred him to the vice principal. Which shows how little I knew.*

*"I'll give him a swat," said the vice principal.*

*Billy came back docile as a whipped puppy and I thought my problem was licked. But after a week, he reverted to his old ways with more cunning than ever. His brother, a successful seventh-grader, often asked me how Billy was doing in class.*

*"Pretty good," I said, figuring Billy needed a censoring sibling about as much as I needed freeway congestion at seven-thirty in the morning.*

*"My father will kill him if he gets in any more trouble."*

*It was Billy's brother who told me that Billy's father believed in corporal punishment way beyond swatting. If corporal punishment worked, Billy would have been a model student.*

*During the school book fair, Billy, who hated to read, stole a book on magic. Instead of returning it, I bought it myself. I read one of the magic tricks to the class and asked them to try it. To the surprise and applause of us all, only Billy could do it. He begged to be allowed to take the book home, promising in exchange to work hard without trouble all week. I might have given him the keys to my car for that. Monday morning he set a table cloth over his desk and put on it six glasses filled to the brim with water.*

*"You wanna see some magic?" he asked us. "You wanna see me take that there cloth off that there table without moving the glasses or spilling the water?"*

*Now there was nothing in Billy's resume to back his claim and nothing available to mop up the water should it spill over the desk and the floor, but it was the first time Billy had volunteered to do anything in class and it might very well be the last.*

*"Abracadabra and hocus pocus," Billy crooned, slowly moving his hands in a wide circle over the table.*

*In the next instant before our very eyes he seized that there cloth out from under those glasses before the water could ripple. That book of tricks got Billy through a month of peaceful behavior. By the time he got bored with it, he could get along with his classmates, who had given him such acclaim. It was magic enough for me.*

✳    ✳    ✳    ✳    ✳

*Some weeks later, the vice principal happened to meet me in the office.*

*"I have to swat a student. Would you be a witness?"*

*It was then I saw that this swatting thing had a ritual dictated by state law and school policy. Apparently, every time it was administered, there had to be an adult witness. Until then, I knew that the school had this punishment, but I hadn't realized how degrading it actually was.*

*"No," I said. "I don't think so." And I didn't.*

*At a committee meeting on school discipline, I suggested we drop the swatting policy.*

*"It served us well all these years," said the vice principal. "I don't see any need for a change."*

*"It's simpler than suspension or detention," said the counselor. "It's over and done in minutes."*

*"But it's absurd," I said. "What does it do for the kids?"*

*"It works for some of them."*

*"It wasn't allowed in the last school where I taught. I think it's illegal in New York."*

*"We have our own system," said the vice principal. "Don't come here, giving us any brilliant ideas from New York."*

*It was the only meeting I ever walked out of in protest. The vice principal and I never became close chums, but the more I realized the magnitude of his problems as school disciplinarian, the more my sympathy for him grew. I also realized how much punitive thinking drove the schools. I never changed the vice principal's mind and he never changed mine, but corporal punishment was illegal in New York and it soon became illegal in California.*

❋   ❋   ❋   ❋   ❋

In his comment on Dade County schools, Joseph Fernandez notes that Black teachers favor corporal punishment and so do Black parents. "They may have a point," he says.[2] Madeline Cartwright, an African-American educator, turned around Blain School by bringing love and hope to its poor African-American children. She used physical punishment when all else seemed to fail.[3] But I believe the use of corporal punishment has nothing to do with Black and everything to do with poor. Poor immigrant families also favored corporal punishment. The biographies of self-made men who came up from poverty are filled with tales of the physical beatings they got as children. The poor children who grew up to be middle-class parents are adamantly averse to the school's use of corporal punishment. Corporal punishment is as demeaning for teachers as it is for children.

## Detention

With the banishment of corporal punishment, the schools' penal system depends on detention, suspension, and expulsion. At Walker, detention was assigned for incomplete assignments, tardiness, cutting class, disrespect, disruption, defiance of authority, insubordination, profanity, threats, throwing objects, and disorderly conduct. Each offense had a number; for example, profanity was fifty-three and tardiness was forty-two. The vice principal and some teachers knew from memory what a code forty-two was. The punishment for not serving detentions was more detention, just as the punishment for truancy was often suspension from school.

Tracy Kidder remarks that at the first faculty meeting of the school he observed for a year, the principal discussed the detention plan.[4] I suspect that the detention plan is on the agenda of the first faculty meeting in every other school in the country. It takes up more time than any other item and sets the mood for code enforcement.

✳    ✳    ✳    ✳    ✳

*With Jan Billings, we had our first faculty meeting in which teachers actually had a choice about supervising schoolwide detention. We had a long, heated debate in which some teachers argued for even stricter detention procedures, like allowing no work to be done in the room, even schoolwork, but having students just sit and stare at the wall. Others argued that by not giving detention, some teachers coddled students and made discipline harder for everyone else. Personally, I believed that if you gave many detentions, there was something wrong with your class management, unless you had all the disruptive students in your classes, which often happened in the remedial classes. In that case, I believed, detention still wasn't the answer. Rethinking remedial classes was.*

*Finally we compromised. All the staff, including administrators, who wanted a schoolwide detention room would rotate the responsibility. Those who didn't take turns in detention supervision could not send students to the detention room, but would have to supervise them in their own rooms. The list of teachers not using the detention hall grew longer every year.*

*I stayed in the computer lab at least forty-five minutes every day after school, but I never gave detention. If I thought it would work, I'd have assigned it in a minute, but I found it as effective as locks on a swinging door. Students who came willingly to detention changed their behavior, turned in their assignments, or atoned for whatever their misdeed was, but they would have done the same if I just spoke to them. Students who came unwillingly didn't change at all. They just became regular detainees.*

*Detention is a discipline tactic designed to succeed least with the students who need it most. These students refused to come. Students who didn't come were assigned a second, longer detention. If they didn't show the second time, they were assigned Saturday work. Some students liked Saturday work because it gave them a chance to meet with their friends, who most likely were there, too. If they didn't show for Saturday work, they got suspension. These were kids who wore detention and suspension with pride and considered those who didn't get them "nerds." These were kids who didn't want to be in school in the first place and probably arranged the scenario so they could get their wish.*

✳     ✳     ✳     ✳     ✳

Parents like detention. Most of them have grown up with it and believe it develops character. Many parents suspect that teachers who don't assign detention are not doing their job. Even some students want it. One year I had two outstanding aides in the computer lab, Jason and Doug. Both of them were conscientious about their education and showed respect and courtesy to their teachers. There were days when we spent more time after school debating detention than we did the wisdom of having Apple computers in the lab instead of IBMs.

## Suspension

The advantages of suspension are that it gets troublemakers out of school, and, because they have to find a place for them, it gets troublemakers' parents more involved in their education. Suspension has serious disadvantages. It frees the student from the obligations of school, which is often his not so secret desire. It also releases an unhealthy number of young miscreants to the streets. It breeds a truancy from which some students never recover.

For the last couple of years, Walker instituted "in-house suspension," in which suspended students had to come to school, but
were not allowed to attend classes or lunch with the rest of their
classmates. Instead, they sat all day in an isolated room with adult
supervision. I don't know what they paid the school aide who sat all
day in that room but it couldn't be enough. It might not be legal. I
heard that some kind of law, maybe state law, said that students
must be under the supervision of a certified teacher at all times. It
was the reason administrators gave as to why teachers had to
supervise detention, lunch, school dances, or wherever else teachers
were needed for—anything but teaching. It could be true. The state
passes some ridiculous laws.

The advantage of in-house suspension is that it gets the miscreants off the streets, but it changed behavior no more than detention
did. Some students spent so many days in the suspension room they
couldn't remember where their regular classes were.

## Expulsion

Expulsion is the last resort and the gravest punishment of the
schools. It is suspension for life. No matter what the school does,
there will always be a few students who will make life and learning
miserable for everyone else. School, after all, is a microcosm of
society. Even as I write, the sociopaths who threaten our streets are
growing up in schools across the land.

A. S. Neill, in whose school lessons were completely voluntary,
admitted that certain students had to be expelled.[5] Joe Clark was
extolled nationwide for expelling 300 students during his first term
as principal. Expulsion is necessary to protect the learning environment, but it doesn't change behavior any more than swats or detention. Jonathan Kozol reports that most of the 300 students Clark
expelled are now in jail.[6]

## Special Education

One of the alternatives to suspension and detention in the last
couple of decades has been special education for the learning disabled, which mushroomed in the schools when parents of children
with learning disabilities demanded that their children be given
equal opportunity for education, a just demand that could not be

denied. When I taught special ed, the majority of my students were learning disabled children who benefited from the smaller classes and individual attention of special ed classes.

I always had a few students, however, who were placed in my class simply because no other teacher on campus could tolerate their behavior. No psychologist ever admitted that students were assigned special ed because of behavior problems. Instead students were said to have a learning disability when tests indicated a four-year gap between their ability and achievement. Under that criterion, disruptive students easily qualified, because their behavior naturally interfered with their achievement. Under that criterion more and more special classes for the learning disabled have become holding tanks for delinquents.

Today there is a movement in the schools to mainstream all special ed students, especially those with learning disabilities; certainly a step in the right direction. Despite the fact that I taught special classes for the learning disabled under one title or another for fifteen years, I always believed that whatever I did for the students was counteracted by the stigma of special education.

✳   ✳   ✳   ✳   ✳

*"And don't say hello to me in the schoolyard," warned Betty, a third-grader in my class. "I don't want anybody knowing I have the special ed teacher."*

*Richard yelled at anybody who left our classroom door open. "Shut that door, you fool. I don't want everybody seeing me in this here fool class."*

*Hank stood all he could as the children debated what class they would be in the following year. Finally he spoke. "What does it matter? You'll still be in special ed. You'll be here next year. When you go to Hackett Junior High, you'll be in special ed. You'll be in special ed the rest of your life."*

✳   ✳   ✳   ✳   ✳

Harold W. Stevenson and James W. Stigler report that there are few special ed classes in Asian schools and declare that there are no hard facts to show that years of special education actually bring a student up to peer progress.[7] As a matter of fact, many students in special ed never get beyond the remedial stage and are not exposed to the enriched learning that comes from peer discussion and inter-action.

✳   ✳   ✳   ✳   ✳

*Jake's parents wanted him to learn the times tables; they insisted that they be included in his Individual Education Plan (IEP). They had been rightly told all their lives that the time tables were the basis for math and were determined to help their son succeed in that area. I would say that Jake majored in multiplication tables his entire seventh grade. We drilled, recited, wrote, and played games to learn the times tables. By June he knew them all. His parents were delighted and Jake was over the moon. When he returned in September, the only tables he remembered were the tens.*

✳   ✳   ✳   ✳   ✳

Special education, like anything else on campus, should not be determined, as it is now, at the district level. It should be designed by the teachers on campus with the input of parents and students. Teachers know which students can be mainstreamed: those who do not disrupt the learning process for everyone else. With smaller classes and teaching more assistance, regular class teachers could accommodate cooperative students even if they have learning dis-abilities.

## Alternatives to Special Education

Special education classes may be the only alternative for chil-dren who are severely physically or mentally handicapped. It has served this population well, providing hope and academic achieve-ment to children who only generations ago would have lived with-out real intellectual challenge. But special education for children who cannot read or those who cannot learn without disrupting a class merits reconsideration.

There is no doubt that students who disrupt classes should be isolated, not only for the benefit of their classmates, but also for their own. Left in the mainstream, they develop low self-esteem because their antisocial behavior elicits rejection from teachers and peers. But special education in classes labeled LD or EH or ED is not the best alternative.

First of all, special education placement requires a time-consuming ritual of reports, analyses, meetings, promises, and affidavits, whereas isolation of disruptive students should be immediate. Furthermore, return to regular classes should be immediate. Students should be allowed to return as soon as they exhibit the desire and ability to do so, no questions asked, no psychological testing, and above all, no weeks of delay for paperwork.

This is crucial because disruptive children are usually average or above average learners. For them, isolated classes can be devastating, leading them to believe that they are slow learners, while keeping them from regular education so that they fall behind and indeed become slow learners. In isolated special ed classrooms, children spend years learning the basics of reading, phonics, and decoding, but they are not exposed to such concepts as metaphors, structuring for a climax, or satire. They do not pit their opinions against their classmates. They are not exposed to ideas beyond their experience, as are children in a large group.

Secondly, special education concentrates on a child's inabilities, rather than on his abilities. Shunting disruptive children to isolated classrooms for individual attention emphasizes their inabililty to read rather than their intellectual capacity. Instead, assignments that show what a child can do should be provided in the regular classrooms. For example, assignments for non-readers should depend, much more than they do now, on oral recitation both among students and between teachers and students. For the first time in the history of education, technology makes it possible for teachers to provide practical alternatives for students who can't read. Instead of reading research for a report, students can watch films or do interviews on tape recorders. Instead of writing a report, students can recite it live or on tape.

What's more, children can use technology in the regular classrooms to learn to read. The hyperlearning advocated by Lewis J. Perelman for learning at home is surely as well placed in the classroom.[8] If technology taught soldiers to read in months, it can teach children in years. While reading and writing remain the ultimate goal, students would not be segregated while they acquire these skills. They would remain in regular classes, learning self control and task completion without the stigma of special education. Above all, they would be contributing members of their classes.

They would know that they are contributing members and they would not have to resort to disruptive behavior either to save face or to voice their frustrations. The millions of dollars now put into isolated special ed classrooms would be far better spent in putting technology in all classrooms.

It may be argued that non-readers would feel inferior in a class of readers, but that is true only if they have no other way to show their abilitlies. In this technological age, children admire audio and video achievements.

It might also be argued that given these alternatives, some students would never aspire to read. But even audio and video tasks require reading and students are not likely to lose their awareness of the need to read. Furthermore, they are more likely to want to read and write when they are surrounded by classmates who read and write than when they are isolated with non-reading peers. Children, like the rest of us, formulate their standards according to the level of their group. There are very few children who do not aspire to do what everyone else is doing. It's the seed of sibling rivalry and the reason neighbors try to keep up with the Joneses. Additionally, their achievements in regular classes would convince children that they can learn, even learn to read, but special ed placement convinces many children that they can't learn.

This is not to say that reading classes would disappear. They would still be available at all grade levels. The difference would be that non-readers would benefit from a full well-rounded education, free from the stigma of special education from which few students successfully emerge. Interventions without stigma should be available as early as possible, before children accept failure as a way of life and delinquency as a badge of honor.

## Programming for Punishment

Schools rely on punishment because they are designed to promote transgression. In the first place, the school day is a rigid regimen that would test the patience of a robot. Stevenson and Stigler said that Japanese students are less disruptive because, although they have a longer day, they have a recess with physical activity every forty-five minutes. American students are expected to sit at their desks all day long with a half-hour break for lunch. Walker students are in class from 7:45 a.m. until 2:30 p.m. with seven classes a day and four minutes between classes. The day is typical of junior high schools. Although elementary school children get more recess time, they have to spend it seated at their desks in inclement weather, chained to their seats by rain, sleet, snow, and cold.

Besides having more recess to work off their energy, Japanese students are allowed to be noisier than American students in class because, whereas Japanese children discuss and solve problems together, American teachers lecture. American teachers lecture because they are under pressure to teach for tests, and lectures are the fastest way to cover all the material for tests. They lecture because the Lancasterian system, in which one adult educated five hundred students, enjoyed great popularity in the schools. They also lecture because preparing for six classes a day, at least half of which are different in context, is easier done by lectures than organizing group learning, which requires much more planning. If American teachers had more time for planning during the day as Asian teachers do, they could more easily implement group learning.

## Rules

Instead of imposing only those rules which are absolutely essential, schools devise a host of petty regulations that are unnecessary and often unenforceable. The more rules abound, the more students will be punished for breaking them. When I taught in parochial schools, the kids had to walk in line in silence to go to the bathroom. In public schools they had to walk in line in silence to go to assembly. At Walker, students walked in groups to assembly but they had to sit by class groups and were not allowed to find seats next to their friends in other classes.

PE teachers have a strict rule about dressing out. Most of the detentions PE teachers give are for not dressing out. When I taught special ed, I had a student who ditched school everyday after lunch because he didn't want to dress out. I heard of kids who didn't graduate high school because they flunked PE for not dressing out.

The no gum rule is grist for legends. Since the invention of Wrigley's spearmint, each generation of students has found a new way to chew gum undetected. Nobody knows better than school children how to swallow a wad of gum in an instant, and nobody knows better than they how amusing it is to pretend before a wary teacher to be chewing gum when you're not. Students knew that I could no more monitor their gum than I could their shoelaces. I didn't care what they had in their mouths as long as it didn't smell or leave droppings about the room. The one time I had trouble with gum on seats, on the floor, and near the computers was the semester I tried to enforce the no gum rule. Cartwright says she did not allow gum and candy in her school because the sugar is not healthy and makes children hyperactive.[9] If she educated the children to the poor nutritional value of gum, it's a gem in her crown, but if she thinks that they stopped chewing because of the no gum rule, the children at Blain were foxier than most.

The rule that is most difficult to enforce is compulsory attendance. The problem with compulsory attendance is that neither the schools nor the legislature have clarified what attendance is worth. Worried about climbing high school absenteeism, the Shenendehowa School District in New York enacted a policy requiring that students attend eighty-five percent of their classes to receive credit for a course. The State Education Commissioner, Thomas Sobol, rendered the policy invalid, ruling that a student receiving a passing grade may not be denied credit for poor attendance. But if attendance doesn't affect grades, why should students go to class? If students can master subjects through independent study, why shouldn't they? If Sobol makes attendance unnecessary, he should make it optional.

The state should allow local sites to make decisions about attendance. In the Anaheim district, a passing grade was based proportionally on homework, tests, and class work. If a student didn't come to class, he didn't do the class work and, therefore, could not get credit. That credit system, at least, provided a reason to come to class. It also gave students a reason for doing homework. If homework didn't affect the grade, many students would not do it. But if students can master a course without doing homework, and we all know many who can, there's no reason they should do it.

To say that schools can be run entirely without the use of penalties is simplistic; nevertheless, schools need to reassess the traditional use of rules and punishment. First of all, there should be as few rules as possible. This not only makes rules easier to enforce, but it also clearly designates their importance. Secondly, punishment should be assigned only for those actions which either disrupt the learning environment or constitute verbal or physical assault. Punishment should not be assigned for violations such as not doing homework, failure to attend class, or any behavior that affects only the individual involved. Such behavior has its own negative consequences. Schools should find ways to encourage student achievement, not police it. Finally, wherever possible, students should be involved not only in the establishment of rules and penalties, but also in their enforcement.

## Punishing Teachers

School schedules are as hard on teachers as they are on students. Little as it is, at least children get a break during recess; but teachers must continue working, supervising students during recess. School officials would be happy to increase recesses for the students, but they would do it by assigning teachers additional recess supervision. Supervising recess is an even more difficult task than teaching, because during recess students are not on task but are free to run around wildly—which they should—and get into mischief—which they will. In class, teachers supervise thirty-five students; during recess, they supervise perhaps nine hundred.

At Walker, teachers were asked to supervise children during the four-minute break between classes. Joe Clark was proud of the fact that instead of letting teachers use the few minutes between classes to get their bearings for the next one, he demanded that teachers stand in the halls directing traffic. Kidder described school recess as a time when annoyed-looking teachers prowled the halls. Annoyed-looking is an understatement. School officials have been traditionally men who see no reason why teachers, mostly women, cannot spend seven hours a days with children without respite.

Detention punishes the teachers as much as the miscreants and degrades them more. During detention, teachers act as wardens, watching prisoners serve time. At the end of a long day, they patrol a detention class full of tired students, the least cooperative in the school, whose only relief from utter boredom is watching the teacher watch them, and whose skill in furtive disruption outclasses that of the artful dodger. While wardens do a whole lot for conformity, they're useless in cultivating trust and love of learning.

Suspension and expulsion are meant to help teachers by removing disruptive students from class. But teachers are not allowed to assign either suspension or expulsion. According to the California Education Code, "A teacher has no power to expel a disruptive or violent student from class or school. The expulsion process can be triggered only by recommendation of the principal or superintendent" (Ed Code #48903). Furthermore, although violent or disruptive students can be involuntarily transferred, a teacher in the school in which the student is enrolled cannot participate in the final decision for an involuntary transfer (Ed Code #48432.5).

Oddly enough, while teachers may not suspend or expel disruptive or violent students from their classes, they are allowed to disarm them. "A teacher is authorized to seize any firearm, knife, razor, switchblade, machine gun or other 'injurious object' capable of inflicting substantial bodily damage from any pupil on school premises" (Ed Code #49331). Frankly, if I haven't the power to expel a student, I'm certainly not going to risk disarming him. I saw only one kid with a switchblade. While he relinquished it to me readily enough, I don't think I would have been as ready to demand his machine gun. I don't know how teachers survive in schools that need metal detectors to keep guns out of school. They deserve purple hearts, all of them.

✳   ✳   ✳   ✳   ✳

*Actually, I never saw any gun at all, but the students in my first period class saw one in Rosemary's bag. When she was suspended and transferred to another school, Rosemary was miffed.*

*"I didn't even take it out at school," she told me. "I only got it for the skating rink after school."*

*She thought the school had no right to interfere with her afterschool activities.*

✳   ✳   ✳   ✳   ✳

Since teachers cannot assign suspension and expulsion, they have to keep disruptive students until the vice principal or principal recommend that students be removed from class. I was not consulted nor could I object to the placement in my class of a student who was transferred from four other classes and had made a career of disruptive behavior.

William K. Kilpatrick extols the days when schools were un-apologetically authoritarian. He says schools today would solve the problem of student behavior if teachers policed bathrooms, play-grounds, corridors, and lunchrooms. He says that teachers don't do this because they don't want to exert the time and energy. They just want to put in as few hours as possible, leave as early as they can, and take no work home with them.[10] Kilpatrick, who speaks safely from ivory towers long notorious for unauthoritarian policies, has it wrong. Teachers want to work; they just don't want to work at policing. If they did, they would have joined the police force.

Where teachers are police, schools are prisons. What's more, teachers who police play an elaborate game of cat and mouse where the odds are stacked against them because mice outnumber the cat thirty-five to one, at least, and the mice have a vast secret network.

Instead of demanding stricter rules and punishment, schools need to finds ways to reduce them. Stevenson and Stigler said that American teachers pay more attention to student behavior than Asian teachers do. Merry White noticed that, unlike American teachers, Japanese teachers are mainly concerned that the children be engaged in their work and not that they be disciplined or docile.[11]

Just as the rising number of young offenders in prison has not had a corresponding decrease in the youth crime rate, so the penal code of the schools has not been a deterrent to truancy, dropouts, and school crime. The *AAUW Report* states that a major cause of dropouts is that students do not consider school a pleasant or worthwhile place to be.[12] Getting better at punishing and policing will not make schools more pleasant or worthwhile.

## Giving Students Responsibility

Most of the time and energy schools spend on devising and implementing punishment would be more effectively spent in find-ing ways to cultivate student cooperation. For instance, schools have never fully utilized the eagerness of students to take on jobs at school. Students volunteer to do chores at school that they would never do at home. They respond like guests who feel more at home at a party when the host asks them to help out.

Bruce Feiler, Stevenson and Stigler, and White, in their separate studies of Japanese schools, remark on the fact that teachers do not call for quiet before beginning lessons, the student in charge does. Students check homework assignments, supervise lunch, and clean their own classrooms. Feiler says that in the school where he taught, every collar, cuff, and curl was supervised by the students themselves.[13]

I have never been in a Japanese school. I never read Feiler or Stevenson and Stigler or White until I retired. I don't think that schools should monitor every collar, cuff, and curl. But I know that students can accept responsibility for their own classrooms and that school becomes more meaningful to them when they do.

✳    ✳    ✳    ✳    ✳

*When I taught special ed, every quarter the students in my class elected a president who called the class to order, announced the order of the day, assigned class chores, settled disputes, and dismissed the class.*

*One day I lost my class keys, a criminal offense in most schools. I think it goes on your permanent record. Administrators complained that women teachers were always losing keys. Of course they were. At that time most of us wore skirts or dresses which, in those days, had no pockets.*

*At any rate, I put the key on my desk for a minute and it disappeared. I asked everyone in the room, but although they all searched and swore they didn't take it, we couldn't find the key.*

*Ronald, our class president, came up to my desk.*

*"Don't worry, Ms. Walsh," he said softly so that no one else would hear. "I'll get it back for you."*

*"How?"*

*"Never mind. Just leave the class for a while. Go outside. I'll tell you when to come in."*

*When I returned, Ronald whispered, "You'll have it before lunch."*

*Amazingly I did. Right after the rest of the class left, Ronald handed me the key.*

*"Where did you get it?"*

*"Roy took it," he said, "but don't say anything to him. I already took care of it."*

*"How did you get him to return it?"*

*"It was easy. I told the class that I would give a ten-dollar reward to the one who found the key. They know I have money, Ms. Walsh. Roy*

*said he it found it by the trash can."*

*"Wow," I said in relief and surprise. "Did you give him the ten dollars?"*

*"Are you crazy, Ms. Walsh? That thief?"*

✳ ✳ ✳ ✳ ✳

*In my computer classes, I assigned a number of points for each job that had to be done in the class and asked for volunteers. There were so many volunteers I had to assign an alternate for each job.*

*Students took attendance, called the class to order, announced dismissal, checked assignments, asked others to pick up their litter, distributed papers, greeted guests, checked equipment, loaded disks, and, of course, tallied points. I printed up the list of all the jobs I had in the class and shared it with Fil. She used it in her class and created a slew of new ones. The more students assumed responsibility for the class, the better they liked it and the more time Fil and I to concentrate on teaching and interacting with students.*

*The only person who ever refused to do her job was the class greeter. Bill Honig, then the California State Superintendent of Public Instruction, came to the class surrounded by the principal and other important looking people. Our greeter took one look at the crowd and got cold feet.*

*The job of making students pick up litter was not a popular one, so it was worth double the points.*

✳ ✳ ✳ ✳ ✳

Stevenson and Stigler note that in Japan children clean their own classrooms.[14] It's a great idea and would do much to eliminate food fights and garbage-strewn lunch areas. At Walker, administrators and counselors actually picked up litter with those ice picks on a stick that I described earlier. I have never seen a more graphic example of teaching students irresponsibility. It is typical of the way the staff is expected to keep schools clean.

✳ ✳ ✳ ✳ ✳

*When I first started teaching, I almost felt I had to apologize for the litter kids left behind.*

*Some object to students cleaning schools because it would take jobs from custodians, but custodians would retain their jobs even with student help. Walker had three custodians to clean the entire school. They barely had time to vacuum, sweep, and clean the boards. The school was dusted and the desks were cleaned once a year in June. By October, most rooms were filthy.*

*When students are responsible for the appearance of the school, they take pride in it. The only time the school bathrooms were free of graffiti was the year the students painted the walls. Fil's foreign language club kept the planter outside her room in blooming flowers all year.*

\* \* \* \* \*

*Elizabeth Jackman was the first principal to let me use students to run the copy machine, a task I considered a colossal waste of time. There I'd be with students waiting to get into class, parent calls to make, meetings to attend, and I'm watching a machine spit out papers. To make matters worse, the copy machine often broke down. Once they were trained to handle its quirks, the students ran the machine with a lot less trouble than I did. Furthermore, they considered it a prestigious responsibility. The word spread quickly as teachers all over the school assigned this task to students.*

*When Jackman came to Walker, she involved students wherever possible. Students read the morning announcements, gave orientations to new students, and planted a garden in the courtyard.*

\* \* \* \* \*

Giving students chores both in class and on campus gives them responsibility, self-satisfaction, and a vested interest in the school. As trite as it is, it is still true that nothing succeeds like success. Students who know they can succeed at one task are more apt to believe they can succeed at others. The satisfaction and esteem students got from their work on campus was reflected in their attention to schoolwork.

### Teacher-Student Collaboration

Involving students in the chores needed to run a school is cost-free and goes a long way toward making school a pleasant place. Another way is to allow students to make their own choices wherever pos-sible. Students in my class chose their own seats. It seems a small thing, but it did more to nourish good will than almost anything else I did. Students sat next to their partners, which they also chose.

Students chose their representatives to the school council. Student council representatives met with parents and teachers and voted on all issues. When Jackman was principal, she met with committees of students on a regular basis and consulted them on issues of campus care, discipline, and school events.

After the Rodney King riots in South Central Los Angeles, the gang leaders held a summit meeting to find solutions to the problems of their neighborhoods. Two years later, Jesse Jackson and other civil rights leaders welcomed gang leaders to their meetings, accepting their help in finding solutions to gang warfare. It makes sense. Nobody knows better how to combat gang violence than gangs do. If gang leaders collaborate in the rebuilding of South Central Los Angeles, they will be far more effective than a stricter penal code. Similarly, the most effective defense of drugs on campus is students themselves. If they had more responsibility for it, students might do more for drug prevention than administrators and teachers combined.

The more the schools collaborate with students, the more students will collaborate with the schools. If teachers and administrators make all the rules in the schools, they alone have full responsibility of enforcing them. But if students have some say about the rules, they are more likely to support them.

For instance, the most difficult school zone to patrol was the locker area because it was periodically the scene of firecrackers, stink bombs, and theft. Before Jackman closed all the lockers at school, she collaborated with a panel of students, who discussed the issue with their peers. Students asked for and got two textbooks for every class so they wouldn't have to carry heavy books back and forth. They also got storage places for their belongings during school dances and lunch. In the end, although the locker closure was not a popular measure, it went into effect with few problems. If Jackman had used her dictatorial powers, students would have responded with damage and mayhem.

Neill, whose school was entirely student-governed, said that while some people believe that sports cultivates team spirit, he discovered that self-government built team spirit.[15] Furthermore, Neill discovered that, with self-governance, students learn by experience that freedom is not license.

School critics like Kilpatrick claim that children can only learn the virtues needed for democracy through authoritarian education. But authoritarian measures have been exhausted in the schools without affecting behavior or inspiring learning. Authoritarian measures force students to obey the rules, but they don't keep students in the schools.

## Student Conflict Resolution

Rita Kramer cites student conflict management as an example of the "frippery" that was part of the teacher education she observed.[16] I cite it as an example of the effectiveness of student collaboration with teachers in the problem of disruptive students. Fighting is a major cause of disruption on campuses and bullying a common fear among students. No matter how well teachers are prepared in the content they teach, they need tools to deal with the fights that inevitably arise when nine hundred or more children share the same campus.

Until about two years ago, if I saw students fighting, I would stand between them. Relieved to have an excuse to quit, they would mutter a parting threat, drop their fists, and swagger away. Today's fighters are surrounded by cheering crowds that make it difficult for teachers to reach them and not too smart to interrupt them. Typically, schools handle fights with suspensions, but such punishment has not reduced the number of fights. In fact, students who get suspension often return with a stronger motive or reason to fight: revenge. What's more, each fighter organizes his own support so that one fight often multiplies into many fights and, consequently, many suspensions. Furthermore, suspension may take fighting off campus, but unless the conflict is resolved, the fight continues on the streets.

The only program I ever saw that reduced fighting on campus was student conflict resolution. In the four years that Fil, Jo Stark, and I organized student conflict resolution, not one dispute reoccurred. Once the disputants came to an agreement, they did not fight again. Moreover, they did not carry the dispute to their friends.

The reason that student conflict resolution worked so well is that students settled disputes without adult interference. This was the most difficult part of selling the program. Most parents, teachers, and administrators cannot trust four young people alone in a room. For one thing, they are afraid the students will waste time and not account for every minute. But, in the four years of the program at Walker, we had only two incidents in which conflict managers set up sessions just so they could talk to their friends and get out of class.

Student conflict managers were serious about their responsibility and believed they had power to make things better. Their pride in seeing conflicts resolved was no less than that of adults would be. They were proud of the fact that they were elected by their peers for such an important task. Moreover, the most frequent fighters on campus were sometimes the most effective conflict managers.

✳ ✳ ✳ ✳ ✳

*There was April. She had been suspended at least three times for fighting. When she was elected, there were some teachers who didn't think she should have the privilege of being in the program. At the beginning of her training, she scoffed and thought the whole thing ridiculous.*

*"What you don't understand, Ms. Walsh, is that some kids have to fight for their pride. If you walk away from a fight, you're considered a fool. Even your parents tell you you should stand up for yourself on your own two feet."*

*By the end of the year, April was explaining the program to a newcomer. "I know you think it's silly. I did too. Now, you know I'm a good fighter. I could never walk away from a fight. But I really learned how to talk things out."*

*There was also Ted. Ted was a strong, tall boy for his age, but he had a cleft palate and an ugly facial deformation that could not be surgically helped until he was fully grown. One day he stormed into the lab after Russell.*

*"I'm going to kill him."*

*Russell's mistake was in believing that because Ted had taken a lot of teasing, he had limitless patience. Now Russell cowered in the back of the room with more daring than muscle, three heads shorter, and twenty pounds lighter than his opponent.*

*"Ted," I said, "can we talk about this?"*

*"No, I've had it," said Ted, circling Russell, contemplating his next*

*move.*

"*Look, let me try this new program I learned where you try to talk it out. If it doesn't work, you can go outside and beat him to a pulp.*"

*Both boys looked at me as if they thought I was leaking brain cells. Because Ted and I were friends, he reluctantly agreed to talk, but he wasn't willing to wait for the student conflict managers so I conducted a quick session myself.*

"*I was just kidding,*" *Russell said.* "*Can't you take a joke?*"

*I said, according to the script,* "*Ted, describe the problem.*"

"*Russell called me pig mouth.*"

"*Russell insulted you. Is there anything else?*"

"*He calls me that all the time.*"

"*Russell, you describe the problem.*"

"*I was just kidding around on the schoolyard. He gets mad and starts chasing me.*"

"*Ted, would you look at Russell and tell him how you feel when he calls you names?*"

"*I feel angry. All my life, since I was in kindergarten, kids called me names. I feel like dirt.*"

"*Russell, tell Ted how you feel when he tells you this.*"

*Russell couldn't do it. He shuffled from foot to foot. He couldn't look at Ted.*

"*I'm sorry,*" *he said.*

"*Tell Ted how you felt when you heard him describe his feelings,*" *I said, reading the script.*

*Ted and I waited in silence for about two minutes. Finally Russell began talking to the ground.*

"*Would you face Ted, please,*" *I said.*

*Russell looked into Ted's face.* "*I didn't know you felt so bad.*"

*It was the turning point of the whole confrontation.*

"*How do you feel?*" *I asked.*

"*I feel bad.*"

"*Russell, what can you do to resolve this conflict?*"

*Now looking at Ted, Russell said,* "*I can leave you alone and not call you names anymore.*"

"*Is this agreeable to you?*" *I asked Ted.*

"*No,*" *said Ted.* "*I don't want to be left alone. I want people to talk to me.*"

"*I can say hello to you whenever we meet,*" *said Russell.*

*Ted accepted that.*

*Russell kept his word. He said hello to Ted every time he came to class. He discovered that Ted was much better on the computer than he was, and was glad when Ted helped him. It was the first time I had a student cease teasing another student, even when there was no adult supervision around.*

## Teacher-Student Partnership

If I hadn't firsthand experience of partnership with students, I might not be as willing to believe it works.

✳    ✳    ✳    ✳    ✳

*When I gave a teachers' workshop presentation on technology, Glen Inanaga set up the disks, laser disk player, computer, and monitor. He described how to interface the equipment, explained how it worked, and demonstrated a program he had designed and written. After Steve Berry and I learned how to interface Logo, a computer language, with Hyperstudio software and incorporate both on a video tape, Steve taught the process to any other student who chose it for a study project.*

*Visiting teachers who watched these seventh-graders at work were impressed with their skill and professional attitude. They thought the boys did so well because they were exceptionally bright, and because kids like technology. But I enjoyed just as able assistance from students who were considered average, below average, and special ed. They helped plan presentations, design flyers, write instructions, and prepare the computer lab.*

✳    ✳    ✳    ✳    ✳

A partnership between teachers and students should be two-fold. Students should assume many school tasks, such as morning announcements, running copying machines, monitoring the halls between classes, supervising lunch, peer tutoring, and assisting custodians. And students should have a voice not only in student activities, but also in discipline, scheduling, and budget.

Teacher-student partnerships should be implemented for two reasons. First of all, students, like teachers and anyone else, support best that which they create and it is time to garner such support for the schools.

Secondly, most scorn for schooling and disruption on campus stems from peer pressure but, if students had ownership in the schools, peer pressure would be used to support the school, not sabotage it. Just as peer pressure can make teachers more accountable, so it can make students more responsible. For instance, gangs are a social and economic problem that schools cannot address alone but, even in schools where there are no gangs, students ape gang mores to gain peer status. The reaction of the schools has been to implement more restrictive regulations and tighter supervision. The more appropriate response is to give youth leaders the power and prestige in the schools that they seek in gangs. At the thirty-second annual Senate Youth Program, Charles B. Redfern, a high school student from Skoki, Illinois, told Madeleine Kunin of the United States Department of Education what he thought should be done about violence on campus: "If anything is going to work, it will be that the students have to take responsibility and say, 'I do not want this in my high school.'"[17]

## Objections to Teacher-Student Partnerships

When I discussed teacher-student partnerships at teacher workshops, elementary school teachers told me that their students were too young; high school teachers told me their students were too jaded. But even small children can accept some responsibility for the school, as they can accept responsibility for family chores. Among secondary students, the response for student community service nationwide indicates that if schools fostered teacher-student partnerships, students would willingly participate. The purpose of community service is to instill in secondary students consideration for others and a sense of obligation toward the community. Teacher-student partnerships would foster such consideration and obligation toward the schools.

Another objection to teacher-student partnership is that it wastes the time of students, who should concentrate only on academic learning. But much time is wasted now on disruptive students, who destroy the learning environment. Partnership between teachers and students would encourage all students to protect the learning environment.

In his discussion of the growing problem of employee theft, Ira

S. Somerson, president of Loss Management Consultants, says that the problem is that employees too often feel that they are treated as adversaries. "Employers think security is a law enforcement issue," he says. "It's not. It's a management issue."[18] Similarly, students are now treated as adversaries. Disruptive student behavior is primarily a management issue, not a rule enforcement issue. If teachers had more time and autonomy in the schools, they could find less punitive ways to deal with disruptive, uncooperative student behavior.

The media is filled with articles, studies, and reports declaring that many children are growing up without meaningful adult relationships. Teachers cannot be expected to feed, dress, or disarm students, but meaningful adult relationships is something teachers can and should provide.

For centuries, schools have assumed that a gap between teachers and students was inevitable and necessary. At best, it led to tyranny in the schools, at worst, to ridicule of schooling and abasement of teachers.

The first item of education reform should be teachers' management of and responsibility for the schools. The second most important step should be students' management of and responsibility for their education. One will not happen without the other.

# Notes

## Introduction

1. Jeff Shear, Charting Success in Virgin Territory, *Insight*, July 8, 1991, p. 26. Richard Branson voiced similar views in an interview on CNN.
2. Susan Dichter, *Teachers: Straight Talk from the Trenches* (Los Angeles, CA: Lowell House, 1989), p. 66.

## Chapter 1

## Out of the Loop

1. Patricia Albjerg Graham, *SOS: Save Our Schools* (New York: Hill & Wang, 1992), p. 142.
2. Tracy Kidder, *Among Schoolchildren* (Boston, MA: Houghton Mifflin, 1988).
3. Emily Sachar, *Shut Up and Let the Woman Teach* (New York: Bantam Dell, 1992).

4. Samuel G. Feldman, *Small Victories: The Real World of a Teacher, Her Students and Their High School* (New York: Harper, 1991).

5. Catherine Collins & Douglas Frantz, *Teachers Talking Out of School* (New York: Little, Brown, 1993).

6. Susan Dichter, *Teachers: Straight Talk from the Trenches* (Los Angeles, CA: Lowell House, 1989).

7. The National Commission on Excellence in Education, *A Nation at Risk: The Full Account* (Cambridge, MA: USA Research, 1984). Carnegie Forum on Education and the Economy, *A Nation Prepared: Teaching for the 21st Century* (New York: Carnegie Forum on Education and the Economy, 1986). California Commission on the Teaching Profession, *Who Will Teach Our Children? A Strategy for Improving California's Schools*, (Sacramento, CA: California Commission on the Teaching Profession, 1985). California Department of Education, *Caught in the Middle: Education Reform for Young Adolescents in California Public Schools* (Sacramento, CA: California Department of Education, 1987). Theodore R. Sizer, *Horace's Compromise: The Dilemma of the American High School* (New York: Houghton Mifflin, 1992).

8. Jonathan Kozol, *Savage Inequalities: Children in America's Schools* (New York: Harper Perennial, 1991), p. 6.

9. Sizer, p. 8

10. Ernest L. Boyer, *High School: A Report on Secondary Education in America* (New York: Harper & Row, 1983), p. 325.

11. Bruce Romanish, *Empowering Teachers: Restructuring Schools for the 21st Century* (New York: University Press of America, 1992).

12. California Commission on the Teaching Profession, p. 59.

13. California Department of Education.

14. President Clinton made the statement at a White House ceremony covered on NBC News honoring Walter Annenberg after The Annenberg Foundation Grant to the schools was announced.

15. William K. Kilpatrick, *Why Johnny Can't Tell Right from Wrong* (New York: Simon & Schuster, 1992), p. 23.

16. Diane Ravitch, *The Great School Wars: New York City, 1805-1973* (New York: Basic Books, 1974), p. xii-xiii.

17. *Ibid.*, p. 134.

18. *Ibid.*, p. 155.

19. *Ibid.*, p. 155.

20. *Ibid.*, p. 144.

21. Diane Ravitch, *The Troubled Crusade: American Education, 1945-1980* (New York: Basic Books, 1983), p. 48.

22. *Ibid.*, p. 54.

23. Ravitch, 1974, p. 132.

24. *Ibid.*, p. 204.

25. *Ibid.*, p. 261.

26. James Nehring, *Schools We Have; Schools We Want* (San Francisco, CA: Jossey-Bass, 1992), p. 81.

27. Louise Booth, *One to Twenty-Eight: A History of the Anaheim Union High School District* (Anaheim, CA: Anaheim Union High School District, 1980), p. 110. All the information on flexible scheduling in the Anaheim secondary school

district is cited from this source.

28. Joseph A. Fernandez, *Tales Out of School: Joseph Fernandez's Crusade to Rescue American Education* (Boston, MA: Little, Brown, 1993), p. 110.

29. Stephanie Grace, Whites, Women Dominate Teaching Corps, *Los Angeles Times*, July 7, 1992, p. A-6.

30. *The AAUW Report: How Schools Shortchange Girls* (Washington, DC: A joint publication of the AAUW Educational Foundation and National Education Association, 1992), p. 6.

31. Kidder, p. 302.

32. Beatrice & Ronald Gross, editors, *The Great School Debate* (New York: Simon & Schuster, 1985), p. 462.

33. John I. Goodlad, *A Place Called School: Prospects for the Future* (New York, McGraw-Hill, 1984), p. x.

34. Mortimer J. Adler, *The Paideia Proposal: An Education Manifesto* (New York: Macmillan, 1982), p. vii.

35. Theodore R. Sizer, *Horace's School: Redesigning the American High School* (Boston, MA: Houghton Mifflin, 1991), pp. 15-19.

36. Rita Kramer, *Ed School Follies: The Miseducation of American Teachers* (New York: The Free Press, 1992), p. 34.

37. *Ibid.*, p. 92.

38. Nehring, p. 13.

39. Kilpatrick, p. 34.

40. Nehring, p. 56.

41. Lee Cantor, Taking Charge of Student Behavior, *National Elementary Principal*, June, 1979, vol. 58, pp. 33-41. Cantor's program was widely used in the schools in the 1980s. The Anaheim Union High School District implemented it in almost all of its junior high schools. In the 1990s, the program seems to be gaining favor in Great Britain. Virginia Makins, Five Steps to Peace in the Classroom: Assertive Discipline Program Developed by L. Cantor. *Times Education Supplement*, November, 1991, vol. 3931, p. 23.

42. Chuck Freadhoff, Schools Give Computers an F, *Investor's Business Daily*, Los Angeles, October 15, 1992, ix, 132, p. 1.

43. Gerda Lerner, *The Creation of Feminist Consciousness from the Middle Ages to Eighteen-Seventy* (New York: Oxford University Press, 1993.), p. 11.

44. Betty Friedan, *The Feminine Mystique* (New York: W. W. Norton, 1963).

45. Susan Faludi, *Backlash: The Undeclared War Against Women* (New York: Doubleday, 1991).

46. Nan Robertson, *The Girls in the Balcony: Women, Men, and the New York Times* (New York: Random House, 1992).

47. *The AAUW Report*, p. 7.

48. Marian I. Hughes, *Standing Tall: Nine Leaders in Education* (Albany, NY: Albany Board of Education, 1984).

49. Faludi, p. 293.

50. Jane White, *A Few Good Women* (New York: Prentice Hall, 1992), p. 20.

51. AUHSD Gang Suppression Unit Captures California Golden Bell, *Reporter*, Anaheim Union High School District, Spring, 1990, p. 1.

52. *Brea Community Accents*, Westlake Village, CA, Fall 1989, p. 12.

53. William J. Bennett, *Our Children & Our Country: Improving Schools and Affirm-*

*ing the Common Culture.* (New York: Simon & Schuster, 1988), p. 222.

## Chapter 2

## Raising Hell

1. Betty Ballantine, *An American Celebration: The Art of Charles Wysocki* (New York: Workman Publishing, 1985), p. 182.
2. Ruth S. Freeman, *Yesterday's Schools: A Looking Glass for Teachers of Today* (Watkins Glen, NY: Century House, 1962), p. 58.
3. William J. Bennett, *Our Children & Our Country: Improving Schools and Affirming the Common Culture.* (New York: Simon & Schuster, 1988), p. 39.
4. Washington Irving, *The Legend of Sleepy Hollow* (Tarrytown, NY: Restorations, 1974), p. 13.
5. *Ibid.*, p. 99.
6. Mark Twain, *Adventures of Huckleberry Finn* (Cutchogue, NY: Buccaneer Books, 1976), p. 11.
7. J.D. Salinger, *The Catcher in the Rye* (Boston, MA: Little, Brown, 1945).
8. Jonathan Tenney asssisted by local writers, *Bi-Centennial Albany* (Albany, NY: W. W. Munsell, 1886), vol. 2, p. 51.
9. Theodore R. Sizer, *The Dilemma of the American High School* (Boston, MA: Houghton Mifflin, 1984), p. 3.
10. Joseph A. Fernandez, *Tales Out of School: Joseph Fernandez's Crusade to Rescue American Education* (Boston, MA: Little, Brown, 1993), p. 24.
11. Susan Dichter, *Teachers: Straight Talk from the Trenches* (Los Angeles, CA: Lowell House, 1989), pp. 61, 66, 81, 94.
12. Harold W. Stevenson & James W. Stigler, *The Learning Gap: Why Our Schools Are Failing and What We Can Learn from Japanese and Chinese Education* (New York: Summit Books, 1992), p. 162.
13, Dichter, p. 122.
14. Alice Walker, *The Color Purple* (New York: Washington Square Press, 1982), p. 19.
15. Virginia Woolf, *A Room of One's Own* (New York: Harcourt & Brace, 1929).
16. Susan Faludi, *Backlash: The Undeclared War Against Women* (New York: Doubleday, 1991), p. 115.
17. Joe Layden, The Shape of Today's Kids, *Times Union*, Albany, NY, Nov. 8, 1992, p. A-3.
18. James Herndon, *The Way It Spozed to Be* (New York: Simon & Schuster, 1968), p. 110.
19. James Nehring, *Schools We Have; Schools We Want* (San Francisco, CA: Jossey-Bass, 1992), p. 87.
20. Bennett, p. 39.
21. Suzanne Fields, Nannygate Shows Need to Change the Law, *Times Union*, Albany, NY, Jan. 26, 1993, p. A-7.
22 Anna Quindlen, Public Relations Preceded Wood, *Times Union*, Albany, NY, Feb. 7, 1993, p. E-6.
23. Molly Ivins, Nannygate's Not the Issue, *Times Union*, Albany, NY, Feb. 12, 1993, p. A-10.

24. Dichter, p. 149.
25. Marilyn Miedzian, *Boys Will Be Boys* (New York: Doubleday, 1991), p. 223.
26. Patricia Albjerg Graham, *SOS: Save Our Schools* (New York: Hill & Wang, 1992), p. 142.
27. Freeman, p. 63.
28. Gary Trudeau, Doonesbury, *Times Union*, Albany, NY, Jan. 21, 1993, p. 11.
29. Stevenson & Stigler, p. 167.
30. *Ibid.*
31. *Ibid.*
32. Bennett, pp. 39, 53.
33. Nina J. Easton, Life Without Father, *Los Angeles Times Magazine*, June 14, 1992, p. 14.

## Chapter 3

## History Repeats Itself

1. Washington Irving. *The Legend of Sleepy Hollow*. (Tarrytown, NY: Restorations, 1974), p. 119.
2. Ruth S. Freeman, *Yesterday's Schools: A Looking Glass for Teachers of Today* (Watkins Glen, NY: Century House, 1962), p. 9.
3. Sheldon S. Cohen, *A History of Colonial Education, 1607-1776* (New York: John Wiley & Sons, 1974), p. 182.
4. Harry G. Good & James D. Teller, *A History of American Education* (New York: Macmillan, 1973), p. 37.
5. Lawrence A. Cremin, *Traditions of American Education* (New York: Basic Books, 1977), p. 23.
6. Marian I. Hughes, *Standing Tall: Nine Leaders in Education* (Albany, NY: Albany Board of Education, 1984), p. 56.
7. Cohen, p. 168.
8. *Ibid.*, p. 171.
9. Good & Teller, p. 301.
10. Cremin, p. 50. Diane Ravitch, *The Great School Wars: New York City, 1805-1973* (New York: Basic Books, 1974), p. 229.
11. Good & Teller, p. 37.
12. Freeman, p. 30.
13. Cremin, p. 60.
14. Jonathan Tenney asssisted by local writers, *Bi-Centennial Albany* (Albany, NY: W. W. Munsell, 1886), vol. 2, p. 51.
15. Ravitch, p. 138.
16 Joseph A. Fernandez, *Tales Out of School: Joseph Fernandez's Crusade to Rescue American Education* (Boston, MA: Little, Brown, 1993), p. 167.
17. Jonathan Kozol, *Savage Inequalities: Children in America's Schools* (New York: Harper Perennial, 1991), p. 27.
18. Growing Opportunities in Tomorrow's Military, *Parade Magazine*, June 6, 1993, p. 4.
19. Chester E. Finn, Jr., *We Must Take Charge: Our Schools and Our Future* (New York: The Free Press, 1991), p. xvi.

20. Whites More Likely to Own Homes, Blacks to Rent, *Times Union*, Albany, NY, June 22, 1993, p. 1.

21. Finn, p. 80.

# Chapter 4

## Indentured Servants

1. Ruth S. Freeman, *Yesterday's Schools: A Looking Glass for Teachers of Today* (Watkins Glen, NY: Century House, 1962), p. 25.

2. Diane Ravitch, *The Great School Wars: New York City, 1805-1973* (New York: Basic Books, 1974), p. 100.

3. Harry G. Good & James D. Teller, *A History of American Education* (New York: Macmillan, 1973), p. 129. In her history of the schools, Ravitch also describes the penury of the Lancaster system.

4. Chester E. Finn, Jr., *We Must Take Charge: Our Schools and Our Future* (New York: The Free Press, 1991), p. 78.

5. Good & Teller, p. 472.

6. Marian I. Hughes, *Standing Tall: Nine Leaders in Education* (Albany, NY: Albany Board of Education, 1984), p. 138.

7. Freeman, p. 108.

8. *Ibid.*, foreword.

9. Hughes, p. 133.

10. Finn, p. 80.

11. *Ibid.*, p. 24.

12. *Ibid.*, p. 290.

13. Harold W. Stevenson & James W. Stigler, *The Learning Gap: Why Our Schools Are Failing and What We Can Learn from Japanese and Chinese Education* (New York: Summit Books, 1992), p. 167.

14. Finn, p. 78.

15. *Ibid.*, p. 79.

16. Stevenson & Sigler, p. 162.

17. Tracy Kidder, *Among Schoolchildren* (Boston, MA: Houghton Mifflin, 1988), p. 330.

18. Thomas Sowell, *Inside American Education: The Decline, The Deception, The Dogmas* (New York: The Free Press, 1993), p. 12.

19. Stevenson & Sigler, p. 205.

20. Chris Carola, Top School Officials Pull in Big Salaries and Lucrative Benefits, *Times Union*, Albany, NY, Feb. 25, p. B-2.

21. Statistics from the Albany Board of Education, 1993.

22. Susan Dichter, *Teachers: Straight Talk from the Trenches* (Los Angeles, CA: Lowell House, 1989), p. 145.

23. Rita Kramer, *Ed School Follies: The Miseducation of American Teachers* (New York: The Free Press, 1992), p. 64.

24. A. S. Neill, *Summerhill: A New View of Childhood* (New York: St. Martin's Press, 1992), p. 27.

25. Sowell, p. 26.

26. Anne C. Roark, The Ghetto of Academe: Few Takers, *Los Angeles Times*, March

14, 1988, p. 1.

27. *Ibid.*

28. *Ibid.*

29. *Ibid.*

30. Stevenson & Sigler, p. 162.

31. Hughes, p. 51.

32. Nancy Hoffman, *Woman's True Profession: Voices from the History of Teaching* (New York: The Feminist Press, 1981), p. 186.

33. Winifred Yu, Guilderland Residents Turn Down School Budget, *Times Union,* Albany, NY, , p. B-11-22.

34. *Wall Street Journal,* Education Supplement, February 9, 1990.

35. Jonathan Kozol, *Savage Inequalities: Children in America s Schools* (New York: Harper Perennial, 1991), p. 78. Kozol discusses the *New York Times* response to the call for money for education reform.

36. Sowell, p. 288.

37. *Ibid,* pp. 27-28.

38. Ravitch, p. 16.

39. Finn, p. 322.

40. Jean Merl, Are Private Schools Any Better? *Los Angeles Times,* March 29, 1992, p. A-1-3.

41. Ronald Bazarini, *Boys: A Schoolmaster's Journal* (New York: Walker & Company, 1988), p. 6.

42. Donald Woutat, Dead Poets Role Model Loses His Job, *Los Angeles Times,* July 25, 1991, p. E-1.

43. Good & Teller, p. 150.

## Chapter 5

## Where Ignorance Was Cheaper

1. Ralph Waldo Emerson, *The Complete Writings of Ralph Waldo Emerson.*(New York: Wm. H. Wise, 1929), p. 1179.

2. Lawrence A. Cremin, *Traditions of American Education* (New York: Basic Books, 1977), p. 68.

3. Harry G. Good & James D, Teller, *A History of American Education* (New York: Macmillan, 1973), p. 226.

4. Sheldon S. Cohen, *A History of Colonial Education, 1607-1776* (New York: John Wiley & Sons, 1974), p. 144.

5. Newton Edwards & Herman G. Richey, *The School in the American Social Order* (Boston, MA: Houghton Mifflin, 1963), p. 576.

6. Good & Teller, p. 233.

7. Edwards & Richey, p. 605.

8. *Ibid.,* p. 577.

9. Good & Teller, p. 306.

10. First Annual Report of the Board of Public Instruction of the City of Albany for the Year ending April 1872 (Albany, NY: The Argus Printers, 1872), p. 9.

11. *Ibid.,* p. 67.

12. Good & Teller, p. 259.

13. Edwards & Richey, p. 577.

14. *Ibid.*, p. 606.

15. Lewis J. Perelman, *School's Out: Hyperlearning, the New Technology, and the End of Education* (New York: William Morrow, 1992), p. 220.

16. Paula S. Fass, *Outside In: Minorities and the Transformation of American Education* (New York: Oxford Univeristy Press, 1989), p. 143.

17. William K. Kilpatrick, *Why Johnny Can't Tell Right from Wrong* (New York: Simon & Schuster, 1992), p. 227.

18. Good & Teller, p. 481.

19. Harold W. Stevenson & James W. Stigler, *The Learning Gap: Why Our Schools Are Failing and What We Can Learn from Japanese and Chinese Education* (New York: Summit Books, 1992), p. 191.

20. Joan Simon, *Susan Rothenberg* (New York: Henry N. Abrams, 1991), p. 11.

21. Good & Teller, p. 481.

22. *Ibid.*, p. 497.

23. *Ibid.*

24. *Ibid.*, p. 498.

25. *The AAUW Report: How Schools Shortchange Girls* (Washington, DC: A joint publication of the AAUW Educational Foundation and National Education Association, 1992), p. 85.

26. Stevenson & Sigler, p. 162.

27. James N. Johnson, *A Quiet Revolution in Teacher Education, Research, & Practice* (San Francisco, CA: Far West Laboratory for Educational Research and Development, Fall 1988), p. 1.

28. Stevenson & Sigler, p. 160.

29. A. S. Neill, *Summerhill: A New View of Childhood* (New York: St. Martin's Press, 1992), p. 87.

# Chapter 6

# Acorns in the Schoolyard

1. Diane Ravitch, *The Great School Wars: New York City, 1805-1973* (New York: Basic Books, 1974), p. 85.

2. Diane Ravitch, *The Troubled Crusade: American Education, 1945-1980* (New York: Basic Books, 1983), p. 133.

3. Ravitch, 1974, p. 87.

4. Martha J. Johnson, Termination Without Stated Cause Leads to Disposable Teachers, *CTA Action*, April 1992. p. 15.

5. Joseph A. Fernandez, *Tales Out of School: Joseph Fernandez's Crusade to Rescue American Education* (Boston, MA: Little, Brown, 1993), p. 200.

6. Susan Dichter, *Teachers: Straight Talk from the Trenches* (Chicago, IL: Contemporary Books, 1989), p. 134.

7. Words spoken to me and other teachers at an Anaheim Union HIgh School District School Board meeting.

8. Karen Nelis, Ukrainian Teacher Visits the United States to See the Schools, *Times Union*, Albany, NY, Jan. 23, 1994, p. C-3.

9. Fernandez, p. 174.

10. Joe Clark, *Laying Down the Law: Joe Clark's Strategy for Saving Our Schools* (Washington, DC: Regnery Gateway, 1989). Madeline Cartwright, *For the Children: Lessons from a Visionary Principal* (New York: Doubleday, 1993). *A Town Torn Apart*, a television docudrama based on a book by Susan Kammer-aad-Campbell, NBC, Nov. 30, 1992.

11. Jay Mathews, A Superior Principal Is Lost, *Los Angeles Times*, Jan. 4, 1989, Part II, p. 13.

12. Patricia Albjerg Graham, *SOS: Save Our Schools* (New York: Hill & Wang, 1992), p. 38.

13. Fernandez, p. 209.

14. Dichter, p. 31.

15. These and and the following references to Joe Clark are from *Joe Clark: The Myth and the Man*, a television report, WWOR-TV, Aug. 8, 1988.

16. James Herndon, *The Way It Spozed to Be* (New York: Simon & Schuster, 1968), p. 17.

17. James Nehring, *The Schools We Have; The Schools We Want* (San Francisco, CA: Jossey-Bass, 1992), p. 101.

18. Tracy Kidder, *Among Schoolchildren* (Boston, MA: Houghton Mifflin, 1988), p. 47.

19. *Ibid.*, p. 256.

20. Dichter, p. 177.

21. *The AAUW Report*, p. 66.

22. Lewis J. Perelman, *School's Out: Hyperlearning, the New Technology and the End of Education* (New York: William, 1992), p. 225.

23. Idea Exchange, *NEA Today*, Dec. 1992, p. 16.

24. Marian I. Hughes, *Standing Tall: Nine Leaders in Education* (Albany, NY: Albany Board of Education, 1984), p. 5.

25. *Ibid.*, p. 169.

26. *Ibid.*

27. Herndon, p. 162.

28. Kidder, p. 113.

29. Perelman, p. 225.

30. Donald Woutat, Dead Poets Role Model Loses His Job, *Los Angeles Times*, July 25, 1991, p. E-1.

31. A.S. Neill, *Summerhill: A New View of Childhood* (New York: St. Martin's Press, 1992), p. 139.

32. Catherine Collins & Douglas Frantz, *Teachers Talking Out of School* (New York: Little, Brown, 1993), p. 215.

33. Hughes, p. 76.

# Chapter 7

# Team Spirit

1. Louise Booth, *One to Twenty-Eight: A History of the Anaheim Union High School District* (Anaheim, CA: Anaheim Union High School District, 1980), p. 42.

2. Tracy Kidder, *Among Schoolchildren* (Boston, MA: Houghton Mifflin, 1988), p. 45.

3. Theodore R. Sizer, *Horace's Compromise: The Dilemma of the American High School* (New York: Houghton Mifflin, 1992), p. 135.

4. *Sixty Minutes*, Don Clapp.

5. J.D. Salinger, *The Catcher in the Rye* (Boston, MA: Little, Brown, 1945), p. 4.

6. Donald R. Bahret, A History of the Anaheim Union High School District. A thesis presented to the Graduate Faculty of Chapman College, Orange, CA, August, 1969. p. 81.

7. Paul Richter & Virginia Ellis, Crusades Show How Perot Gets Things Done, *Los Angeles Times*, June 14, 1992, p. A-1.

8. Joseph A. Fernandez, *Tales Out of School: Joseph Fernandez's Crusade To Rescue American Education* (Boston, MA: Little, Brown, 1993), p. 103.

9. Booth, p. 241.

10. *Ibid*. The photos include the 28 schools of the district.

11. Lewis J. Perelman, *School's Out: Hyperlearning, the New Technology, and the End of Education* (New York: William Morrow, 1992), p. 336.

12. Louis L'Amor, *Education of a Wandering Man* (New York: Bantam Books, 1989), p. 5.

13. *The AAUW Report: How Schools Shortchange Girls* (Washington, DC: A joint publication of the AAUW Educational Foundation and National Education Association, 1992), p. 45.

14. Derrick Z. Jackson, Sports No Panacea for Today's Youths, *Times Union*, Albany, NY, Oct. 27, 1993, p. A-13.

15. *The AAUW Report*, p. 73.

16. People, *Times Union*, Albany, NY, July 1, 1993, p. A-2.

17. Gerda Lerner, *The Creation of Feminist Consciousness from the Middle Ages to Eighteen-Seventy* (New York: Oxford University Press, 1993.), p. 258.

18. Holly Favino, Talking Dirty in Zulu or Yiddish, *Times Union*, Albany, NY, August 16, 1993, p. C-1.

19. Nancy Hoffman, *Woman's True Profession: Voices from the History of Teaching* (New York: The Feminist Press, 1981), p. 179.

20. Steve Bornfield, Straight to Hell, *Times Union*, Albany, NY, Jan, 3, 1993, p. I-1.

21. *The AAUW Report*, p. 82.

22. Suzanne Fields, Sex Harassment Nothing if Not Ambiguous, *Times Union*, Albany, NY, p. A-11.

23. William K. Kilpatrick, *Why Johnny Can't Tell Right from Wrong* (New York: Simon & Schuster, 1992), p. 182.

24. *Sixty Minutes*, January 9, 1994.

# Chapter 8

## My Student Myself

1. Gerda Lerner, *The Creation of Feminist Consciousness from the Middle Ages to Eighteen-Seventy* (New York: Oxford University Press, 1993), p. 197.

2. *The New York Times Book Review*, Oct. 4, 1992, p. 13.

3. Marian I. Hughes, *Standing Tall: Nine Leaders in Education* (Albany, NY: Albany Board of Education, 1984), p. 54.

4. Madeline Cartwright, *For the Children: Lessons from a Visionary Principal* (New

York: Doubleday, 1993), p. 42.

5. *A Town Torn Apart*, a television docudrama based on a book by Susan Kammer-and-Campbell, NBC, Nov. 30, 1992.

6. *The AAUW Report: How Schools Shortchange Girls* (Washington, DC: A joint publication of the AAUW Educational Foundation and National Education Association, 1992), p. 67.

7. William K. Kilpatrick, *Why Johnny Can't Tell Right from Wrong* (New York: Simon & Schuster, 1992), p. 149.

8. James Herndon, *The Way It Spozed to Be* (New York: Simon & Schuster, 1968), p. 37.

9. Holly Favino, Talking Dirty in Zulu or Yiddish, *Times Union*, Albany, NY, August 16, 1993, p. C-1.

10. Kilpatrick, p. 70.

11. *Ibid.*, p. 69.

12. William J. Bennett, *Our Children & Our Country: Improving Schools and Affirming the Common Culture.* (New York: Simon & Schuster, 1988), p. 100.

13. Kilpatrick, p. 70.

14. Joe Clark, *Laying down the Law: Joe Clark's Strategy for Saving Our Schools* (Washington, DC: Regnery Gateway, 1989), p. 95.

15. Margaret Mead, *Sex and Temperament in Three Primitive Societies* (New York: Willliam Morrow, 1963), p. xii.

16. *Ibid.*, p.x.

17. *Ibid.*, p. xiv.

18. Mary Gordon, *Good Boys and Dead Girls and Other Essays* (New York: Viking, 1991), pp. 3-13.

19. Julie Hatfield, Makeup Can Mark Rite of Passage, *Times Union*, Albany, NY, Apr. 1, 1993, p. C-1.

20. *The AAUW Report*, p. 11.

21. Kilpatrick, p. 156.

22. *Ibid.*, p. 157.

23. Herndon, p. 180.

24. *The AAUW Report*, pp. 73, 82.

25. Kilpatrick, p. 148.

26. *Ibid.*, p. 80.

27. *Ibid.*, p. 199.

28. *The AAUW Report*, p. 68.

29. Kidder, p. 261.

30. Ruth S. Freeman, *Yesterday's Schools: A Looking Glass for Teachers of Today* (Watkins Glen, NY: Century House, 1962), p. 64.

31. A.S. Neill, *Summerhill: A New View of Childhood* (New York: St. Martin's Press, 1992), p. 33.

32. Joseph A. Fernandez, *Tales Out of School: Joseph Fernandez's Crusade to Rescue American Education* (Boston, MA: Little, Brown, 1993), p. 80.

33. Lerner, p. 204.

34. Should There be Special Schools or Classes for Black Males? *NEA Today*, Oct. 1991, p. 31.

35. *Ibid.*

36. Kilpatrick, p. 234.

37. Stephanie Grace, Whites, Women Dominate Teaching Corps, *Los Angeles Times*, July 7, 1992, p. A-6.

38. *The AAUW Report*, p. 73.

39. Martha Grant, Far Beyond White Gloves and Teas, *Newsweek*, Oct. 1994, p. 158.

40. Youssef M. Ibrahim, France Bans Muslim Scarf in Its Schools, *The New York Times*, Sept. 11, 1994, p. 4.

# Chapter 9

## Schoolhouse Keepers

1. Joseph A. Fernandez, *Tales Out of School: Joseph Fernandez's Crusade to Rescue American Education* (Boston, MA: Little, Brown, 1993), p. 80.

2. *A Town Torn Apart*, A television docudrama based on a book by Susan Kammerand-Campbell, NBC, Nov. 30, 1992.

3. Madeline Cartwright, *For the Children: Lessons from a Visionary Principal* (New York: Doubleday, 1993).

4. William J. Bennett, *Our Children & Our Country: Improving Schools and Affirming the Common Culture* (New York: Simon & Schuster, 1988), p. 39.

5. Chester E. Finn, Jr., *We Must Take Charge: Our Schools and Our Future* (New York: The Free Press, 1991), p. 25.

6. Joe Clark, *Laying down the Law: Joe Clark's Strategy for Saving Our Schools* (Washington, DC: Regnery Gateway, 1989), p. 81.

7. Cartwright, p. 152.

8. *Joe Clark: The Myth and the Man*, a television report, WWOR-TV Aug. 8, 1988.

9. Tracy Kidder, *Among Schoolchildren* (Boston, MA: Houghton Mifflin, 1988), chap. 3.

10. Clark, *Laying Down the Law*, p. 195.

11. *Joe Clark: The Myth and the Man*.

12. Bennett, p. 38.

13. *Ibid.*, p. 42.

14. *Joe Clark: The Myth and the Man*.

15. Clark, *Laylng Down the Law*, p. 44.

16. *Joe Clark: The Myth and the Man*.

17. *Ibid.*

18. *Ibid.*

19. *Ibid.*

20. *Ibid.*

21. *Ibid.*

22. Clark, *Laying Down the Law,* p. 58.

23. *Ibid.*, p. 39.

24. *Ibid.*, p. 196.

25. *Ibid.*, p. 200.

26. *Ibid.*, p. 197.

27. *Ibid.*, p. 203.

28. Susan Dichter, *Teachers: Straight Talk from the Trenches* (Los Angeles, CA: Lowell House, 1989), p. 245.

29. *A Town Torn Apart.*

30. Clark, *Laying Down the Law*, p. 36.

31. Kidder, p. 70.

32. James Nehring, *The Schools We Have; The Schools We Want* (San Francisco, CA: Jossey-Bass, 1992), p. 148.

33. Cartwright, p. 194.

34. James Herndon, *The Way It Spozed to Be* (New York: Simon & Schuster, 1968), p. 37.

35. Patricia Albjerg Graham, *SOS: Save Our Schools* (New York: Hill & Wang, 1992), p. 158.

36. Fernandez, p. 98.

37. Cartwright, p. 64.

38. Betty Friedan, *The Second Stage* (New York: Summit Books, 1993), p. 246.

39. Cartwright, p. 181.

40. Elaine Woo, Tired of Having Little Say, Teachers Pushing for Shared Authority, *Los Angeles Times*, Apr. 23, 1989, Part I, p. 3.

41. Janet Bryant Quinn, Small, Medium-Sized Firms Replace Larger, Inefficient Companies, *Times Union*, Albany, NY, Feb. 8, 1993, p. A-12.

42. Joyce M. Rosenberg, Same Parade, but a New Macy's, *Times Union*, Albany, NY, Nov. 25, 1992, p. B-8.

43. Tina Lam, Experts Criticize Postal Service's Management Style, *Times Union*, Albany, NY, May 11, 1993, p. A-4.

44. Carla Lazzareschi, Under the Big Gray Cloud at IBM, *Los Angeles Times Magazine*, Feb. 2, 1992, p. 24.

45. *Ibid.*, p. 42.

46. David Perkins, *Smart Schools: From Training Memories to Educating Minds* (New York: The Free Press, 1992), p. 205.

47. Wayne Johnson, Los Angeles Teachers Strike, *Los Angeles Times*, Apr. 16, 1990, p. B-5.

48. Lee C. Deighton, editor, *The Encyclopedia of Education* (New York: Macmillan & The Free Press, 1971), vol. I, p. 202.

49. Thomas Sowell, Protecting Jobs at Cost Of Education, *New York Times*, October 16, 1993, p. A-7. Bennett, p. 42.

50. Clark, *Laying Down the Law*, p. 36.

51. Theodore R. Sizer, *Horace's Compromise: The Dilemma of the American High School* (New York: Houghton Mifflin, 1992), p. 199.

52. Nehring, p.72.

53. Fernandez, p. 168.

54. Terry Frith, *Secrets Parents Should Know About Public Schools* (New York: Simon & Schuster, 1985), p. 27-32.

55. Clark, *Laying Down the Law*, p. 178.

56. Ernest L. Boyer, *High School: A Report on Secondary Education in America* (New York: Harper & Row, 1983), p. 219.

# Chapter 10

# Beyond the PTA

1. Ruth S. Freeman, *Yesterday's Schools: A Looking Glass for Teachers of Today*

(Watkins Glen, NY: Century House, 1962), p. 14.

2. Madeline Cartwright, *For the Children: Lessons from a Visionary Principal* (New York: Doubleday, 1993). pp. 172-173.

3. Susan Dichter, *Teachers: Straight Talk from the Trenches* (Los Angeles, CA: Lowell House, 1989), p. 267.

4. Harold W. Stevenson & James W. Stigler, *The Learning Gap: Why Our Schools Are Failing and What We Can Learn from Japanese and Chinese Education* (New York: Summit Books, 1992), p. 171.

5. Speaking Out: What Must Be Done, *Ebony*, August, 1989, p. 155. The article contains four Black leaders' opinions on government's anti-drug efforts. In his many speeches on staying in school, Jesse Jackson often exhorts parents to get to know their children's teachers.

6. Cartwright, p. 244.

7. Terry Frith, *Secrets Parents Should Know About Public Schools* (New York: Simon & Schuster, 1985), p. 58.

8. Cartwright, p. 244.

9. William K. Kilpatrick, *Why Johnny Can't Tell Right from Wrong* (New York: Simon & Schuster, 1992), p. 89.

10. Diane Ravitch, *The Great School Wars: New York City, 1805-1973* (New York: Basic Books, 1974), p. 49.

11. Thomas Sowell, *Inside American Education: The Decline, The Deception, The Dogmas* (New York: The Free Press, 1993), p. 37.

12. Chester E. Finn, Jr., *We Must Take Charge: Our Schools and Our Future* (New York: The Free Press, 1991), p. 95.

13. Stevenson & Sigler, pp. 28-30.

14. Merry White, *The Japanese Educational Challenge: A Commitment to Children* (New York: The Free Press, 1987), p. 76.

15. Stevenson & Sigler, p. 59.

16. White, p. 166.

17. Bruce S. Feiler, *Learning to Bow: An American Teacher in a Japanese School* (New York: Ticknor & Fields, 1991), p. 167.

18. This anecdote about MacArthur is part of West Point folklore and is related by tour guides at the Academy.

19. A significant portion of both Feiler's and White's books discuss the fact that working men in Japan spend little time at home in domestic involvement.

20. Mia B. Moody, Learning Center Says Dads Aren't Doing Enough, *Times Union*, Albany, NY, Oct. 25, 1993, p. C-4.

21. William J. Bennett, *Our Children & Our Country: Improving Schools and Affirming the Common Culture.* (New York: Simon & Schuster, 1988), p. 35.

22. Sowell, p. 259.

23. Diana B. Henriques with Dean Baquet, Evidence Mounts of Bid-Rigging in Milk Industry, *Times Union*, Albany, NY, May 23, 1993, p. 1.

24. Marilyn Miedzian, *Boys Will be Boys* (New York: Doubleday, 1991), p. 187.

25. Lewis J. Perelman, *School's Out: Hyperlearning, the New Technology and the End of Education* (New York: William Morrow, 1992).

## Chapter 11

## Children Should Be Seen and Not Hushed

1. Diane Ravitch, *The Great School Wars: New York City, 1805-1973* (New York: Basic Books, 1974), p. 100.
2. Joseph A. Fernandez, *Tales Out of School: Joseph Fernandez's Crusade to Rescue American Education* (Boston, MA: Little, Brown, 1993), p. 101.
3. Madeline Cartwright, *For the Children: Lessons from a Visionary Principal* (New York: Doubleday, 1993), p. 83.
4. Tracy Kidder, *Among Schoolchildren* (Boston, MA: Houghton Mifflin, 1988), p. 70.
5. A. S. Neill, *Summerhill: A New View of Childhood* (New York: St. Martin's Press, 1992), p. 61.
6. Jonathan Kozol, *Savage Inequalities: Children in America's Schools* (New York: Harper Perennial, 1991), p. 163.
7. Harold W. Stevenson & James W. Stigler, *The Learning Gap: Why Our Schools Are Failing and What We Can Learn from Japanese and Chinese Education* (New York: Summit Books, 1992), p. 205.
8. Lewis J. Perelman, *School's Out: Hyperlearning, the New Technology and the End of Education* (New York: William Morrow, 1992)
9. Cartwright, p. 117.
10. William K. Kilpatrick, *Why Johnny Can't Tell Right from Wrong* (New York: Simon & Schuster, 1992), p. 229.
11. Merry White, *The Japanese Educational Challenge: A Commitment to Children* (New York: The Free Press, 1987), p. 67.
12. *The AAUW Report: How Schools Shortchange Girls* (Washington, DC: A joint publication of the AAUW Educational Foundation and National Education Association, 1992), p. 49.
13. Bruce S. Feiler, *Learning to Bow: An American Teacher in a Japanese School* (New York: Ticknor & Fields, 1991), p. 77.
14. Stevenson & Sigler, p. 63.
15. Neill, p. 34.
16. Rita Kramer, *Ed School Follies:: The Miseducation of American Teachers* (New York: The Free Press, 1992), p. 11.
17. Charles J. Lewis, A Lesson in School Violence, from Kids in the Know, *Times Union*, Albany, NY, Feb. 13, 1994, p. C-13.
18. Lini S. Kadaba, Stealing from Work a Symptom of Anger, *Times Union*, Albany, NY, April 11, 1993, p. H-1.

# Index

# About the Author

**Edwina Walsh**, a writer and education consultant, lives in Albany, New York. She is a graduate of Fordham University, holds a masters degree in English, and has studied in the state universities of New York and California in the the fields of special education and computer education. Walsh has taught thirty-two years in public and parochial schools in New York and California in special and regular education classrooms at the elementary, junior high, and senior high school levels. She has experience teaching every track from elementary through high school, including special education, advanced placement, and computer labs. For eight years, Walsh worked for school reform in a California junior high school where she was department chair in special education, a resource teacher, and the computer coordinator. She also served as executive director of the Anaheim Secondary Teachers Association and district chairperson for site-based management. Her writing has appeared in professional journals in special education, reading, and computer training for teachers. She is presently preparing a book about special education at the elementary level.